Cooking with SEITAN

Cooking with SEITAN

Delicious Natural Foods from Whole Grains

by Barbara and Leonard Jacobs

Japan Publications, Inc.

© 1986 by Barbara and Leonard Jacobs
Illustrations by Barbara Jacobs

Published by
JAPAN PUBLICATIONS, INC., Tokyo and New York

Distributors:
UNITED STATES: *Kodansha International | USA, Ltd., through Harper & Row, Publishers, Inc., 10 East 53rd Street, New York, N. Y. 10022.* SOUTH AMERICA: *Harper & Row, Publishers, Inc., International Department.* CANADA: *Fitzhenry & Whiteside Ltd., 195 Allstate Parkway Markham, Ontario L3R 4T8.* MEXICO AND CENTRAL AMERICA: *HARLA S. A. de C. V. Apartado 30–546, Mexico 4, D. F.* BRITISH ISLES: *International Book Distributors Ltd., 66 Wood Lane End, Hemel Hempstead, Herts HP2 4RG.* EUROPEAN CONTINENT: *Fleetbooks—Feffer and Simons (Nederland) B. V., 61 Strijkviertel, 3454 PK De Meern, The Netherlands.* AUSTRALIA AND NEW ZEALAND: *Bookwise International, 1 Jeanes Street, Beverley, South Australia 5007.* THE FAR EAST AND JAPAN: *Japan Publications Trading Co., Ltd., 1–2–1, Sarugaku-cho, Chiyoda-ku, Tokyo 101.*

First edition: January 1987

LCCC 85–80537
ISBN 0–87040–637–X

Printed in U.S.A.

Foreword

After I met George Ohsawa and learned about food's important role in the health and well-being of all peoples and societies, I found that those delicious traditional Japanese foods I had known since childhood were healthful and nutritious. In combination with whole grains and vegetables they can form the basis for healthy daily eating for everyone.

When my husband, Michio, and I began teaching macrobiotics in the United States in the 1950s we encouraged the importation of traditional-quality Japanese foods and are happy that now most of them are available at natural foods stores around the country. When we started the Seventh Inn Restaurant in Boston in 1971, we encouraged the preparation of these foods in various ways that were more suitable for the American taste. Through the creativity of the many cooks in this restaurant, we learned how to prepare many traditional Japanese foods for American people's taste.

One food that we introduced through this restaurant was "seitan." George Ohsawa had popularized this food in Japan, especially among macrobiotic people. I had thought the preparation of seitan might be too complicated for many people to learn. But when one of our friends came to help with the cooking in the Seventh Inn, she taught the chefs how to make seitan in delicious and healthful ways. They also adapted the traditional Japanese method of preparing this food into many American styles.

Leonard Jacobs was one of the chefs at the Seventh Inn during this period. He and his wife Barbara learned how we prepared seitan in Japan and became interested in how to introduce this unusual food to more people. Since Barbara has a large family, she developed many tasty ways of cooking to satisfy her family and friends. Barbara has also cooked for hundreds of people who have studied with her, and she has always managed to create delicious and nutritious meals using a variety of healthy ingredients.

Seitan is one of the many traditional Japanese foods we hope you will use. It is possible to prepare this food in your home kitchen. There are also many natural foods stores which sell already cooked seitan that has either been imported from Japan or made by people in the United States. (In Europe there are also many companies making seitan for sale through natural foods stores.) I am happy that Americans have been able to use their ingenuity and imagination to develop so many variations on our traditional way of preparing foods. We have seen the development of tofu, miso, and now seitan shops in this country. There are also people collecting and harvesting sea vegetables in North America. This is a sign that macrobiotic foods can really be adapted to an international cuisine and can be integrated into the various cooking styles of all peoples. The formation of businesses that make and distribute these foods is important to the work of Michio and myself. We hope you will be encouraged by the work of all the people involved in such enterprises.

The Jacobs have used their understanding and enthusiasm to write this book. They have been directing the *East West Journal* for the past ten years. Their work on this magazine has helped them understand the needs of many people. *East West Journal* is dedicated to presenting the basic principles of maintaining total and complete health through proper diet and cooking. This new book is another way of presenting these same basic principles. I hope it will help you discover how easy it is to use seitan, and how delicious and healthful it is.

November, 1985

AVELINE KUSHI

Acknowledgments

While creating these recipes, we searched for and tested many types and brands of flours, natural soy sauces, soymilks, and oils. We were looking for those foods that were manufactured with the consumer's good health in mind, as well as foods that tasted great and were readily available. During this research period, we decided to use products noted for their high quality and consistent reliability in cooking. Although you may use products other than the brands recommended here, the recipes in this book were created with the following products: Arrowhead Mills whole winter wheat flour, Ohsawa America Organic Shoyu, and Eden Foods "Edensoy" soymilk and safflower oil. For their wonderful products we thank Arrowhead Mills and the Ohsawa America Company. Special gratitude also goes to Peter Milbury, Mike Potter, and Cliff Adler for their continued work in ensuring the availability of healthful foods, and their support and encouragement toward the development of this book.

The recipes in this book were tested by many people with a wide range of cooking experience—yet they all shared one ingredient—an enthusiasm and sense of adventure toward new ideas in cooking. We would like to especially thank those people who tested the early versions of new recipes, offering honest constructive criticism designed to make the final recipes simpler to prepare and more delicious. Those cooks who spent their precious time include: Martha Felt, Suzy Whittlesby, Jeanne Sloan, Maria Cohen, Fern Israel, Joanne Goldman, Jacqui Ozon, Denise Barrak, Pamela Fuller, Linda Roszak Elliot, Merridee La Mantia, Joanne Saltzman, Malli Gero, and Helen Sandler. Like many of you, some of them had never heard of seitan before.

We also thank our children Jesse, Daria, Joshua, Molly, and Sean for being there for each other while we were cooking and typing. They were the main objects of what we began to refer to as "The Great Seitan Caper," and their sense of humor, honest enthusiasm, and reactions to new dishes will always be appreciated.

We all appreciate Yumie Kono, whose introduction to making and tasting seitan laid the foundation, 17 years ago, for this book.

BARBARA and LEONARD JACOBS

Contents

Navy Bean Soup with Hickory Seitan
Almost Instant Clear Soup with Fu and Greens
Golden Squash Potage

Main Dishes and Casseroles, 85

Seitan Stroganoff
Stuffed Red Peppers
Mushroom Lasagne Au Gratin
Pan-Fried Cutlets with Mushroom Sauce
Sweet and Spicy Stew with Dried Fruits
Creamed Corn and Cutlet Casserole
Apricot-Glazed Seitan "Roast"
Seitan Rolls Braised in Saké Sauce
Shepherd's Pie
Chili
Polenta "Al Forno"
Tricolor Pilaf
Seitan Stew Provençale
Pastichio—Greek-Style Macaroni Casserole
Baked Vermicelli with "Pepperoni Seitan"
Seitan Kebabs
Casserole with Mashed Potatoes and Seitan "Pepperoni"
Old-Fashioned Stew in White Sauce over Egg Noodles
Yeasted Pizza Dough
Deep-Dish Neapolitan Vegetable Pie
Fennie's Dutch Casserole
Country-Style Pot Pies
Creamy Fettucine with Crispy Seitan Strips
Aunt Ruth's "Turkey" with Couscous Stuffing
Couscous Stuffing
Spanish Rice

Side Dishes, 113

Cutlets Braised in Peanut Sauce
Filled Noodle Nests
Red-Simmered "Roast"
Baked Sauerkraut with Spicy Seitan Patties and Apples
Barbecue Robai Cutlets
Piroshki
Filled Crepes with Orange-Shallot Sauce
Orange-Shallot Sauce for Filled Crepes
Sweet and Sour Chinese Vegetables and Seitan Cubes
Vegetarian Sausage Links or Hot Dogs
Onion-Caraway Balls with Sauerkraut

Seitan Cubes in Garlic Sauce
Carrots and Daikon with Fu Rings
Baked Buttercup Treasure Chest
Old-Fashioned Hickory Baked Beans
Curried Seitan Cubes
Enchiladas
Broiled Breaded Seitan Cutlets
Seitan Cutlets Romano
Garden Vegetables with Seitan Strips
Barbecued Baked Cutlets
Savory Stuffed Tomatoes
Pan-Fried Cutlets with Onion Rings
Cutlets Scallop
Easy Szechuan-Style Sweet and Sour Cubes
Stir-Fried Seitan Strips with Romaine
Home-Style Stew
Five-Spice Seitan with Green Beans and Sesame Seeds
Baked Seitan and Vegetables in Dill Sauce
Whole Onions Filled with Seitan and Sauerkraut
Spring Rolls
Pouches II
Burgers
Carrots in Blankets
Filled Turnip Cups
Seitan and Green Beans Baked in Mustard Sauce

Salads, 147

Watercress and White Mushroom Salad with Golden Seitan Strips
Green Bean and Walnut Salad
Fu with Dandelion Greens
Savory Seitan Salad
Two-bean Salad with Hickory Slices
Wild Rice Salad
Carrot Greens and Cabbage Salad with Sesame
Chinese Pasta Salad
Broccoli Rabe Salad with Tiny Croquettes
Seitan and Escarole Salad with Anchovy-Tarragon Vinaigrette
Hearty Seitan "Roast" Salad with New Red Potatoes
Mediterranean Vegetable Medley
Large-Shell Macaroni Salad with Walnut and Pimiento Dressing
Confetti Rice Salad
Winter Salad with Radishes
Spring Salad with New Potatoes and Snow Peas
Flint Corn Salad

Sauces, Dressings, and Marinades, 165 —————————

Mustard Sauce
Barbecue Sauce I
Barbecue Sauce II—Mild
Barbecue Sauce III—Hickory
Barbecue Sauce IV
Apricot Butter
Red Chiles Marengo
Basic Tomato Sauce
Mediterranean Marinade
Teriyaki Marinade
Thick Marinade with Miso
Little Cream Sauce
Quick Gravy Using Seitan Broth
Easy Garden Vegetable Sauce for Pasta
Creamy Umeboshi Dressing
Miso-Lemon Dressing
Basic Vinaigrette
Anchovy-Tarragon Vinaigrette
Sweet and Sour Dressing
Creamy Chive Dressing
Spicy Miso-Orange Dressing
Tamari-Lemon Dressing with Tarragon
Creamy French Dressing
Mustard Dressing
Ume-Orange Dressing

Condiments, 175 —————————————————

Nori Sprinkles and Spirals
Savory Seitan Spread with Miso
Hickory Strips
Seasoned Seitan "Bits"
Seitan Paté with Ginger, Onion, and White Miso

Sandwiches, 179 —————————————————

Hot Barbecued Seitan Sandwich
Seitan Sandwich with Tangy Miso-Tahini Sauce
Tangy Miso-Tahini Sauce
Hot Super-Sandwich
Tofu Spread with Variations
Seitan-Tofu Paté

Desserts, 183

Coconut-Lemon Cookies
Choco-Carob Fudge Sauce
Banana Dream Pudding
Chewy Date-Walnut Cookies
Almond Essence Whip
Divine Fresh Fruit Shake
Maple-Walnut Custard
Cinnamon-Chestnut Puffs
New "Good Old Chocolate Pudding"
Date-Nut Filled Puffs

From the Pantry, 191

Basic Crepes
Flint Corn
Tofu "Feta Cheese"
Whole Wheat Bread with Hickory Bits
Corn Bread
Millet
Millet "Mashed Potatoes"
Chunky Mushroom Gravy
Bill's Dills
More Summer Vegetable Pickles
Homemade Sauerkraut
Pesto
Pasta with Pesto
Couscous
Sweet and Sour Marinated Beet Salad
Sunshine Mint Tea
Wakame Sea Vegetable with Onions and White Miso
Glazed Carrots with Sesame
Steamed Greens—Kale, Collard, and Mustard
Toasted Nori Strips
Brown Rice
Brown Rice Rolls (*Norimaki Sushi*)
Bulgur
Kasha
Arame Sea Vegetable with Natural Soy Sauce
Special Baked Apples
Marinated Cucumbers and Watercress Salad
Miso-Tahini Sauce or Spread
Kukicha Tea
Basic Bean Cookery

Sample Lunch and Dinner Menus, 211 ─────

Appendix, 215 ─────

Introduction

Flour power for the Eighties! Cooking with seitan, a succulent, versatile food made from wheat, is an excellent way to reduce cholesterol, fat and calories in your diet. Its full-bodied, hearty flavor and familiar texture remind many people of meat; thus it is a very good food to use when making the transition to a meatless or less-meat diet. For these same reasons, seitan makes an exciting introduction or satisfying addition to any natural foods diet.

Seitan is a food with a long history. Although not widely known in the West, it was traditionally eaten in China, Korea, Japan, Russia, the Middle East, and probably many other countries that grew wheat. In America, the Mormons and the Seventh Day Adventists made gluten and used it on a regular basis. This is a food with tradition, and a food that satisfies nutritional and taste needs without disrupting the ecology. The name *seitan* comes to us from the Japanese, who have prepared cooked wheat gluten for hundreds of years. However, only during the past ten to fifteen years has this method of preparing whole wheat been discovered by people using natural foods. Since many people are aware of the potential health risks of eating fatty foods and high cholesterol animal foods, seitan, with its chewy, meat-like texture and excellent nutritional profile, is destined for widespread popularity. Some natural foods industry insiders think seitan will become the "tofu of the '80s."

Seitan is made from gluten extracted from wheat flour, which has first been made into a dough-like consistency, similar to bread dough. (Also known simply as gluten, or wheat meat, we prefer to use the Japanese name even though technically *seitan* refers to gluten that has been cooked in soy sauce.) Even though this new old food is easy to prepare and remarkably nutritious, some people are reluctant to use it because it is a partially refined food. While preparing the gluten, most of the bran and starch is removed and often discarded. In the recipes that follow, there are suggestions for using the starch, and even the bran need not be thrown away. In many cases you can include the bran and starch in the same meals in which you serve seitan. Thus seitan can be a whole food, and is, in fact, a more complete food than either soymilk or tofu.

Seitan was introduced to the U.S. natural foods industry about sixteen years ago when a Japanese variety, shrink-wrapped and quite dry and salty, was first imported. There had been several other varieties available from vegetarian groups, primarily the Seventh Day Adventists and the Mormons. Chinese restaurants have also been preparing wheat gluten for many years. The Chinese call it *mien ching*, or *yu mien ching*. Chinese restaurants often refer to this as "Buddha food," claiming that it was developed by Buddhist monks as a meat substitute. There is also a dried wheat gluten available in Oriental food markets called *fu* by the Japanese and *k'ao fu* or *kofu* by the Chinese.

Within the past two to three years, there has been some success in getting seitan distributed to a few supermarkets, but the vast majority of all seitan commercially prepared is sold through natural foods stores and restaurants. Upcountry Seitan in Lenox, Massachusetts, is the largest manufacturer we located in a recent survey (June 1985) of the industry. It makes 600 pounds each week and distributes through six states. The smallest enterprise we came across makes about ten pounds and sells to only one store. Extrapolating from existing figures, it appears that in the U.S. about 2,500 pounds of seitan are made commercially each week, or about 130,000 pounds per year.

All the companies we contacted (with one exception) make the seitan from 100 percent organic whole wheat flour. There are mixed feelings regarding whether hard red winter or spring wheat is the best. The taste and texture of seitan depends upon such factors as the type of wheat, its freshness, how finely ground it is, the farm it comes from, how it was cooked, and so forth. Nutrition will be affected somewhat by these factors as well. However, the biggest difference among seitan makers that we discovered is in the quantity of gluten extracted from the flour. This ranges from a low of 50 percent to a high of about 110 percent. (Absorption of water and soy sauce accounts for the possibility of getting more seitan than the amount of flour started with.)

Although the seitan industry is still in its infancy, today there are more companies in the natural foods industry making seitan than there were companies making tofu ten years ago when *The Book of Tofu* by Bill Shurtleff and Akiko Aoyagi was published. Among today's seitan makers are:

• Upcountry Seitan, begun three and a half years ago by Win Donovan, is now owned and operated by Wendy Rowe and Sandy Chianfoni. Sales have increased by 200 percent over the past two years and Upcountry is currently making 600 pounds of seitan each week. The kneading and rinsing processes are automated, but the remaining steps are done by hand. Upcountry achieves a 50 percent extraction of gluten from the wheat flour, but because the gluten absorbs a considerable amount of water and soy sauce in the cooking, 90 pounds of flour result in 120 pounds of seitan. Chianfoni has been experimenting with several desserts that use the starch water from the washing process. This starch has the same thickening properties as cornstarch and can be used to prepare custards and puddings.

• Michael Vitti of Rising Tide Natural Market in Long Island has been making seitan commercially for six years. He has seen a 400 percent increase in his sales over this time. He makes several different varieties of seitan, using a number of spices in addition to a plain soy sauce base. About one-third of his production is bought by another company for use in making sandwiches.

• Ron Harris of the Grain Dance Company in San Francisco has been making seitan for the past eight years. He is currently selling 250 pounds each week in eight ounce packages. He does everything by hand and has distribution throughout the West Coast. He has noted a 200 percent increase in sales over the past several years.

• Yaron Yemini of Creative Kitchens in Miami has been making seitan for three years. He has seen a five-fold increase during this time and currently makes

120 pounds each week. Yaron produces approximately seventy pounds of cooked seitan from 100 pounds of whole wheat flour. He sells seitan in bulk, packaged, and in a variety of sandwiches, salads, and sauces.

• Steve Lepenta of the Bridge Company in Middletown, Connecticut, claims sales of seitan through his shop have doubled in the past two years. He is currently producing 400 pounds of cooked seitan each week. He has established distribution into 90 retail stores throughout New England. This seitan is sold in both small plastic tubs as well as in bulk. All the seitan produced at the Bridge is made from 100 percent whole wheat spring flour. A Hobart mixer is used for the kneading of the flour, but the washing and shaping is all done by hand. Most of the seitan from the Bridge is cooked in a broth of soy sauce, kombu and ginger, but they do provide unflavored seitan for special orders.

• Rosemary Whittaker of Maritime Foods in Portland, Maine is currently producing 50 pounds of seitan each week. Practically all the distribution of this seitan goes to the Portland market. She also makes fresh soymilk, but has great hopes for increasing the distribution of seitan. Maritime Foods uses local Maine kombu in the seitan and grinds flour fresh for each batch of seitan. Rosemary has been experimenting with various alternatives to chunk seitan. This company also supplies seitan "wheat balls" and "prepared breaded-cutlets."

• Sharon Warren of Real Foods in Towson, Maryland, has been making seitan for six years. She has noted an increase of 25 percent over the period January 1984 to June 1985. Sharon currently makes 150 pounds of seitan each week from 100 percent organic hard red winter wheat. Some of her seitan is sold to another company which uses it for seitan burgers and salads. However, the majority of the seitan from Real Foods is sold bulk in the Baltimore and Washington, D.C. areas.

Other manufacturers confirmed the growing consumer interest in seitan. Many feel that there is a much larger market still untapped. Shelf life for the commercially prepared seitan ranges from two to three weeks, depending on the amount of salt used in the cooking and the storage temperature. Among the makers we contacted, retail prices range from a low of $1.69 per ½ pound to a high of $3.50 per ½ pound. Although each company noted a dramatic increase in their sales over the past several years, it is unclear whether this is due more to an increased number of outlets for their product or an increased demand in each outlet.

As the companies gain in expertise and business savvy, they will be able to find more distributors and sandwich makers interested in purchasing their product. Many makers feel that a real increase in the demand for seitan itself will result only when there is a greater awareness of its healthfulness and versatility. Seitan's versatility could be enhanced, one noted, by creating an uncooked variety. Although this would allow for considerably more uses for the gluten, the shelf life is much shorter if it is not cooked first with soy sauce. If a method for storing the cooked (or uncooked) gluten could be achieved (possibly by freezing it), most of the manufacturers were confident many more products could be prepared at home.

We hope you will experiment with this unique, delicious and nutritionally rich food. It provides remarkable possibilities for expanding on your cooking repertoire and will add a new dimension to your culinary arts.

About Wheat: Wheat (*Triticum*) has been known since prehistoric times. The oldest grains, dating from 6750 B.C., were found in excavations in the upland of eastern Iraq (the area known as the "fertile crescent"). In ancient times, wheat became the most important cereal, a position that it still occupies in almost all countries of the Western World. The history of cultivated wheat and that of human civilization have been closely interwoven. A large proportion of our essential nutrients is contained in the wheat grain. These are: carbohydrates (60–80 percent, mainly as starch); proteins (8–15 percent, which contain adequate amounts of all essential amino acids except lysine, tryptophane, and methionine); fats (1.5–2.0 percent); minerals (1.5–2.0 percent); and vitamins such as the B complex and vitamin E.

In addition to its high nutritive value, the low water content, ease of transport and processing, and good storage qualities have made this crop the most important staple food of more than one billion people or 35 percent of the world's population. Currently, the main producers of wheat are the U.S.S.R., the U.S.A., Canada, and China.

An enormous variation has developed with wheat. Some 17,000 different varieties have been produced. The wheat plant can grow from northern Finland and Norway to southern Argentina. One type of wheat, called *einkorn*, has been known since the Stone Age and was developed from the wild wheat which still grows wild in Asia Minor and Southeast Europe. Einkorn wheat is no longer of any importance and is grown only rarely, mainly in the mountainous regions of Spain, where it is sown chiefly as a fodder plant. The name einkorn (German: "one-seeded") refers to the fact that the spikelets contain only one seed.

Another variety of wheat, *emmer*, is also grown on only a limited basis, mainly in Ethiopia, Iran, and Russia as well as a few mountainous regions of Germany. Emmer was the prominent cereal in the early farming villages of the Near East, and eventually spread throughout Europe, Central Asia, and India. One variety of emmer wheat is *durum* which grows best in warmer regions. Durum wheat has become important as the source of semolina flour, most suitable for the production of pastas. The Italians claim the best wheat for this purpose is grown in the region around Rome.

The most widespread type of wheat grown throughout the world is from a different family—known technically as *T. vulgare*, or *common wheat*. It is used mainly for bread making.

Wheat can withstand low temperatures during its growth, but it does require a summer sufficiently long to allow it to flower and produce grain. Since such summers do not occur in extreme northern regions, it was the Russians who became particularly interested in trying to induce wheat sown in early spring to flower earlier. This method has enabled wheat to be cultivated in areas where this would not have otherwise been possible.

Wheat is grown in hard and soft varieties. The hard wheats contain higher levels of protein than the soft wheats, and the soft wheats contain higher levels of carbohydrates. Both hard and soft wheats are further classified as being spring or winter varieties. This refers to the season in which they are planted. Wheat is also classified by color—usually as red or white.

The hard wheats, because of their higher gluten (protein) content, are the basic seitan and bread wheats. In classical Roman times, the hard wheat was referred to as *triticum* and the soft as *siligo* so the distinction is by no means of recent origin. Generally the hard spring wheats have a bit more gluten than the hard winter wheats.

Because they do not rise as well as the hard wheats, soft wheat varieties are used in making pastries, biscuits, or blended with the harder varieties for bread baking. Pastry wheat, a white spring variety that is very low in gluten content, is used for crackers or pastry dough. Some of this type of wheat is exported to Japan for making *udon* noodles.

Botanically, there are no distinguishing features to enable a clear identification of the two types of wheat—hard and soft. Although it is true that hard grains generally exhibit a flinty, vitreous appearance of the endosperm, while the endosperm of soft wheat is mealy and white, this is not an infallible guide. The two types can be identified with certainty only at the milling stage by the types of flour that they produce. It appears that the difference between hard and soft wheat varieties lies in the protein fraction of the endosperm. Chemical analysis reveals clearly that there is a difference in the amounts of protein, as can be seen in the following chart:

Type of Wheat	Protein (%)	Starch (%)	Sugar (%)	Fat (%)	Ash (%)
Hard Red Spring	16.5	61.2	3.19	2.00	2.04
Durum	16.0	63.0	3.58	2.19	2.19
Hard Red Winter	15.3	63.5	2.84	1.67	1.92
Soft Red Winter	12.4	66.5	2.90	1.66	2.07
White	11.2	66.6	4.02	1.80	1.86

Thus the hard varieties contain larger amounts of protein than the soft varieties. Yet this is not in itself sufficient to explain the very great differences in the baking properties of the two types of flour, which is attributed to differences in the nature of the proteins in the endosperm. There is evidence that in the soft wheat endosperm, there is a higher ratio of soluble proteins to insoluble proteins than in the endosperm of hard wheat. This means that hard wheat contains more of the insoluble fraction or gluten than the soft wheats. However, the difference is not really understood completely.

Gluten: The *endosperm* (starch) of wheat consists of thin-walled cells which are embedded in a protein called *gluten*. This elastic protein found only in wheat (and to a limited extent in rye) is the source of *glutamic acid*, which is in turn the source of *monosodium glutamate*. Gluten is made up of *gliadin* and *glutenin*, a chainlike molecule that creates an elastic network.

When wheat flour is first mixed with water, the proteins are in big knotted clumps. Kneading the dough breaks up these clumps and straightens out the strands, working the proteins into a thin, strong, resilient fabric referred to as the gluten sheet. The most effective kneading is repeated stretching and folding, always in the same direction, in order to best develop the gluten sheet. The kneaded dough is like a cellulose sponge, with the holes sealed by the elastic and absorbent gluten.

Bakers say that gluten is the skeleton of the dough and largely determines its physical character. Glutenin gives solidity to the gluten. It is a longer molecule, has little taste, and is a negatively charged molecule. The gliadin is a soft, sticky substance that is responsible for the binding. Gliadin is positively charged. It sticks to the glutenin and prevents it from being washed away in the process of the gluten extraction. The glutenin and gliadin contain all the amino acids of the wheat.

Bakers determine the total protein content of flour by a chemical test known as the *Kjeldahl process*. But this only determines quantity and not the quality of the gluten. The traditional test for gluten that can also be used to choose the best flour for seitan is as follows. First weigh out 20 grams of flour and add sufficient water to make a ball of dough. Place the dough ball in a cup of cold water, completely immersed for one hour to mature the gluten. Knead this dough ball under running water to wash away the starch. Weigh the wet gluten on filter paper. Then dry the gluten on the filter paper over night in the oven at 200°F. until quite dry. Weigh the gluten again. As a rule, wet gluten weighs about three times more than dry gluten. If this ratio is less, the gluten is of a higher concentration. While wet, it is also possible to evaluate the quality of the gluten. Factors to consider include stretch, runniness, and its short or snappy tendency. Satisfactory flours for seitan usually possess 10 percent or more dry gluten.

Analysis of Gliadin and Glutenin

Amino acid	Gliadin (%)	Glutenin (%)
glycine	0.0	0.9
alanin	2.0	4.6
valine	3.3	0.2
leucine	6.6	5.9
proline	13.0	4.2
phenylalanine	2.3	2.0
tyrosine	3.1	4.2
serine	0.1	0.7
cystine	1.9	1.6
aspartic acid	0.8	2.0
glutamic acid	43.7	25.7
arginine	2.9	4.7
histidine	1.5	1.8
lysine	0.6	1.9
tryptophan	1.1	1.7

Commonly Asked Questions About Seitan: These are questions that people who have never made seitan may ask when considering preparing this new food.

1. What is *seitan*?
Seitan is the cooked and flavored gluten which has been extracted from wheat flour. It is very rich in protein while being extremely low in fat and calories. Seitan can be prepared in a variety of ways, achieving a wide range of textures and flavors suitable for many traditional foods.

2. What is so special about it?
Seitan is easy to prepare and can serve as an excellent vegetarian source of protein. It has been a special dish used by many cultures throughout history.

3. Is seitan available in supermarkets?
Seitan is only recently being sold through several select supermarket chains. It is widely available in natural foods stores.

4. Is homemade seitan better?
The seitan you prepare at home can be inexpensively made into a wide variety of textures and seasoned with a wide variety of seasonings. Nevertheless, you may prefer the convenience of purchasing already cooked seitan at your local natural foods store.

5. Is seitan hard to make?
The first time you make seitan from "scratch" it may seem a bit complicated. But once you understand the basics, you will find it is possible to make seitan from start to finish in a little more than 30 minutes. In addition, seitan freezes well, so you can make large batches and always have some at hand.

6. What if I am allergic to wheat?
Since seitan concentrates the gluten of the wheat, you may have a reaction to seitan if you are sensitive to wheat gluten. However, some people who are sensitive to wheat gluten have found that once seitan is cooked with natural soy sauce and *kombu* sea vegetable, they have little or no allergic reaction.

7. Is seitan good for people on weight-control diets?
Seitan has practically no fat and is very low in calories, so it is an excellent food for people on weight-control diets.

8. How can athletically-inclined people benefit from eating seitan?
Because seitan provides such a high concentration of protein with low amounts of fat, it is an extremely digestible food. It can be a great supplement for anyone who is physically active.

9. Can seitan be prepared in elegant ways, suitable for entertaining?
You will find that seitan can be made into a wide variety of dishes suitable for

entertaining, or simply for making into lunches or snacks.

10. How can I convince my kids to eat seitan?
You do not have to convince your children to eat seitan—just serve it to them. Practically everyone who tastes seitan will love its flavor and texture.

11. Is seitan a meat substitute?
Seitan can be used as a substitute for meats, but it is most often enjoyed simply as a food on its own, or used as an ingredient in other food preparations.

12. Is seitan economical?
One third of a pound of seitan provides 92 percent of the minimum daily requirement of protein for less than $0.75. It is possible to serve four to six people with one quarter pound of seitan each for a total cost of $1.28.

Getting Started

When I first tasted seitan, about 17 years ago, I was fascinated by its delicious flavor and chewy texture. I had begun eating whole, natural foods, and the idea of using a grain-based product having the qualities of seitan was an appealing one. There were a few problems, however. The only seitan available at that time was expensive and salty, and the pieces of seitan, as they came out of their package from Japan, were tiny and hard. Perfect for beer-snacks, but not really useful for other purposes.

Some years later, a Japanese woman working at a natural foods restaurant in Boston taught me how to make seitan. That knowledge became a wonderful gift that has benefited many people, including my family. Consuming seitan as a staple food has given us great varieties in taste as well as nutritional benefits.

Now that you are about to embark upon a new adventure, be prepared for an interesting, exciting, and rewarding experience. Making seitan has been a form of cooking that I have always enjoyed. The transformation of flour into seitan is one that is a pleasure to participate in—and, while making the seitan, you can plan what form it will take when it is finished.

I will first present a simplified version of gluten extraction so the first time you make seitan you will have a general idea of what to expect. This will be followed by detailed information explaining more completely how to extract gluten and how to prepare seitan. The recipes in this section have been selected for their simplicity and adaptability to a wide variety of needs.

To make seitan, whole wheat flour is made into dough, kneaded, and then washed to remove the starch (carbohydrate) and bran, thus concentrating the gluten (protein) of the wheat. The gluten is then slowly simmered in a broth seasoned with natural soy sauce.

Basic Seitan: Combine 4 cups whole wheat flour and 4 cups unbleached white flour with about 3½ cups water in a large mixing bowl. Knead the dough for about 50 strokes. If dough is too stiff, add about ½ cup more water while kneading. Cover the bowl with a cloth and let the dough rest for about 20 minutes to allow the gluten to develop.

Add warm water to the dough in a gentle stream. Knead the dough slowly and carefully in the water as the bowl fills, and then pour off the creamy liquid. Continue this process, alternating between warm and cold water rinses, kneading each time to extract the cream-colored starch. (The milky, somewhat thick "starch water" from the first few rinses can be saved—it is excellent in bread recipes and as a thickener for stews, sauces, etc.) At first the dough may seem to be falling apart. Sometimes a batch of flour disintegrates in the washing, instead of separating into starch, bran, and gluten. In this case you will have to try again with a different type of whole wheat flour.

After about 6 rinses, the dough should become rubbery gluten. Remaining specks of bran or starch can be rinsed away under the tap by pulling the gluten apart and exposing the inside. Pull off balls, or form gluten into patties, and drop them into a broth made of water, soy sauce, and kombu sea vegetable. You may also add a variety of seasonings to the broth in order to add additional flavors to the cooked seitan. (More information on these seasonings is presented in chapter, "Using the Seasonings.") You can expect 1″ balls of gluten to require 20 to 30 minutes of cooking to absorb the seasonings and finish cooking.

A wide variety of textures and flavors can be obtained with seitan. This is due to the many types of gluten and seasonings you can use. Another determining factor in your success with seitan will be the method of cooking you choose.

For most types of seitan, slow simmering is best. Heat that is too high, resulting in

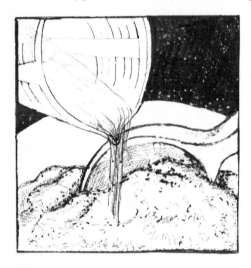

Fig. 1   Add water to the flours and mix.

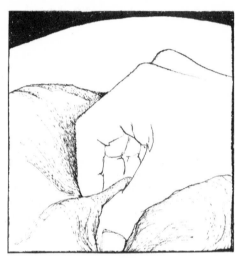

Fig. 2   Knead the dough.

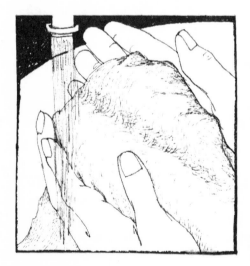

Fig. 3   Pick up a section of dough with both hands, squeezing gently under running water.

Fig. 4   Pour the starch water into a measuring cup.

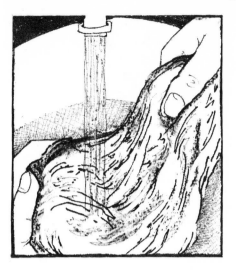

Fig. 5   Gluten and water in the bowl—
midway through the process of
extracting gluten from wheat
flour.

Fig. 6   Pull and stretch the gluten
vigorously under running water.

Fig. 7   Knead the finished mound of
gluten in a colander.

boiling, will create a more spongy seitan. Although this type of seitan is usable, many people find a chewy texture (produced by slow simmering) more delicious.

The following recipes were selected for their ease of preparation and adaptability to many types of meals.

Simmered Cutlets or Cubes

    2 cups uncooked seitan

For the Broth:

    4 cups water
    1/4 to 1/2 cup natural soy sauce (for stronger tasting broth use 1/2 cup)
    3″ piece kombu
    1 tablespoon sesame oil
    4″ to 6 1/8″ slices fresh ginger root

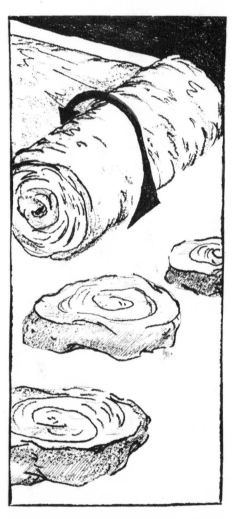

Fig. 8   **Stretch out the uncooked seitan.**

Fig. 9   **Roll up the uncooked seitan into a cylinder, then slice it.**

- Slice the seitan into 6 slices each ½″ thick, or 10 to 12 slices each about ¼″ thick. When cooked, these will be almost doubled in thickness.

Note: Uncooked seitan may also be cubed before cooking, when it is to be used in stews or skewered dishes, or other recipes calling for cubes. Their edges are sharper looking than those cut from larger pieces of precooked seitan. The taste is not affected, but when I plan ahead for kebabs or stew, I usually cut the seitan into cubes before cooking. It gives a better appearance to the dish as a whole and in this way improves the flavor.

- Bring the water and kombu to a boil and remove the pot from the heat. Add the sesame oil, soy sauce, and ginger.

- Heat the seasoned broth to a low boil and Reduce the heat. And add the seitan slices one by one. The seitan may also be cut up into small pieces.

- Partially cover the pot and simmer the seitan for about 2 hours. Very few bubbles should be evident in the simmering broth. Boiling the cutlets will result in a texture which is "spongy." Stir the pieces occasionally by lifting and repositioning them gently. After about 2 hours, most or all of the broth will be absorbed into the cutlet pieces. If any remains, save it for flavoring gravies or other sauces or soups. Even when the pieces are well-cooked, they may be fairly soft and tender. At this point they are still very fragile, so handle them carefully—they will become more firm as they cool. This is best done by allowing the seitan pieces to remain in the broth until they are cool, so it will be easier to remove them without breaking them.

Easy Pinto Bean Soup with Seitan Dumplings ────────

The seitan cooks right in the soup for a hearty crowd-pleaser.
Serves 8 to 12 (and freezes well)

1 cup uncooked seitan 1, 2, or 3

4 cups cooked pinto beans
6 cups broth from cooking pinto beans OR
2 cups uncooked pinto beans and
7 to 8 cups water (see cooking instructions for beans, below)
2″ piece kombu
2 1/2 tablespoons sesame oil
2 garlic cloves, crushed and minced
1 to 1 1/2 cups yellow onion, diced (1 medium)
2 cups celery, diced (2 stalks)
1 to 1 1/2 cups carrot, diced (1 medium to large carrot)
1 teaspoon salt
1 teaspoon basil
1 tablespoon natural soy sauce
1 cup collard greens, with stems (leaves cut 1/2″ square, stems cut 1/4″, tightly packed)

Cook the Beans: Soak the beans overnight in water to cover. Drain, and cook with 7 to 8 cups water and the kombu. Cooking may be by boiling for about 1½ hours, or pressure cooking 45 minutes to 1 hour. Do not add salt until specified.

• In a heavy soup pot, heat the oil and garlic briefly, then add the onion. Sauté over a medium heat until the onion is slightly browned. Add the celery and carrots and sauté together for about 5 minutes. Add the broth and the cooked beans, and the salt, basil and natural soy sauce. Bring to a slow boil.

• Holding the seitan in one hand, use the other to break off very small pieces no larger than ½". Roll each piece between thumb and fingers before gently dropping into the slowly boiling soup. Stir occasionally while adding the seitan to prevent the pieces from sticking together in the soup. (Stir after adding each 10 pieces.)

• Reduce the heat, cover and simmer 20 to 30 minutes or more. About 10 minutes before serving, add the cut up collard greens to the soup. Do not mix them in, but let them rest on top of the soup in order to steam. Mix through once, just before serving.

Make a great meal with Pinto Bean Soup, a fresh salad and some crusty French bread.

Minnesota-Style Seitan Salad ─────────────────

This is the salad to use in sandwiches or to stuff into a juicy tomato, resting on a bed of tender Boston or Bibb lettuce. This is an easy and delicious way to use your leftover "roast" or seitan cutlets.
Serves 4

> 2 cups cooked seitan, cutlets or cubes
>
> 1 1/2 cups celery, diced
> 1/2 cup onion, diced
> 1/2 cup sweet red pepper, diced
> 2 tablespoons pimientos, diced 1/4" pieces
> 6 pitted green olives, sliced thin crosswise rounds
> 1/4 cup parsley, minced

For the Dressing:

> 1/2 cup prepared mayonnaise
> 2 teaspoons lemon juice

- Place all the salad ingredients in a mixing bowl. Combine the mayonnaise with the lemon juice. Mix lightly to coat seitan and vegetables with the dressing.

- Serve on Boston or Bibb lettuce, or in sandwiches. A quick and delicious way to use your leftover "roast" or seitan cutlets.

Oven-Braised Stew

This easy-to-prepare stew is really one-pot cooking. The seitan is cooked with the vegetables, eliminating any previous preparation. Serve it at the table from its own cooking pot, with rice or pasta, or in a bowl all by itself accompanied by a crusty whole grain sourdough bread and a crisp green salad.
Serves 4 to 6

2 cups uncooked seitan

1 pound whole small white onions (about 10, 2" onions)
1 tablespoon sesame oil
3 carrots, cut in half lengthwise, then crosswise in 1" pieces
4 cups water
3" piece kombu, broken into tiny pieces
1/4 cup natural soy sauce or to taste
1 tablespoon Seasoning Mix as desired (optional, see Chapter 3)
3 tablespoons thick starch from preparing seitan
1/4 cup minced parsley
2 teaspoons *mirin* or wine (optional)

Note: After you have poured off the starch water during the seitan-making process, let it sit at least 2½ hours, then carefully pour the thin, yellow-colored water into a separate container. This is referred to as "thin starch." What is left in the container is the "thick starch."

- Preheat the oven to 350° F. If the onions are larger than 1" diameter, cut them in half.

- Heat a flameproof, covered baking dish and add the sesame oil. Add the onions, then the carrots and sauté with a medium heat for a few minutes, stirring frequently. Add the water, kombu, and seasonings and bring to a boil. Add the seitan in unformed, broken-off pieces of about 1" diameter. Cover and place the casserole in the oven for about 45 minutes, or until the vegetables are tender. Mix gently at 15 minute intervals.

- Replace the casserole on the stove over a low heat, and add in the starch, parsley, and mirin. Continue to stir gently until the sauce becomes thick and glossy.

Chewy Coconut Puffs ━━━━━━━━━━━━━━━━━━━━━━━━━━━━━

Makes 15 or more. I couldn't keep them around long enough to count.

1 cup uncooked seitan

1/2 cup barley malt syrup
1/4 to 1/2 cup shredded coconut unsweetened

- Preheat the oven to 400° F.

- Cut the seitan into 1″ pieces, and place on a lightly oiled cookie sheet. Bake the puffs for 10 minutes, then turn them over and bake the second side for 10 to 15 minutes or until the puffs feel light inside. Test one—it should resemble a puff made with egg.

- Heat the barley malt and cook on a medium heat for 15 to 20 minutes, stirring frequently to prevent sticking. When the puffs are cooked, dip each one in the hot barley malt, and then roll it immediately in the coconut. Let stand for 5 minutes.

Variation: Add carob powder and vanilla to the barley malt.

Creating Seitan from Wheat Flour

Seeing is deceiving. It's eating that's believing.—James Thurber (1894–1961),
Further Fables for Our Times

Although commercially made seitan is available, and in fact can be used in many delicious dishes, there are many advantages to making your own seitan. In addition to the economic advantage (commercial seitan will cost at least three times more than homemade), there is the advantage of flexibility. By choosing your own combination of flours, you have a much greater variety of seitan available.

Seitan is always, by definition, made from a high-gluten wheat flour, but this flour may be in the form of whole wheat flour, unbleached white flour, or extracted gluten flour. These flours may be used alone or in combination, but the initial seitan preparation follows the same general process regardless of the flour used.

You will find that, with the many combinations of flours given, you will be able to create a vast array of flavors and textures that is not possible when using precooked, commercially prepared seitan.

Choosing the correct flour to use for making seitan is essential to the success of your seitan making experience. I have found that hard red winter wheat flour works well, but other cooks will recommend spring wheat flour. Whole wheat flours that are available in supermarkets are generally adequate. If you prefer an organic flour, request it from your natural food store managers. Some stores have a bulk "bread flour" which may be good for bread but for various reasons may not be suitable for making seitan.

I have had many experiences in which an entire batch of seitan has failed because the flour was not right. The safest thing to do is to buy one or two cups of several types of wheat flour (except pastry flour—it has practically no gluten at all), labeling each one to identify its type and place of purchase, and then make a small sample batch of seitan from each one. When you do this, you don't have to cook them separately—the purpose of the experiment is only to determine how well each one "sticks together" when uncooked, and which gives you the smoothest texture. After determining which flour yields the firmest, smoothest gluten, as well as which gives you the largest quantity of gluten for the amount of flour used, make a note of it for future purchases.

Preparation of the gluten for making seitan occurs in four phases: 1) mixing the flour with water, 2) kneading the flour and water into a dough similar to bread dough, 3) resting the dough, and 4) rinsing the dough to separate the starch and bran from the gluten. Most commonly, the gluten is cooked soon after its preparation, and this is the substance called "seitan." For simplicity, I usually refer to the uncooked gluten as "uncooked seitan."

Using Seitan in the Recipes

The recipes given in chapters, "Appetizers" through "Desserts," utilize most of the various types of seitan listed below. If you do not have on hand the exact amounts of whole wheat and unbleached white flours to make a particular type of seitan, try it anyway. In most cases, slight variations in proportions will not make a major difference in the end result.

Most of the recipes in this book suggest a type of seitan to be used, but these are generally interchangeable. The few cases where substitution is not recommended will be indicated as such.

Various Types of Seitan

Seitan Number	Contains These Flours	Most Often Used In
1	Whole wheat and unbleached white flour	Cutlets, cubes, grinding and deep-frying
2	Unbleached white flour only	Pouches, or other dishes needing a very stretchable type of gluten to be used as a "wrapper"
3	Whole wheat flour only	Cutlets, cubes, grinding and deep-frying
4	Whole wheat, unbleached white and gluten flour	Cutlets, cubes, pan-frying and deep-frying (more chewy texture than (1 or 3) Best gluten to be used in recipes calling for "ground seitan"
5	Unbleached white flour, gluten flour	Use in place of 4 when either whole wheat or white flour is unavailable
6	Whole wheat flour, gluten flour	
7	Gluten flour only (very stiff dough)	Braised seitan "pepperoni"
8	Gluten flour only (less stiff than 7)	Use as 6
9	Gluten flour only (very soft dough)	Deep-fried puffs and dumplings, seasoned or unseasoned (unless otherwise indicated), and which may or may not be cooked in a broth
10	Gluten flour only—with soymilk (soft type dough)	
11	Use equal parts gluten 2 and 3	Braised seitan "roasts"

Note: "Featherweight" and "Walnot Acres" brands of gluten flour are not recommended for these recipes.

Making Seitan Using Whole Wheat Flour, Unbleached White Flour, or Both

Seitan 1

Using both whole wheat and unbleached white flour, this is an all-purpose gluten usually specified in recipes using cutlets, cubes, grinding, and deep-frying.

Makes $2\frac{1}{2}$ cups uncooked seitan

      4 cups whole wheat flour
      4 cups unbleached white flour
      3 1/2 to 4 cups water

Makes 5 cups uncooked seitan

      8 cups whole wheat flour
      8 cups unbleached white flour
      7 to 8 cups water

Seitan 2

Using unbleached white flour only, this type of seitan is specified in recipes for pouches, or other dishes needing a very stretchable type of gluten to be used as a wrapper. It is usually not interchangeable.

Makes $2\frac{1}{2}$ cups uncooked seitan

      8 cups unbleached white flour
      4 to 5 cups water

Makes 5 cups uncooked seitan

      16 cups unbleached white flour
      8 to 9 cups water

Seitan 3

Using whole wheat flour only, this is another all-purpose seitan which is specified for dishes using cutlets, cubes, grinding, and deep-frying.

Makes $2\frac{1}{2}$ cups uncooked seitan

      8 cups whole wheat flour
      5 1/2 cups water

Makes 5 cups uncooked seitan

> 16 cups whole wheat flour
> 11 cups water

Note: All the varieties of gluten made from whole wheat flour, unbleached white flour, or both are made in basically the same way.

For preparing gluten, or "uncooked seitan," it will be helpful to use a mixing bowl which is at least four inches taller than the size of the dough it is to contain, although it should be able to fit into your kitchen sink for most efficient processing. A large stainless steel mixing bowl (12 qt) is adequate for making the larger amounts of seitan listed above, and will be very comfortable for the smaller amounts, but smaller bowls of course may be used. Do not use a wooden bowl as it could be damaged by the time it spends in water.

Put all the flour for the batch of dough into the bowl. For seitan 1, which uses two types of flour, the flours should be well blended with a fork prior to adding the water. Add the water 1 to 2 cups at a time, and mix well with a spoon or paddle after each addition. When all the water has been added, begin to mix with one hand while holding the bowl steady with the other. Doing this in the sink will make it easier to add more water as needed it to prevent excessive dough from sticking to your mixing hand.

Begin to knead and continue for 50 or 60 strokes using a motion in which a generous handful of the dough is scooped up from the bottom of the bowl and placed on top of the dough in the bowl, to be pushed down firmly with the mixing hand. Rotate the bowl a few inches between kneading strokes to achieve thorough mixing.

Let the dough rest for 20 to 30 minutes. If you have to leave the dough for a longer period of time, cover the dough with a damp cloth, as if leaving bread to rise. It is during this time that the gluten undergoes further development, so be sure to allow *at least 20 minutes* at this point. If the gluten does not develop well, much of it may simply turn into batter and wash away in the next phase. After the resting period, knead the dough again, with damp hands, for 20 strokes. You should be able to notice that the consistency of the dough, while still fairly soft, is much more dense than before.

It is during the rinsing that you will actually separate the gluten from the starch and bran. Put the bowl in the sink and run lukewarm water into the bowl at the edge of the mound of dough. Fill the bowl with water.

Begin to manipulate the dough by lifting a section of it in both hands and compressing it gently but firmly between the palms. Repeat this about 15 times, then run more water slowly into the bowl. Repeat this squeezing motion under the stream of water, picking up a new section of dough every so often and squeezing it under the running water. Turn off the water, or direct it away from the bowl, and continue to pick up dough from the bottom and compress it a few times between the palms. The water should now be very thick and white. Pour it off into a large measuring cup and pour from the measuring cup into a large glass jar. If you have extra jars, you can save up to 3 to 4 gallons of this "starch water" which will, in about 2 hours time, separate into layers, the top of which may be poured off. Repeat this method of filling the bowl with water, squeezing the dough thoroughly, and pouring off the milky starch water. You may want to save only the water from the first 1 or 2 bowlfuls. (See Appendix for extensive information on "Saving and Using Wheat Starch.")

After two complete cycles, the dough can be treated much more vigorously. Continue to squeeze the dough under gently running water. As you observe the developing gluten, which you can recognize by its stringy, elastic qualities, increase the strength of the water stream and the vigor of your squeezing until you are really stretching and pulling the gluten in all possible directions. You may alternate water temperatures, are warmer water makes the gluten softer and cold water makes it more rubbery. The gluten will develop into a cohesive mass more quickly as more clear water is worked into the dough, so keep the water running or change it often. As soon as you feel the separate pieces of gluten holding together, the rest should stick to it.

Note: If you feel the dough break up into what feels like lumpy batter, the gluten is not so strong, so you will have to be very gentle with the dough in order to make the gluten stay together. Watch it carefully as you knead it; within a few minutes after beginning to wash the dough, you should be able to observe the stringy gluten appearing. If it does not look this way, wash the dough only by small handfuls, very carefully directly under slowly running water, and put whatever amount of gluten you are able to salvage directly into a colander. When the whole amount of dough has been treated in this way and all the gluten is in the colander, proceed to wash the gluten all together with a little more strength. In this way the gluten should be able to proceed normally. If it does not, and you lose the whole batch, don't be discouraged. Try again with a different type of flour, or knead it a little more, or let it rest a little more, or use a little less water when mixing the dough initially.

When the gluten has formed a fairly solid mass, and instead of any small loose pieces floating about, it is all quite elastic and holding together well, put it into a colander with large holes (not a strainer) and finish the rinsing process this way, as most of the starch and bran has been either saved or discarded. The remaining kneading is to remove any traces of starch or bran which are still evident. Squeeze the seitan firmly, away from running water. Any water which comes out of it should be almost clear. When it is ready to use, the gluten will be shiny and have a firm, somewhat rubbery consistency. If there is much starch present in the finished seitan, the texture will not be as good when it is cooked.

In spite of the length of this description, the total time for rinsing need not be more than 20 minutes for a double batch (5 cups seitan), once you have practiced it once or twice.

Making Seitan Using Whole Wheat Flour, Unbleached White Flour, and Gluten Flour ————————————

Seitan 4

Using whole wheat flour, unbleached white flour, and gluten flour, this seitan is very similar to seitan 1, but the firmer texture makes this variety better-suited for recipes using ground seitan. This type of gluten is also excellent to use in cutlets, cubes, pan-frying and deep-frying.

Makes 2 cups uncooked seitan

> 1 1/3 cups whole wheat flour
> 1 1/3 cups unbleached white flour
> 2/3 cup gluten flour
> 2 to 2 1/2 cups water

Makes 6 cups uncooked seitan

> 4 cups whole wheat flour
> 4 cups unbleached white flour
> 2 cups gluten flour
> 6 to 7 1/2 cups water

Seitan 5

Use this type of seitan in place of seitan 6, when whole wheat flour is unavailable.

Makes 3 cups uncooked seitan—a very soft, sticky dough

> 3 cups unbleached white flour
> 3/4 cup gluten flour
> 3 3/4 cups water

Seitan 6

Use this type of seitan in place of seitan 5, when unbleached white flour is unavailable.

Makes 1½ cups uncooked seitan

> 3/4 cup whole wheat flour
> 3/4 cup gluten flour
> 3/4 cup water

Seitan 4, 5, and 6 are all made in the same way. Combine the flours with a fork until they are well blended. Add the water gradually while mixing vigorously. Knead for 50 strokes, wetting your hands frequently to prevent sticking. Let the dough rest for about 20 minutes, then proceed to rinse and knead the dough as indicated in the general directions.

Making Seitan Using Only Gluten Flour ——————————

Seitan 7—a very stiff dough

This type of seitan is most often recommended to be used in "Braised Seitan Pepperoni." It has a very firm, chewy texture.

Makes 2½ cups uncooked seitan

>   2 cups gluten flour
>   1 1/4 cups water or cool, seasoned stock

Seitan 8

Use this type of seitan in deep-fried puffs and dumplings, seasoned or unseasoned.

Makes 2 cups uncooked seitan

>   2 cups gluten flour
>   2 cups water or cool, seasoned stock

Seitan 9

Use this type of seitan in deep-fried puffs, and seasoned or unseasoned dumplings.

Makes 3½ to 4 cups

>   2 cups gluten flour
>   4 cups water or cool, seasoned stock

Seitan 10

Use this type of seitan in deep-fried puffs, and seasoned or unseasoned dumplings.

Makes 3 cups soft uncooked seitan

>   2 cups gluten flour
>   1 cup plain soymilk
>   2 cups water or cool, seasoned stock
>   3 tablespoons natural soy sauce
>   1 tablespoon sesame (or other) oil

When making seitan 7, 8, 9, or 10, which all use only gluten flour, make a well in the center of the flour and add the combined liquids all at once. When any season-ings or oil are indicated to be used in making the gluten, mix them in with the gluten flour before adding any liquids.

Mix immediately and vigorously with a fork. When the dough is too thick or stiff to continue mixing with the fork, use your hands to knead or mix it for 10 to 15 strokes. Let the dough rest 2 to 5 minutes, then knead it again for just a few strokes. With gluten flour there is nothing to wash away, because the gluten has already been isolated. Allow the dough to rest about 15 minutes before cooking.

Using a Food Processor to Make the Dough

Some people prefer to prepare the dough in a food processor or other kneading machine rather than by hand. This is fine, and in fact will give you excellent results. But although it allows you to knead the dough more quickly, it may take almost as long to clean the machine afterwards as it does to knead the dough by hand. If you do use a food processor, make the batch of seitan in two parts; simply divide all the ingredients in half and do it twice.

The following recipe is for half-proportions—you will have to follow the directions twice to make the usual 2 to 2½ cups of uncooked seitan for use in subsequent recipes.

Half-Proportions for Mixing in a Food Processor

Makes 1 to 1¼ cups uncooked seitan

> 2 cups whole wheat flour
> 2 cups unbleached white flour
> 1 3/4 to 2 cups water

Put the flours into the bowl of the machine and turn it on and off once to mix the flours before adding the water. Add 1¾ cups of water and mix for about 1½ minutes. Stop the machine and push down the dough as needed. Add water up to 2 cups total (including what is already in the dough) and process for about 30 seconds more.

Note: These are very general directions. Methods may vary according to the type of food processor you use. What you want to achieve is a smooth, elastic dough, not too firm and not too soft. Amounts of water needed will vary according to the machines and flours being used.

Using the Seasonings

Our apothecary's shop is our garden full of potherbs, and our doctor is a clove of garlic.—Anonymous, *A Deep Snow*, 1615

Much of seitan's versatility is due to its ability to accept any type of seasoning. Depending upon the seasonings and cooking method you choose for the dish you are making with your cooked or uncooked seitan, you will be able to recreate many of your favorite dishes using this remarkable no-cholesterol, high protein food.

The traditional Japanese way of seasoning seitan is to cook it in a broth using kombu sea vegetable, natural soy sauce, and fresh ginger root. This was the first seitan flavor I encountered and is the one taken for granted as the standard "seitan flavor" by commercial seitan makers and most people who are familiar with seitan. This soy sauce seasoning is a good basic seasoning for seitan, as it imparts a slightly salty, robust flavor upon which many variations may be built. Proportions for this basic natural soy sauce broth can be found at the beginning of chapter, "Additional Methods of Cooking."

Included in this section are the proportions for five other seasoning variations. Using these five types of seasonings in your seitan repertoire will vastly increase the variety of tastes and textures you can achieve. These seasonings are usually used as additions to the basic cooking broth. However, other uses include mixing the seasonings into ground seitan and using the seasoning mixes to flavor sauces, cornmeal breadings, and batters. The method needed for each dish is specified in each individual recipe.

Salt-Free, Milder Seasoning

In those instances when you want a less salty or unsalted seitan, such as for people on salt-free diets or for young children, just omit all or part of the natural soy sauce and use kombu sea vegetable and ginger for the seasoning. This will not have as strong a flavor as the fully-seasoned seitan, but all of the same dishes can be prepared, and the textures will not be affected. The taste will be mild and somewhat "wheat-y," and this in itself is also very pleasant.

About the Seasoning Mixes

Each of the following seasoning mixes is presented in three forms. The first set of ingredients refers to the amount recommended to season 2 cups of uncooked seitan, which is the amount most often used in a given recipe.

The second set of ingredients for each seasoning mix refers to making bulk amounts of that seasoning mix. Some recipes call for varying amounts of seasoning. You may want to mix up a bulk amount from which to take the amount you need for a given recipe. The ingredients for these bulk seasonings will total one cup. The amounts of each mix needed to season 2 cups of seitan vary, and are indicated in each seasoning recipe.

The third set of ingredients for each seasoning mix refers to using the mix in a broth, in place of or in addition to the basic natural soy sauce broth. In these cases, you will not be using as much soy sauce, because there is additional salt in the seasoning mix itself. If you are using seitan that has already been cooked in Natural Soy Sauce Broth and you wish to add another seasoning, just simmer it briefly in an unsalted version of the seasoning mix added to water, then proceed with your chosen recipe.

Spicy Seasoning Mix

To season 2 cups uncooked seitan:

> 1/4 teaspoon crushed red pepper
> 2 1/2 teaspoons sage
> 1/2 teaspoon nutmeg
> 1/2 teaspoon dry mustard
> 1/2 teaspoon black pepper
> 4 teaspoons paprika
> 1 1/2 teaspoons salt

Spicy Seasoning Mix—Bulk

Makes 1 cup

For 2 cups seitan, use 3 tablespoons plus ¾ teaspoon seasoning mix, or to taste:

> 1 1/4 teaspoons crushed red pepper
> 4 tablespoons plus 1/2 teaspoon sage
> 2 1/2 teaspoons nutmeg
> 2 1/2 teaspoons dry mustard
> 2 1/2 teaspoons black pepper
> 6 1/2 tablespoons paprika
> 2 tablespoons plus 1 1/4 teaspoons salt

Spicy Seasoning Broth

Add 3 tablespoons and ¾ teaspoon Spicy Seasoning Mix to the following broth:

> 2 cups water
> 3″ piece kombu

2 tablespoons natural soy sauce
2 tablespoons oil, except when deep-frying

Hearty Seasoning Mix

To season 2 cups uncooked seitan:

4 teaspoons parsley flakes
1/2 teaspoon salt
1/2 teaspoon celery seed
1 teaspoon basil
4 1/2 teaspoons paprika
1 1/2 teaspoons thyme
1/4 teaspoon garlic granules OR
1 teaspoon fresh garlic, minced

Hearty Seasoning Mix—Bulk

Makes 1 cup

Use ¼ cup (4 tablespoons) for each 2 cups of seitan:

5 tablespoons plus 1 teaspoon parsley flakes
2 teaspoons salt
2 teaspoons celery seed
1 tablespoon plus 1 teaspoon basil
6 tablespoons paprika
2 tablespoons salt
1 teaspoon garlic powder or granules

Hearty Seasoning Broth

Add 4 tablespoons Hearty Seasoning Mix to the following broth:

4 cups water
4" piece kombu
4 to 6 tablespoons natural soy sauce, or to taste
2 tablespoons oil, except when deep-frying

Savory Seasoning Mix I

To season 2 cups uncooked seitan:

1/2 teaspoon black pepper
1 teaspoon coriander powder
1 teaspoon thyme
1 teaspoon tarragon
1 tablespoon nutritional yeast
1 1/2 teaspoons salt

3/8 teaspoon garlic granules OR
1 1/2 teaspoons minced garlic

Savory Seasoning Mix I—Bulk

Makes 1 cup

Use 2 tablespoons plus 2 teaspoons of the following for each 2 cups of seitan:

1 tablespoon black pepper
2 tablespoons coriander powder
2 tablespoons thyme
2 tablespoons tarragon
6 tablespoons nutritional yeast
3 tablespoons salt
3 1/4 teaspoons garlic granules or garlic powder (or add 1 1/2 teaspoons fresh,
minced garlic to each portion used)

Savory Seasoning Broth I

Add 2 tablespoons plus 2 teaspoons Savory Seasoning Mix I to the following broth:

6 cups water
4" piece kombu
2 tablespoons natural soy sauce
2 tablespoons oil, except when deep-frying

Savory Seasoning Mix II

To season 2 cups uncooked seitan:

1/2 teaspoon black pepper
3/4 teaspoon thyme
1/8 teaspoon tumeric
1/4 teaspoon celery seed
1/4 teaspoon sage
1 teaspoon coriander powder
1/4 teaspoon rosemary
1/4 teaspoon oregano
1 1/8 teaspoons salt

Savory Seasoning Mix II—Bulk

Makes 1 cup

Use 1½ tablespoons for each 2 cups seitan:

1 tablespoon plus 2 1/4 teaspoons back pepper
2 tablespoons plus 2 3/4 teaspoons thyme
1 1/2 teaspoons tumeric

2 3/4 teaspoons celery seed
2 3/4 teaspoons sage
3 tablespoons plus 2 1/4 teaspoons coriander powder
2 3/4 teaspoons rosemary
2 3/4 teaspoons oregano
4 tablespoons plus 3/4 teaspoon salt

Savory Seasoning Broth II

Add 1½ tablespoons Savory Seasoning Mix II to the following broth:

4 cups water
2" piece kombu
1 tablespoon natural soy sauce
2 tablespoons oil, except when deep-frying

Aromatic Seasoning Mix

To season 2 cups uncooked seitan:

3/4 teaspoons salt
1/4 teaspoon black pepper
1 teaspoon cumin
1 teaspoon coriander
1/4 teaspoon garlic granules OR
1 clove fresh garlic, minced
1 teaspoon lemon juice

Aromatic Seasoning Mix—Bulk

Makes 1 cup

Use 1 tablespoon of the following for each 2 cups of seitan:

4 tablespoons salt
1 tablespoon plus 1 1/2 teaspoons black pepper
5 tablespoons plus 2 teaspoons cumin
5 tablespoons plus 2 teaspoons coriander powder
1 tablespoon plus 1 teaspoon garlic powder or granules (or
    add 1 clove garlic, minced, to each individual recipe)
1 teaspoon lemon juice—to be added to each individual recipe

Aromatic Seasoning Broth

Add 1 tablespoon Aromatic Seasoning Mix to the following broth:

4 cups water
2" piece kombu
2 tablespoons natural soy sauce
1 tablespoon oil, except when deep-frying

Additional Methods of Cooking

Cooking is like love. It should be entered into with abandon or not at all.—Harriet van Horne, 1920–

This section concerns the wide variety of cooking methods beyond the basic simmering preparation. Among them you will find variations on basic simmered cutlets, variations of braised seitan "roasts," braised seitan "pepperoni," and recipes for using ground seitan. There is also a detailed section on deep-frying, with information on how to deep-fry uncooked as well as cooked seitan and recipes for various types of batter.

Many recipes will use more than one cooking method. It is through these various methods of cooking that an amazing variety of tastes and textures is made possible. These recipes begin with the requirement for either simmered seitan or uncooked seitan. For this reason, it is convenient to have some seitan on hand to use when you become inspired. After you have made seitan a few times you will have the experience and confidence to make it "from scratch"—at the spur of the moment if need be. In this way, you will easily be able to incorporate homemade seitan into your regular menus.

Simmered Cutlets or Cubes is the easiest method of cooking if you want to make seitan to have on hand, but are not exactly sure how you will be using it.

Thin Pounded Cutlets, a variation of simmered cutlets, produces a different texture altogether.

Braised "Roast," also called "Seitan 11," is a combination of two types of gluten made from whole wheat and unbleached white flours. This method refers to oven-braising, a long, slow method of cooking which results in a very firm loaf that can be thinly sliced or used in other ways.

Spiral Cutlets and Cubes made from Seitan 11 will give you very firm seitan used in dishes requiring ground seitan or seitan which is to be broiled or deep-fried. It is interchangeable with other cutlets and cubes.

"Pepperoni" Seitan refers to cooking and seasoning seitan 7 to result in a vegetarian pepperoni-style sausage.

Pressure-Cooked Seitan can be made when you are in a hurry. By combining it with a few vegetables and using the starch water as a thickener, you can create a nearly instant stew. The only disadvantages to this method are a slightly more spongy texture (from the high heat) and slightly less penetration of seasoning into the seitan (from the shorter cooking time).

Basic Baked Seitan Slices are used as cutlets or fillable pouches.

Ground Seitan is used in cocktail croquettes, patties and burgers, and many types of casserole dishes. Ground seitan is usually made from baked or simmered seitan.

Deep-Frying is useful for a multitude of dishes. It makes the seitan more crispy, more chewy, or more tender depending upon how it is utilized. See the section on Deep-frying and recipes throughout the book for examples. Deep-frying the uncooked seitan before simmering will result in a richer flavored seitan with a texture very different from that of plain simmered seitan.

Simmered Cutlets or Cubes in Natural Soy Sauce Broth ─────────────────────────────

> 2 cups uncooked seitan

For the Broth:

> 4 cups water
> 1/4 to 1/2 cup natural soy sauce (for stronger tasting broth use 1/2 cup)
> 3″ piece kombu
> 1 tablespoon sesame oil
> 4 to 6, 1/8″ slices fresh ginger root

- Slice the seitan into either 6 slices, each ½″ thick, or 10 to 12 slices, each about ¼″ thick. When cooked, these will almost double in thickness.

Note: Uncooked seitan may also be cubed before cooking, to be used in stews or skewered dishes, or other recipes calling for cubes. Their edges are sharper looking than those cut for kebabs or stew, I usually cut the seitan into cubes before cooking. It gives a better appearance to the dish as a whole and in this way improves the flavor.

- When the broth is to be seasoned with one of the seasoning mixes, you will not need the soy sauce and ginger listed above. Bring the water and kombu to a boil, remove the pot from the heat and add the necessary seasonings. Allow the broth to stand for 5 minutes before adding the seitan, then proceed as follows:

- Heat the seasoned broth to a low boil. Reduce the heat and add the seitan slices one by one. The seitan may also be cut up into small pieces.

- Partially cover the pot and simmer for about 2 hours. Very few bubbles should be evident in the simmering broth. Boiling the cutlets will result in a texture which is "spongy." Stir the pieces occasionally by lifting and repositioning them to minimize breakage. After about 2 hours, most or all of the broth will be absorbed into the cutlet pieces. If any remains, save it for flavoring gravies or other sauces or soups. Even when the pieces are well-cooked, they may be fairly soft and tender; at this point they are still very fragile, so handle them carefully. They will become more firm as they cool, which is best done by allowing the seitan pieces to remain in the broth so they will be easier to remove.

Thin Pounded Cutlets in Natural Soy Sauce Broth —————

A variation on Simmered Cutlets

Use slices of uncooked seitan about 3" in diameter by about 1/4" thick.

For the Broth: See Simmered Cutlets or Cubes in Natural Soy Sauce Broth (page 28)

- Use the outside edge of your fist or the palm of your hand to pound the surface of the cutlet lightly with a horizontal sliding movement. This motion doubles the surface area of the cutlet, while making it about half its original thickness. As you pound the seitan, shape the cutlets whichever way you want. Oval or triangular shapes look more interesting after cooking than do round shapes.

- Heat the seasoned broth to boiling, then reduce the heat to *very low*. This very low heat is maintained throughout the cooking time, usually about 1 to 1½ hours. If the heat is too high, the texture of the cutlets will be "spongy." If time allows, let the cutlets remain in the broth to cool at room temperature. Otherwise, refrigerate to cool them.

- A very firm texture is best for deep-fried cutlets that will be cooked again in other recipes calling for pan-fried, or baked cutlets. These firm cutlets will become more tender in the second cooking.

Braised "Roast" Seitan 11 ——————

For the Broth:

    4 cups water
    4" piece kombu
    2 bay leaves
    2 1/2 teaspoons paprika
    1 teaspoon parsley flakes

1/2 cup natural soy sauce
3 tablespoons oil

2 cups uncooked seitan 2 (white flour gluten)
2 cups uncooked seitan 3 (whole wheat flour gluten)

Note: If one of the seasoning mixes is required in a given recipe, omit the bay leaves, paprika, parsley, natural soy sauce, and oil, and use the proportions indicated for the seasoned broth of your choice (see Seasoning Mixes). Increase the seasonings to 1½ times the usual amount.

- Put all the ingredients except the gluten into a flameproof casserole and bring to a boil. Cover and reduce the heat to simmer.

- Knead the two types of gluten together to create a "marbled" effect. This is done by laying the seitan 2 gluten on the work surface and stretching it into a 8″×10″ rectangle. Do the same for seitan 3 gluten, and lay it on top of seitan 2. Roll them together into a cylinder, then start at one end to roll the cylinder into a very tight ball. Pull and twist the gluten, pulling from the inside and firmly "wrapping" it around and over the outside. An elaborate network of gluten will develop. Finally, the white part of the gluten is to be pulled around and over the entire piece in a ball-like shape.

- Preheat the oven to 275° F.

- Place this ball into the hot stock. Simmer the seitan for ½ hour, turning it frequently but other wise keeping the pot covered. Place the pot in the 275° F. oven.

- After 1 hour, make cuts in the gluten 1″ deep and 2″ long. Turn the piece of seitan over and do the same on the other side. Cover and continue to braise for 1 hour. Turn again. Continue to braise for a total of 3½ hours, adding a little water (½ to 1 cup) to the stock as needed. Bast the seitan frequently with the broth.

- At the end of the cooking time, remove the "roast" and reserve any remaining stock, kombu, etc., for use as a seasoning for gravies, sauces, or soups.

Variations on Braised "Roast" Seitan 11 ————

Hickory Roast

2 cups uncooked seitan 2
2 cups uncooked seitan 3

4 cups water
4″ piece kombu
4 tablespoons Liquid Hickory Smoke

        2 tablespoons Spicy Seasoning Mix
        3 tablespoons natural soy sauce

• Form the "roast" according to directions above, and, using the above ingredients for broth, proceed according to directions for Braised "Roast" Seitan 11.

Garlic Roast

        2 cups uncooked seitan 2
        2 cups uncooked seitan 3
        6 cloves garlic, slivered
        3" pickled daikon radish (Japanese *takuan* pickle), slivered (optional)

For the Broth:

        4 cups water
        4" piece kombu
        2 bay leaves
        2 1/2 teaspoons paprika
        1 teaspoon parsley flakes
        1/4 to 1/3 cup natural soy sauce
        3 tablespoons sesame oil

• Form the "roast" according to Braised "Roast" 11. Make a few deep cuts in the seitan, and insert the slivers of garlic and daikon pickle. Proceed to simmer and cook in broth as for Braised "Roast" 11, above.

Spiral Cutlets and Cubes Made from Seitan 11 ────────────

        1 or 2 cups uncooked seitan 2
        1 to 2 cups uncooked seitan 3
        2 to 4 cups broth for simmering, seasoned as desired

• Lay out the unbleached white flour seitan 2 and stretch it to form a rectangle about 8"×10" (if using 1 cup seitan). Place the whole wheat seitan 3 on top of it, and roll tightly away from you, always stretching the white seitan over the whole wheat seitan at the ends. Roll it into a cylinder about 12" long by 3" in diameter. Let the seitan roll rest on a damp surface or plate (it may stick to a dry or rough surface), seam side down, for about 10 minutes while the broth is being prepared.

• Cook the cutlets using one of the following methods:

1. Slice into rounds ½" thick, and pound or press flat with the palm of your hand. Cook as for simmered cutlets in the broth of your choice.
2. Cut into 1" cubes (or cut 1" slices and quarter each one), and cook as for simmered cubes, to be ground or used in stews, and kebabs.

3.   Deep-fry without batter, then blot with paper towels and simmer in the broth of your choice. Use as cutlets, or in sandwiches. This method makes very rich-tasting, juicy cutlets.

Seitan Pepperoni 7

Makes 4, 8″ to 9″ spicy seitan "sausage links"

>   2 cups gluten flour
>   1 recipe (or 3 tablespoons plus 3/4 teaspoon) Spicy Seasoning Mix
>   8 tablespoons (1/2 cup) oil
>   1 cup water
>   4 yards cotton string

For the Stock:

>   4 cups water
>   2 tablespoons natural soy sauce
>   4″ piece kombu

● Combine the spices with the gluten flour. Drizzle the oil over the surface of the seasoned flour and mix in well with a fork. Pour the water slowly over the flour-oil

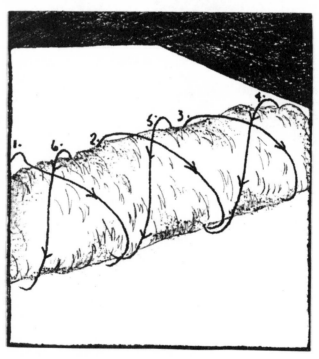

Fig. 10   **Wrap a cotton string around the uncooked seitan, following arrows 1 to 6.**

mixture, working rapidly with a fork so all the ingredients are moistened. Knead well to blend. Divide both the dough and string into 4 equal parts.

● Flatten and then roll up each of the 4 pieces of seitan into a cylinder. Wrap each piece of uncooked seitan with the string to maintain the cylindrical shape. Wrap the string around the cylinder in a spirallic line, then cross it in the opposite direction using the same winding motion. See illustration Fig. 10.

● Preheat the oven to 400° F.

● Heat the broth to a low boil in a heavy covered flameproof casserole. Reduce the heat to low, add the seitan and simmer 20 minutes to ½ hour.

● Bake for 20 minutes then lower the oven heat to 275°F. Turn the links every 20 minutes until most of the broth is absorbed. When turning for the last time, dribble 1 teaspoon of oil over the top of each one. Remove the cover and bake 15 minutes more, turning every 5 minutes for even browning. Very little broth should remain.

● These cylinders will more than double in size while cooking, so select a pot large enough to accommodate the finished pieces. Allow the seitan to cool thoroughly before carefully removing the string.

Pressure-Cooked Seitan

This method of cooking gives a more soft-textured seitan.

> 4 cups uncooked seitan
>
> 6 to 8 cups water
> 4" piece kombu
> 1" fresh ginger root, sliced thin
> 1/2 cup natural soy sauce

● Bring all broth ingredients to boil, and add the seitan in pieces about the size of golf balls. Pieces may also be larger, smaller, or sliced, as you wish. When pressure has been reached, reduce the heat to a simmer and cook about 1 hour.

● Reduce the pressure by placing the pot in the sink and running cold water over the top. Do not remove the weight or open the cover until all pressure has been released. Allow the seitan to cool in the broth for 20 to 30 minutes. The seitan will become firmer as it cools.

Variation:

● For a quick stew, pressure-cook the seitan in bite-size pieces or balls 2" in diameter. After cooking, release the pressure and add vegetables of your choice. Simmer until the vegetables are tender, or pressure-cook once more for 2 to 5 minutes, depending upon the vegetables you use.

- Add about ¼ cup thick wheat starch flavored with mirin, garlic, and natural soy sauce, to taste. Stir over a medium heat until thick and garnish with slivered scallions. Adjust the thickness with more starch or more water as needed.

Baked Seitan Slices

Use as fillable pouches, cutlets, or grind for patties or croquettes.

2 cups uncooked seitan 4

- Preheat the oven to 400° F.

- Form the seitan into a cylinder and cut it into 8, ½″ slices. Place the slices on a lightly oiled cookie sheet and bake about 10 minutes. Turn the pieces over, lightly oiling the cookie sheet under each one before replacing it. Bake 15 minutes more.

Pouches: Cut a baked seitan slice in half crosswise, and open it out. Fill with one of the seitan "patés" or a mixture of vegetables and grains. Filling baked seitan pouches is a good way to use leftover grains and vegetables.

- After filling the pouch, pinch the edges together and secure with 1 or 2 tooth-picks, as if sewing the pouch shut.

- Place the pouches on a steamer over ½″ water, and steam for 5 minutes. Pouches can be served simply in packed lunches and picnics, or more elaborately with a sauce.

Cutlets: Simmer the baked slices in the broth of your choice for 15 minutes, then bake or broil them. These may be served chilled, and used in sandwiches or salads, or added to cooked vegetables.

Ground Seitan: Bake small pieces, or cut up baked slices. Use a blender or food processor to make a coarse, crumbly texture. Be careful not to over-process; the seitan should not be too fine. Use seasonings and further instructions according to the results desired.

Ground Seitan Cocktail Croquettes ━━━━━━━━━

Makes about 20, 1″ croquettes

> 2 cups cooked seitan 4, (see Simmered Cutlets with Natural Soy Sauce Broth)
>
> 1 tablespoon seasoning mix, or to taste
> 2 tablespoons whole wheat pastry flour
> 1/4 cup (4 tablespoons) chickpea flour
> 2 tablespoons oil (if baking) OR
> Oil for deep-frying

- Grind the cooled, cooked seitan. Mix the ground seitan with the remaining ingredients. Do not use oil in the mixture if you intend to deep-fry the seitan balls.

- Form the seasoned seitan mixture into 1″ balls and deep-fry until golden-brown. Then place on a few paper towels to remove excess oil.

- If you are planning to bake the croquettes instead of deep-frying them, preheat the oven to 350° F. Bake for 20 minutes, until brown and firm. They may seem somewhat dry, but this is because they are intended for use as follows:

  - with a dip

  - in a salad

  - as garnish in a soup

  - served with a sauce

  - mixed with steamed vegetables

Ground Seitan "Sausage Patties" ━━━━━━━━━

Makes about 16 small patties

> 1 1/2 cups uncooked seitan 6
>
> 2 cups water
> 1 tablespoon natural soy sauce
> 2″ piece kombu
> 3 tablespoons plus 3/4 teaspoon Sausage Seasoning Mix (or use single-use proportions)
> 2 tablespoons sesame oil (if baking)
> 5 tablespoons chickpea flour
> Oil for deep-frying

- Cut the uncooked seitan into small pieces and simmer in the water, natural soy sauce, and kombu for about ½ hour or more. Drain the seitan and allow it to cool to room temperature (it may be refrigerated and stored in the broth for future use).

● Grind the drained seitan coarsely in a blender or food processor. Combine it with the sausage seasoning mix, sesame oil, and chickpea flour.

Three Methods of Cooking the Seitan Patties:

1.   Shape into the desired size and deep-fry. Remove when golden-brown and place on paper towels to drain.

2.   Shape into the desired size and bake at 400° F. for 25 minutes. Turn the patties over and continue to bake 5 minutes more.

My favorite way is:

3.   Bake as above, then pan-fry in 1 to 2 tablespoons sesame oil for a few minutes on each side. Add ½ to ¾ cup water and steam over a medium-low heat for 2 to 5 minutes or until all the water is gone. This gives a delicious texture, along with a "steamed-in flavor."

About Deep-Frying

Deep-frying can be done easily, neatly, and healthfully if a few simple procedures are followed. Most importantly, be organized. Make the batter (if batter is used) and have all food to be deep-fried ready to cook before you heat the oil. A cookie tray with 3 or 4 layers of paper towels on it is essential to have on hand, ready to receive the hot cooked foods. Try to plan your first attempt at deep-frying for a time when there will be a minimum of distractions.

Clean-up is also easy if you wipe up any oil spatters on your stove as soon as you finish cooking. A wet, soapy sponge will remove all traces of the oil and you can dry the stove with a sheet of paper towel or a cloth.

The oil should be kept fresh, that is, not used more than twice or, at the most three times if cooking sessions are brief. To ensure the freshness of the oil, do not overheat it. If it becomes very dark, thick and "sticky," it should be discarded.

Fig. 11   Saving used deep-frying oil in a jar.

One way to prolong the life and usefulness of your deep-frying oil is to not allow it to smoke during use. Another method of oil preservation is to strain it after each use. (See illustration.) Use one sheet of *strong* paper towel attached with a rubber band to a clean glass jar or plastic container. Attach the paper towel loosely, so when you pour in the oil the paper towel will automatically form a cone shape and the oil will easily drip down into the jar. Do not pour too much oil in at once. When you are done, remove the paper towel, cover the container and refrigerate.

This strained oil may be used in baking, sautéing, and in salad dressings if it does not have a strong taste.

Deep-Frying Uncooked Seitan Without Batter

Determining the Temperature of the Oil:

Use 2 to 4 inches of safflower or a light corn oil for deep-frying.

To test the temperature of the oil, drop in a tiny piece of the seitan. The oil is the correct temperature if the seitan sinks to the bottom and *immediately* rises to float and spin gently on the surface of the oil, surrounded by tiny bubbles. Food which is deep-fried in fresh oil of the correct temperature will be crispy (not burned or soggy) on the outside and tender (not raw or wet) on the inside. Excess oil will be absorbed by the paper towels, and the food will be very lightly oiled, not greasy.

If the piece of food does not rise immediately but lays on the bottom of the pot, the oil is too cool. If this happens food will not be crispy on the outside and cooked on the inside; instead, it will be damp and soggy throughout and saturated with oil.

The oil is too hot if it is smoking, or if the piece of food stays on top and spins or moves around very fast. This will not only ruin the oil, but the food will become overdone on the outside and undercooked in the center.

To Deep-fry the Uncooked Seitan:

1. Squeeze *uncooked seitan* firmly to remove excess water. Sometimes it may be necessary to pat it quickly with a paper or cloth towel.

2. Lower the seitan carefully into the oil—don't drop it in.

3. Hold the seitan under the oil for a minute with a pair of forks or chopsticks. Uncooked seitan will puff up dramatically in all directions, but will deflate somewhat as it cools. The shape may be controlled while the seitan is cooking in the oil by gently pulling outward from the center, with one fork or chopstick in each hand. Further instruction on shaping in this way is indicated in the various recipes. (See Robai.)

4. Turn the piece over and repeat as in step 3.

5.   Cook in the hot oil approximately 1 to 1½ minutes on the first side, and ½ to 1 minute on the second side.

6.   To test for doneness, open a piece and examine the center. In a cutlet-sized piece it will be neither dry nor wet but will slightly resemble the inside of a popover—somewhat moist and elastic looking. The outside should be a golden-brown color.

Deep-Frying Using Batter

Test oil for the correct temperature by dropping about 1 teaspoon of the batter into the hot oil. If it sinks and immediately rises to spin gently over the surface of the oil, the oil is ready to use. Do not overheat the oil or allow it to smoke.

1.   Chill the batter for a more crispy coating.

2.   Remove the excess liquid from cutlets or cubes to be deep-fried by draining them, then pressing firmly between 2 pads of paper towel. This can only be done with cooked seitan.

3.   Cook 1 cutlet at a time (or 5 to 8 cubes, depending upon their size). Coat the seitan well with the batter and carefully lower it into the hot oil. Deep-fry *approximately* 3 minutes on the first side and 2 minutes on the second side, or until crispy and golden. Remove to blot on a pad of paper towels.

Deep-Fried Cutlets

Pounded, deep-fried, simmered briefly, breaded, then broiled—it sounds like a lot, but it's really quite simple.

Makes 4 to 8 thick cutlets

>   2 cups uncooked seitan (your choice of seitan)

For the Broth:

>   4 to 5 cups seasoned broth
>   1/4 to 1/2 cup starch from preparing seitan (more or less, as desired)

• Form the seitan into a cylinder and cut it into 4 to 8 slices each ½" thick. Use the outside edge of your fist to stretch each cutlet, pounding with a sliding motion. Drop ¼ teaspoon natural soy sauce on the cutlet surface, fold over, and continue to pound and stretch. Repeat 3 or 4 times. The final size will be about 2½"×4", and ⅛" to ¼" thick.

- Lower the cutlet carefully into the hot oil. It will expand up to ½" thick. (See Instructions for Deep-Frying.)

- Heat the broth. Set aside the starch to use for thickening the broth which remains after cooking the cutlets. Partially cover the cutlets, and simmer for 10 to 15 minutes. Remove, drain, and chill the cutlets.

- Dredge the chilled cutlets in corn meal or corn flour, seasoned as you desire.

- Broil the cutlets 1 minute. Press down on the cutlet with your spatula, turn, and broil 1 minute on the other side. Repeat for ½ minute on each side.

- If you have 1 to 1½ cups of broth left, heat it and add the wheat starch, stirring constantly until it is smooth. Adjust thickness and seasoning to taste.

Batter for Deep-Frying—Whole Wheat and Corn Flour

Makes 2 to 2¾ cups batter

1 cup whole wheat pastry flour
1/2 cup corn flour
1 teaspoon salt
1 tablespoon arrowroot flour
1 1/4 cups water

- Blend all the dry ingredients well with a fork. Mix in the water. Refrigerate the batter for 10 to 30 minutes. When you are ready to use the batter, add a little more water as needed to make a batter that will evenly coat the seitan or vegetable to be deep-fried.

Batter for Deep-Frying—Whole Wheat Flour

Makes about 2½ cups batter

1 1/3 cups whole wheat pastry flour
1 1/4 cups water
1/2 teaspoon salt

- Mix all ingredients together, and let rest 5 minutes before using.

Seasoned Batter for Deep-Frying

Use with 2 cups uncooked seitan or 6 to 10 prepared, simmered cutlets, ¼" to ½" thick.

1 1/2 cups whole wheat pastry flour
3 tablespoons arrowroot flour
2 tablespoons seasoning mix of your choice (if the prepared cutlets are
    cooked with a seasoning mix, use the same one)
1 1/2 cups water

- Blend all the dry ingredients well with a fork. Add the water and mix—a few lumps will not be a problem. Chill the batter for 5 minutes, while the oil is heating.

- Test the oil for correct temperature before using. (See the Basic Instructions for Deep-frying Without Batter.)

Robai

Robai is a type of seitan traditionally used in Japanese temple cooking. It is prepared similarly to seitan deep-fried without batter, but the addition of a small amount of sweet rice flour prevents it from deflating after cooking. You will find the two varieties to be interchangeable in some recipes, but they have qualities which make them very individual as well.

For each 1/2 cup of uncooked seitan 1, use 1 tablespoon very fine sweet rice
    flour (*mochiko,* Japanese white sweet rice flour, is available in Oriental food
    stores and is ideal for this purpose)
Oil for deep-frying.

- Sprinkle the piece of uncooked seitan and the kneading surface with the sweet rice flour. Vigorously knead the flour into the seitan, until all the flour from the kneading surface has been absorbed. Let the dough rest 5 minutes.

- Heat the oil, and stretch the seitan to about 7″ in diameter. Do not worry about any holes that may develop—they will become crispy as they cook. Lower the piece of seitan into the oil. Use two chopsticks or two forks, one in each hand, to stretch the dough to about 9″ in diameter as it cooks. This should be done fairly quickly, within the first 30 seconds or so of cooking. The dough will puff up quickly, and then continue to expand more slowly in all directions. When one side looks golden, turn the entire piece over to cook the second side. This step may then be repeated to ensure thorough cooking.

Appetizers

Strange to see how a good dinner and feasting reconciles everybody.—Samuel Pepys, 1633–1703, *Diary*

Corn Doggies

Delicious and easy to make, these treats are a favorite with snackers of all ages. Serve them alone, or with a dip of your choice.

Makes 20 pieces

> 2 cups cooked seitan (your choice), cut into 2" cubes
> Oil for deep-frying

For the Batter:

> 3/4 cup whole wheat pastry flour
> 1/4 cup corn flour
> 2 tablespoons arrowroot flour
> 1/2 cup water
> 1 medium egg

For Dredging:
- After dipping each piece in the batter, coat it with the following mixture.

> 1 cup cornmeal, seasoned WITH
> 1 teaspoon Aromatic Seasoning Mix (optional), OR
> 1/2 teaspoon salt

- Pat the pieces of cooled, cooked seitan between pieces of paper towel to dry them.

- Combine all the batter ingredients until smooth, and allow the batter to rest for 10 minutes or so. During this time, heat the oil for deep-frying and mix the dry ingredients.

- Dip the seitan, 1 piece at a time, in the batter. Gently shake off the excess batter, and immediately roll the piece of seitan in the seasoned cornmeal. Lower it into the hot oil. Proceed with 4 or 5 pieces at a time, depending upon the size of the deep-fry pot. Add the seitan to the oil one piece at a time. Pay careful attention to the temperature of the oil so the cornmeal coating does not burn.

- Remove the pieces from the oil when they are golden and crispy. Do not brown them, as this will give a bitter flavor.

- Serve with Barbecue Sauce IV or other dip.

Barbecue Sauce IV ——————————————————

Use this sauce as a dip for Corn Doggies.

Makes about 1 cup

> 1/4 cup red or mugi miso
> 1/4 cup tomato paste
> 1/4 cup grated onion (about 1/2 medium onion)
> 2 cloves garlic, crushed and minced well
> 2 tablespoons olive oil
> 1/4 cup cider vinegar
> 1/4 cup barley malt syrup
> 1/4 teaspoon dry mustard
> 1/4 teaspoon allspice

- Combine the miso, tomato paste, and grated onion, mixing thoroughly. Mix in the garlic and olive oil, then the cider vinegar. Add the barley malt syrup, mixing vigorously. Blend in the mustard and allspice.

- Allow the sauce to remain at room temperature for ½ hour before using, to allow the flavors to blend.

Green and Golden Spirals ——————————————

Crispy and chewy, these spiral rolls make good snacking any time.

1 cup of uncooked seitan makes 24 pieces

> 1 cup uncooked seitan 1
>
> 4 leaves bok choy, swiss chard, or spinach (each about 4″×4″)
> Oil for deep-frying
> 1/2 cup Mustard Sauce for dipping (see page 165)

- Wash the vegetable leaves and pat dry. Remove any stem portions, including those which extend into the green part of the leaf, and reserve them to be used in other dishes.

- Divide the seitan into 4 equal sections. Working with one section at a time, carefully stretch the seitan to a shape approximately 4″×4″. Hold the seitan flat with the palm of one hand (or it will immediately curl up), pick up one leaf with the other hand and place it on the surface of the seitan piece, while you keep the seitan stretched flat with your fingers.

- Immediately roll the filled seitan away from you, into a tightly formed cylinder. Tucking in any pieces of protruding leaf while you roll. Press the edges together and lay the cylinder, seam side down, on a plate while you continue in the same way to prepare the three remaining leaves and pieces of seitan.

- Heat the oil and deep-fry all the rolls, one by one, until they are bubbly and golden. Remove them to drain on paper towels. When all the rolls have been cooked this way, start with the first one done and make crosswise slices approximately ½″ wide. You should be able to get 6 to 8 pieces per roll.

- Return each slice to the hot oil to cook once again. This time the inside section will puff up a little and, in some cases, puff up out far beyond the cut edge. Keep turning each piece as it fries to insure even cooking. The pieces are done when they are cripsy and golden.

Serve the warm spirals as soon as possible with Mustard Sauce (see page 165) as dip.

Dolmadakia—Stuffed Grape Leaves ——————

These small, savory roll-ups are a traditional Greek dish with a new twist. Serve the grape leaves hot or cold as appetizers, or serve 3 or 4 per person as a side dish. Stuffed grape leaves may be prepared a day in advance of serving, and will keep well for 2 or 3 days after preparation if covered and refrigerated.

Makes about 30 small rolls

One, 8 oz. jar grape leaves in brine (available at Middle-Eastern markets, some natural food stores, and some supermarkets)

For the Filling:

2 cups cooked seitan 4, seasoned with strong natural soy sauce broth

1 cup long grain brown rice
2 cups warm water
1/2 medium onion, chopped very fine
4 tablespoons Hearty Seasoning Mix
2 tablespoons paprika
4 tablespoons crumbled, dried mint leaves
1/4 teaspoon black pepper, or to taste
2 tablespoons natural soy sauce, or to taste
3 cups boiling water (more if necessary)
Olive oil

64

For the Sauce:

    1 tablespoon kuzu
    1 cup water (or, add enough water to the remaining broth to make 1 1/4
        cups total)
    3 tablespoons lemon juice

Make the Filling:
- Soak the rice in the warm water for 2 hours. Remove and drain the grape leaves, then carefully unroll and separate them in a bowl of cold water. The leaves are quite delicate, so rinse and drain them carefully.

- Grind the seitan with a hand grater, meat grinder, blender or food processor. Combine with the chopped onion, 2 tablespoons Hearty Seasoning Mix, and all the other seasonings. Drain the rice and add it to the seitan mixture.

Fill the Leaves:
- Lay a leaf on your work surface, vein side up, with the stem end pointing to you. Place about 2 tablespoons of the filling in the center of the leaf near the stem end. Pick up the lower edge and begin to roll it away from you, snugly folding the left and right sides of the leaf over the filling. Continue to roll to the end of the leaf.

- Oil a heavy covered saucepan or deep skillet and place a few of the unfilled leaves flat in the bottom of the pot. As the rolls are completed, layer them, seam side down, over the flat leaves. When all the rolls are assembled, spoon a little olive oil over their surface.

- Make a broth with the boiling water and 2 tablespoons of the Hearty Seasoning Mix. Pour the broth around the rolls (it should come just to the top of the grape leaf rolls), then cover the rolls with a layer of 4 or 5 flat grape leaves.

- Place a plate on top of the flat leaves to prevent the rolls from opening up as they cook. Bring to a boil, then simmer 1¼ hours.

- Remove the rolls carefully and place them on a platter to chill. Save any remaining broth to use in the sauce.

- Serve at room temperature with the following sauce.

Make the Sauce:
- Dissolve the kuzu in about ¼ cup of the reserved broth. Bring the remaining broth to a low boil, and add the lemon juice. Add the kuzu, stirring constantly. When the sauce is thick, taste it and adjust the seasonings. If it is too thick add a little water and adjust the seasonings if necessary. When it is just right, it should run off a metal spoon with a slow, syrupy consistency.

Seitan Bandito ───────────────────

Use ready-made corn tortillas for these filled rolls. Save a few to pack in lunchboxes.

Serves 6—makes 12 tortilla rolls

> 12 corn tortillas
> Oil for deep-frying

For the Filling:

> 1 1/4 cups seitan 1, 2, or 3, seasoned with natural soy sauce
>
> 1/2 pounds firm tofu, mashed with a fork
> 1 tablespoon prepared Dijon-style mustard
> 1 tablespoon seasoning mix of your choice

- Combine the filling ingredients and begin to heat the oil for deep-frying.

- Place 1½ tablespoons of the filling across one third of a tortilla, shaping the filling into a rectangle about 1″ × 3″, and ½″ thick. Pack the filling down firmly so it will stick together. Leave about 1″ between the filling and the edge of the tortilla.

- Begin to roll the tortilla, tucking it very tightly over and around the filling. Continue to roll the tortilla around to the end. Hold the "package" closed between your thumb and index finger, then transfer it to a pair of long chopsticks or tongs held in the other hand.

- Lower the tortilla roll into the hot oil, continuing to hold it together with your utensils for a count of 10 seconds. After this time it should stay together without being held, and you can assemble the next roll. Be careful to maintain the correct temperature in the oil.

- Remove the tortilla roll when it is crispy and golden. Drain it at 45° angle on paper towels.

- Serve with a seasoned sauce such as "Red Chiles Marengo." (See page 167.)

Deep-Fried Seitan Cubes in Velvet Dill Sauce ──────────

Very rich tasting—a little bit goes a long way. For a variation, omit the dill sauce and try Mustard Sauce as a dip.

Serves 4

1 cup gluten flour
2 to 4 tablespoons prepared, dehydrated vegetable broth mix (if using one
    with salt, 2 tablespoons should be enough)
1 cup water
Oil for deep-frying

For the Sauce:

1 1/2 cups plain soymilk
1 tablespoon kuzu, dissolved in 1/4 cup water
2 tablespoons dry white wine (or saké)
2 teaspoons dill, chopped very fine

Make the Seitan Nuggets:
• With a fork, blend the gluten flour and dehydrated vegetable broth very well. Make a well in the center and add the water all at once, mixing vigorously with a fork. Let the dough rest 10 to 20 minutes. Deep-fry small pieces—cut or break ½″ pieces off from the main piece and drop them carefully into the hot oil (see Instructions for Deep-Frying). Blot on paper towels.

Make the Sauce:
• In a saucepan, heat the soymilk then add the seitan and simmer about 20 minutes, stirring occasionally.

• Dissolve the kuzu in ¼ cup water. Add the kuzu mixture to the hot soymilk and stir until creamy. Mix in the wine and dill and simmer 10 minutes more. Adjust the seasonings. If an unsalted vegetable broth mix was used, you may want to add a little salt.

Savory Filo Strudel ——————————————————————

Using a glaze of barbecue sauce over the flaky layers of filo dough makes this an appetizing addition to any buffet.

Serves 4 to 6 as appetizer, 2 to 3 as side dish

2 cups cooked seitan 4 or 3, simmered in natural soy sauce broth as
    cutlets or cubes

1 tablespoon aromatic seasoning mix
2 tablespoons chickpea flour
4 leaves filo dough at room temperature (if frozen, defrost according to package
    instructions)
Sesame oil
1/4 cup barbecue sauce of your choice

Note: Chickpea flour and filo dough are available at Middle-Eastern or gourmet food shops. Chickpea flour is also called "Besan" or "Gram Flour" when found among Indian foods.

- Chill the cooked seitan thoroughly.

- Preheat the oven to 350° F.

- Grind the cooked seitan in a blender, food processor, or meat grinder. Combine the ground seitan with the seasoning mix and chickpea flour.

- Brush some sesame oil over the surface of 1 sheet of the filo dough. Filo dough is very thin and fragile so be gentle with it. Lay the second sheet on top of the first sheet, and brush it with oil also. Repeat with the remaining 2 sheets of dough.

- Arrange the filling in a narrow rectangle about 2″ deep, on the lower third of the dough. Leave margins of 2″ on the bottom edge, (the edge closest to you), and 1″ on each side edge. Roll the bottom edge of the filo up over the edge of the filling. Fold in the left and right edges and roll over again to enclose the filling within the roll. Continue to roll to the edge of the dough. Lift the roll carefully and place it seam side down on a cookie sheet.

- Bake 20 minutes. Brush or spread the barbecue sauce over the top surface. Bake 10 minutes more. Allow the roll to cool before slicing it into ¾″ to 1″ pieces.

Quick and Easy Seitan Cubes in Mustard Sauce ——————

Prepare this dish well ahead of serving time—the flavor will only improve. Great sandwiches can be made by using slices of seitan instead of cubes. It will keep well refrigerated.

Serves 4 to 6 as appetizer

> 2 cups cooked seitan, cut into 1″ cubes
>
> Oil for deep-frying
> 1 1/2 cups, or 1 recipe Mustard Sauce
> 1 scallion, sliced thin

- Cook the seitan cubes according to instructions for Deep-Flying without batter. Cook the cubes until crispy, then blot on paper towels.

- Heat the mustard sauce and add the seitan cubes. Mix to coat the seitan pieces with the sauce.

- Simmer about 5 minutes or until the cubes are heated through. Add the scallions. Serve hot or cold as an appetizer, side dish, or in sandwiches.

Note: Prepare this dish in advance by cooking the seitan pieces well ahead of serving time. The mustard sauce may also be prepared well in advance of serving. With this method, the only step remaining is to heat the two together with the scallions.

German-Style Cocktail Croquettes ──────────

Makes 20, 1″ balls

For the Croquettes:

>2 cups cooked seitan (Seitan 4 is best, Seitan 1 or 3 are suitable)
>
>1 tablespoon Spicy Seasoning Mix
>2 tablespoons whole wheat pastry flour
>4 tablespoons chickpea flour (available in Middle-Eastern food stores)
>Oil for deep-frying OR
>2 teaspoons oil in mix if baking instead of deep-frying

For the Gravy:

>1/4 cup chickpea flour
>2 tablespoons corn oil
>3/4 cup soymilk
>1/2 cup water
>2 tablespoons cider vinegar
>1/4 cup grated onion
>1/4 teaspoon allspice
>1/4 teaspoon black pepper

Prepare the Croquettes:
- Preheat oven to 350° F. Grind the seitan and combine it with the seasonings and flours, working all ingredients together well with a fork.

- Form the mixture into 1″ balls, wetting hands as needed to prevent sticking. Bake on a cookie sheet for about 20 minutes, or deep-fry.

Prepare the Gravy:
- Heat the oil in a sauce pan. Sprinkle the chickpea flour over the oil, stirring constantly. Cook together over a low heat for 2 to 3 minutes, continuing to stir constantly.

- Slowly add the soymilk and water, mixing with a wire whisk. Simmer, stirring constantly as the sauce thickens. Add the grated onion, allspice, pepper, natural soy sauce, and vinegar. Continue to simmer for 20 minutes.

- Put the croquettes into the gravy and heat through to serve hot.

Herbed Seitan Paté

Makes about 2 cups paté for crackers or sandwiches.

> 1 1/4 cups uncooked seitan 4
>
> 3 1/2 cups water
> 2" piece kombu
> 2 garlic cloves
> 1 teaspoon thyme
> 1/2 teaspoon black pepper
> 1 teaspoon basil
> 1 tablespoon parsley
> 2 teaspoons paprika
> 2 tablespoons olive oil
> 3 tablespoons natural soy sauce
> 1 teaspoon lemon juice
> 2 tablespoons chickpea flour (available in Middle-Eastern food stores)

● Preheat the oven to 375° F.

● Bring the water to a boil with the kombu. Break off tiny pieces of the seitan and drop them one by one into the water. Reduce the heat and simmer uncovered 15 minutes, stirring occasionally. Drain and cool the cooked seitan pieces and the kombu.

● Put the cooked seitan and kombu into a blender or food processor with all the remaining ingredients except the chickpea flour. Process until they are well ground but not mushy. Turn this mixture out into a mixing bowl and add the chickpea flour, mixing well to evenly distribute in the seitan.

● Bake the paté in one or two small oven-proof dishes for 20 to 30 minutes. Serve warm or cool as a spread for crackers or sandwiches.

Savory Nuggets

Use these seitan bits as an appetizer, snack, or side dish with a light sauce.

Makes 20 pieces, 1" × 2"

> 2 cups uncooked seitan 2

For the Broth: (Use with uncooked seitan only)

> 3" piece kombu
> 2 teaspoons Savory Seasoning Mix II
>
> 1 egg
> 1/4 cup plain soymilk
> 1 cup cornmeal
> 2 tablespoons arrowroot flour

1/8 teaspoon salt
1/2 teaspoon paprika
Oil for deep-frying

- Cut the uncooked seitan into 20 pieces and simmer with the kombu and seasoning for 30 to 50 minutes, according to the procedure for Simmered Cutlets and Cubes. Remove the pieces from the broth and chill thoroughly.

Note: If you are using pre-cooked, chilled seitan begin here.

- Beat the egg and soymilk together. In a separate bowl combine the cornmeal, arrowroot, salt and paprika.

- Heat the oil, and pat the seitan pieces as dry as possible with a paper towel.

- Dip each piece of seitan in the egg mixture, then dredge in the seasoned cornmeal. Dip and dredge again in both, then lower the seitan into the hot oil to cook until golden. Dip and dredge the pieces one at a time, but 3 or 4 may be cooked together depending upon the size of the pot.

Seitan Jerky Chips

2 cups uncooked seitan (preferably one containing gluten flour)

2 tablespoons Spicy Seasoning Mix, or other seasoning of your choice
1/4 cup natural soy sauce
2 teaspoons Liquid Hickory Seasoning
5 cups water

Note: You may replace the uncooked seitan and seasoning with Seitan Pepperoni 7 if you have it already made. If you are using Seitan 7, you only need to slice it into $\frac{1}{8}$" rounds before deep-frying.

- Mix the seasoning mix well into the uncooked seitan. Form it into a cylinder approximately 10" long $\times$ 2" in diameter. Wrap and tie it as for Seitan Pepperoni, or as for Hot Dogs. (See page 52.)

- Simmer for one hour then remove the seitan from the broth. When the seitan is cool to the touch, unwrap it. It can be refrigerated to cool faster. Return the seitan to the broth and continue to simmer for 2 hours more.

- Chill the cooked seitan and slice it into $\frac{1}{8}$" thick rounds. If you have the "seitan pepperoni" already made, use it now.

- Deep-fry the seitan slices without batter until crispy.

Seitan Jerky Chips may be served with or without a dip.

Five-Spice Pouches

These little pouches, packed full of goodies and glazed with a faintly sweet, aromatic sauce, are great as appetizers or as a side dish.

Makes 12 filled pouches
Serves 4 to 6

Note: Because of the length of this recipe, places have been noted which are useful "stopping places" if you choose to make this dish in stages.

> 1 cup uncooked seitan 2
>
> 1 cup broccoli flowerets
> 2 tablespoons chickpea flour
> Oil for deep-frying
> 1 cup water
> 1 1/2 tablespoons natural soy sauce
> 3 tablespoons crushed pineapple (unsweetened, in its own juice)
> 1 teaspoon Chinese 5-flavor spice (available at natural food stores or super-
>   markets)
> 1 tablespoon thick starch from preparing seitan

Make the Filling:
- Steam or parboil the broccoli for about 3 minutes. Refresh in cold water. Drain and mince the broccoli. Add the chickpea flour and mix well.

- Divide the uncooked seitan into 4 equal pieces, then divide each of those pieces into thirds. Let the seitan pieces rest 2″ away from each other on a damp smooth surface, so they don't stick together. These 12 pieces will become the individual pouches. Each pouch will enclose 1 tablespoon of the broccoli filling.

Form the Pouches:
- Place one of the seitan pieces on the work surface. Using a rotating motion, begin to press and flatten it with the palm and heel of your hand until it is about 3″ square and very thin. Hold it open with one hand so it does not roll up.

- Place 1 tablespoon of the filling about 1″ away from one of the corners. This works best if you face the seitan as a diamond with one corner pointing toward you. Continue to hold the seitan open and flat. Use the other hand to fold the corner nearest the filling up and over the filling.

- Fold over the left and right corners as well, stretching them slightly while wrapping to make a tightly sealed package.

- Pick up the last corner and, again stretching slightly, bring it up and over the top, toward you. Don't be concerned if the wrapping seems to extend too far over into the rest of the pouch—more layers of a thin, tight wrapping are better than fewer layers of thick, loose wrapping.

- Place the pouch seam side down on a plate, and prepare all the remaining pouches in the same way. These few minutes of setting time will help to ensure a good seal on all the edges.

Steam the Pouches:
- Put about 1″ of water in a sauce pan and bring it to a boil. Place a steamer inside the pot. (For very large quantities, a bamboo Japanese steamer used with a wok or a large frying pan will be more efficient.) Wet a clean, smooth textured cloth such as a linen dish towel, and squeeze it well. Use this damp towel to line the steamer.

- When the water is boiling, place the pouches seam side down on the towel. Cover the pot and steam the pouches for 8 to 10 minutes. You may want to lift up any protruding edges of the towel and place them on top of the pot.

- Remove the cooked pouches carefully and let them cool on a plate.

Note: Stop here if necessary. When the pouches are at room temperature, cover and refrigerate them.

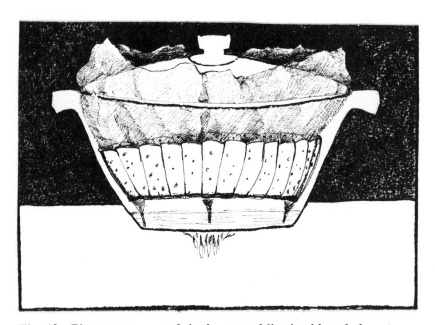

Fig. 12   Place a steamer rack in the pot and line it with a cloth.

Deep-fry the Pouches:
- Heat the oil for deep-frying. Gently lower the pouches into the hot oil and let them cook until they are golden and crispy. After one side is cooked, turn them over. Do not cook more than 3 pouches at a time—they sometimes have to be held down after turning or they may bounce back to side one. Blot on paper towels.

Note: Stop here if necessary. The pouches may be loosely covered with a cloth, paper towel, or a bamboo mat and kept at room temperature for a few hours.

Cook Pouches in the Sauce:
- Prepare a broth with the water, natural soy sauce, pineapple, and 5-spice powder. Bring to a boil and reduce the heat. Immerse the pouches and simmer, uncovered, for about 10 to 15 minutes. Turn the pouches often.

- Remove the pouches carefully with a slotted spoon and arrange them on a platter. Add the thick starch to the remaining hot broth and, stirring constantly, heat until thick and glossy.

- Simmer the sauce for about 20 minutes or until reduced to $\frac{1}{4}$ cup. Stir occasionally.

To Serve:
- Spoon the sauce onto a plate and place the pouches on top, or spoon the sauce over the pouches. Garnish with watercress, orange slices, cut red radishes, or other colorful garnishes of your choice.

Variations on Fillings:
- Baked seitan, ground and seasoned with one of the seasoning mixes

- Chinese dried shrimp, soaked and chopped (or mix them in with the broccoli filling)

- As a dessert with the date-nut filling. Glaze the deep-fried, filled pouches with hot maple syrup. Or, roll then in maple granules (maple sugar) immediately after deep-frying

Easy Preparations of Small Amounts of Uncooked Seitan
—Most Suitable for Snacks, Additions to Salads, or Used as Appetizers or in Sandwiches ━━━━━━━━━━━━━━━━━━━━━

Broiling:
- Marinate $\frac{1}{2}$" to 1" pieces of uncooked seitan in a thick marinade for 15 minutes, turning 2 or 3 times.

- Place the marinated pieces on an oiled baking sheet and broil 2 minutes on each side. Watch carefully—the pieces should be 6" below the broiler flame.

- Serve with or without a dip.

Deep-frying:
- Carefully drop 1" pieces of uncooked seitan into hot oil and deep-fry until crispy and doubled in size. Drain on paper towels.

- Marinate, using the salad dressing, sauce, or marinade of your choice.

- Place on a cookie sheet and broil 6″ below the flame.

- Serve with or without a dip. Mustard sauce is good as a marinade or dip if you like a tangy, pungent taste.

Soups

To make a good soup, the pot must only simmer or "smile."
—French Proverb

Vegetable Soup with Savory Dumplings and Lemon ——————

In an easy half-hour, you can prepare this delightful fresh vegetable soup accented with succulent dumplings.

Serves 6

For the Soup:

>8 cups water
>3" piece kombu
>1 cup onion slices
>1 carrot, sliced into 1/8" thick ovals or rounds
>1/2 head cauliflower, cut into medium size flowerets
>1 teaspoon salt
>1 tablespoon natural soy sauce
>1 lemon, sliced crosswise into 1/8" thick rounds
>Watercress sprigs or fresh dill for garnish

For the Seitan Dumplings:

>3/4 cup gluten flour
>2 tablespoons Savory Seasoning Mix I
>1 cup plain soymilk
>1 teaspoon sesame oil

Make the Soup: Simmer the water and kombu together for 5 minutes, then remove the kombu. Cut the kombu into thin strips and return it to the soup. Add the onion, carrot, cauliflower, salt and natural soy sauce.

Make the Dumplings: Separately combine dry ingredients and liquid ingredients. Add the soymilk/oil mixture all at once to the seasoned flour, mixing it in vigorously with a fork. Mix well and knead until it has a uniform consistency. Allow this mixture to rest for 5 minutes.

- Break off 1″ pieces of the uncooked seitan dumplings and drop them one by one into the hot soup. Stir after adding 5 or 6 to prevent them from sticking together. Simmer for 15 to 20 minutes and adjust seasonings.

To Serve: Place one of the thin lemon rounds in the bottom of each bowl. Pour the soup over the lemon, and garnish with the watercress or fresh dill.

Hot and Sour Cabbage Soup

Warm up with this traditional Chinese taste.

Serves 6

> 1/2 cup uncooked seitan 2, cut into small strips, 1″ x 1/4″
>
> 1/3 to 1/2 medium green or white cabbage
> 2 tablespoons sesame oil
> 1 medium onion, sliced thin
> 1 1/2 teaspoons salt
> 8 cups water or stock
> 1 pound tofu
> 1/4 teaspoon pepper OR
> 1/2 teaspoon Chinese Hot Pepper Oil
> 4 tablespoons natural soy sauce
> 4 tablespoons lemon juice
> 2 tablespoons arrowroot or kuzu
> Scallion greens, slivered, to be used as garnish

- Remove the cabbage core. Cut the cabbage in thirds lengthwise, then shred finely crosswise.

- Using a heavy sauce pan or soup pot, pan-fry the seitan strips with sesame oil, using a medium heat. Stir constantly to prevent sticking. When the seitan is browned, add the onions and sprinkle the salt over them. Add the cabbage and continue to sauté until the vegetables are translucent.

- Add enough hot water or stock to almost cover the vegetables, and bring to a low boil. Cut the tofu into ½″ cubes and add it to the broth. Season the soup with pepper or hot pepper oil and simmer for 20 minutes.

- Combine the natural soy sauce and lemon juice, and dissolve the arrowroot or kuzu in it. Mix this thickener into the hot soup, stirring to avoid lumps. The soup will thicken slightly.

- *Do Not Overheat* the soup or its glaze-like quality may be lost. Serve immediately, garnished with the scallion slivers.

Black Bean Soup

Thick and rich with memories of South American cuisine. Serve this hearty soup with steaming corn bread and crisp, cool greens.

Serves 6

2 cups cubed seitan 11 "roast" AND/OR
1 1/2 pieces pepperoni seitan 7 sliced 1/4" thick

2 cups black beans
2 quarts water
2" piece kombu
6 or 7 cups water for cooking beans (see below)
6 tablespoons olive or sesame oil
1 medium onion, diced
4 garlic cloves, crushed and minced
2 cups water
2 teaspoons salt

1 tablespoon cumin	1 sweet red pepper, diced
3/4 tablespoon oregano	1 1/2 tablespoons mirin
1 bay leaf	1 tablespoon barley malt syrup
1/4 teaspoon cayenne	2 tablespoons lemon juice
1 tablespoon natural soy sauce	1/4 cup parsley, chopped fine

Cook the Beans—Using one of the following methods:

1.   Soak the beans overnight in 2 qt. water. The following day, drain the beans and add 6 to 7 cups of water. Bring to a boil with the kombu. Reduce the heat and simmer, covered, 1 to 1½ hours or until the beans are tender.

2.   Do not soak the beans. Pressure-cook the beans and kombu with 6 cups water for 40 minutes to 1 hour. Bring the pressure down by placing the entire pot in the sink and running cold water over it.

Make the Soup:

• In a soup pot, heat 3 tablespoons of the oil and sauté the onions and garlic over a low heat until the onions are translucent. Add the cooked beans with their cooking liquid to the onions. Add 2 cups water and the salt, cumin, and oregano, bay leaves, and cayenne. Simmer together, uncovered, for about 1 hour. Stir occasionally.

• Use the remaining 3 tablespoons of oil to pan-fry the seitan cubes and/or pepperoni slices for about 5 minutes. Sprinkle the natural soy sauce over them and continue to cook until they are well-browned and somewhat crispy.

• Add the hot cubes with their cooking oil to the bean soup; add the red pepper pieces, mirin, barley malt, lemon juice and parsley. Simmer together for 15 to 30 minutes.

Hearty Garden Soup with Chickpeas and Golden Dumplings

This easy soup is enhanced by the seitan dumplings becoming chewy and juicy in the broth.

Serves 6 to 8

For the Seitan: Makes about 12 tablespoons of uncooked seitan which will each become a nugget 2″ in diameter after deep-frying.

> 2/3 cup gluten flour
> 1/2 cup water
> 2 tablespoons plain soymilk
> Oil for deep-frying

For the Soup:

> 1 tablespoon sesame oil
> 1 medium onion, diced
> 1 cup celery, diced
> 2 cups carrots, diced
> 8 cups water
> 6″ piece kombu, broken into 1/4″ pieces
> 4 cups cooked chickpeas
> 1 teaspoon salt
> 1 cup zucchini, half-rounds 1/4″ thick
> 1 cup green beans, cut into 1″ lengths
> 2 tablespoons natural soy sauce
> 3 tablespoons fresh chives, use for garnish

Make the Seitan:
- Combine the liquids. Add all the liquid at once to the gluten flour and mix vigorously with a fork. The mixture will be fairly soft. Let the dough rest for 10 to 15 minutes.

- To make the seitan dumplings, heat the oil and deep-fry the gluten flour mixture by tablespoons, until golden and crispy. (See Instructions for Deep-Frying.)

Prepare the Soup:
- Heat the sesame oil and sauté the onions until they are translucent. Add the celery and carrots and continue to sauté for 5 minutes. Add the water, and break up the dry kombu into it. Add the cooked chickpeas and salt, and bring to a boil. Reduce the heat and simmer for about 30 minutes.

- Add the seitan dumplings to the soup and gently press each one against the side of the pot to flatten it somewhat. Stir the soup occasionally, pushing the seitan pieces against the sides of the pot. Add the zucchini and green beans to the soup and simmer 10 to 15 minutes more until they are just tender but not overcooked.

To Serve:
• Adjust the seasoning by adding natural soy sauce to taste. Garnish each bowl of soup with 1 teaspoon minced fresh chives sprinkled over the top.

Miso Soup with Fu and Wakame

This is a Japanese style light miso soup, whose delicate aromas and light color will stimulate the senses. Half of the enjoyment of this soup comes from watching the fu float to the top of the soup and unfold as it absorbs the soup, accompanied by the mingling aromas of the lemon, scallion, and miso.

Serves 6

2 pieces flat fu
6 to 7 cups water
6″ wakame
3 tablespoons miso—white, light barley, or "mellow"
1/4 cup water
1 lemon
1 scallion

• Break each piece of fu into 6 equal pieces. Bring the water to a boil.

• Soak the wakame 10 minutes in water to cover, or according to package directions. Squeeze the wakame gently, checking to see that no hard parts remain. Cut the wakame lengthwise in half or thirds, then crosswise in ¼″ slices. Add the wakame to the boiling water, reduce heat and simmer 10 minutes.

• Make a paste of miso with ¼ cup water. Carefully peel the lemon, using only the yellow outer layer. Mince the lemon peel. Cut the scallion in half lengthwise, then crosswise in 1″ lengths. Use these pieces to make lengthwise slivers.

• Remove the soup from the heat and add the miso, to taste. The soup should have a slightly salty taste.

To Serve:
• Place 2 pieces of fu in each soup bowl along with a pinch of lemon peel and a few green and white scallion slivers. Ladle the soup over these and serve immediately.

"Just Like Grandma's" Noodle Soup ——————————

Thin strips of deep-fried seitan give this soup the rich warming taste loved by fans of noodle soups.

Serves 6

4 large or 6 small thin, cooked seitan cutlets (or slices of seitan "roast")

8 cups water
3" piece kombu
1 onion, quartered
1 carrot, quartered lengthwise
1 stalk celery, quartered
1 1/2 teaspoons powdered coriander
1 teaspoon chervil
2 teaspoons salt
1 tablespoon natural soy sauce

Oil for deep-frying
3 cups cooked pasta
2 tablespoons parsley, minced

- Combine the first 9 ingredients (not including seitan) to make the soup stock. When it begins to boil, reduce the heat, cover, and simmer 20 to 30 minutes. While the stock is simmering, prepare the seitan cutlets.

- Heat the oil for deep-frying the seitan. Blot the cutlets with paper towels and cut them into thin strips, about 2" long, $\frac{1}{8}$" wide, and $\frac{1}{8}$" thick. Deep-fry the strips until they are crispy but not hard. Drain on paper towels.

- Ten minutes before serving, remove the vegetables from the soup and adjust seasonings. Add the precooked pasta, the seitan strips and the parsley. Cover to allow the pasta and seitan to soften slightly in the soup.

Navy Bean Soup with Hickory Seitan ——————————

This soup is a hearty puree with the added dimension of hickory.

Serves 6

2 cups cooked seitan cutlets or seitan 11 "roast," cooked with Spicy Seasoning Mix, OR
2 links (1/2 recipe) seitan 7 cooked with Spicy Seasoning mix

1 1/2 cups navy beans
Water to cover beans, for soaking, OR
5 cups water, for pressure cooking beans
2" piece kombu

For the Soup:

      1 tablespoon corn oil
      2 large cloves garlic, crushed and minced
      1 onion, diced
      2 carrots, diced
      1 bay leaf
      1/2 teaspoon thyme
      7 cups water or 2 cups water (depending on how beans are cooked—see
         below)
      1 cup green beans, cut into 2" lengths
      2 teaspoons salt
      1/4 cup parsley, minced
      1/2 cup sweet red pepper, diced fine (to be used as a garnish)

For the Hickory Marinade:

      1 1/4 cups water
      1 tablespoon Liquid Hickory Smoke
      2 tablespoons natural soy sauce
      2 tablespoons sesame oil

Cook the Beans by One of the Following Methods:

1. Soak the beans for 8 hours or overnight in water to cover. Drain the beans then add them directly to the soup as directed below.

2. Pressure-cook the beans, kombu, and 5 cups water together for 20 minutes. Then cook the beans in the soup as follows.

Prepare the Soup:

- Heat the corn oil and sauté the garlic and onions over a medium heat for 4 to 5 minutes, or until the edges of the onion are lightly browned. Add the carrots, bay leaf, thyme, and parsley. Cover, and continue to cook over a low heat for 10 minutes more.

- If the beans have been soaked but are not cooked, drain them and add to the vegetables along with the kombu and 7 cups of fresh water. If the beans have been partially cooked by pressure cooking, add them to the vegetables along with their cooking liquid plus 2 cups fresh water.

- Bring the soup to a boil, then reduce the heat and simmer until the beans are tender. This will take ½ to 2 hours, depending upon how long they were already soaked or cooked.

- When the beans are tender, add the salt. Remove the bay leaf and puree the soup in a blender or food processor. Return the pureed soup to the cooking pot and keep hot until serving time. Adjust the seasonings.

- Cut the cooked seitan into ½″ cubes or ¼″ rounds, depending upon which type of seitan you are using. If a hickory-flavored seitan is desired, marinate the pieces in the Hickory Marinade Mixture while the beans are cooking. Drain the seitan and pat it dry with a paper towel before pan-frying.

- Pan-fry the seitan cubes or slices in the sesame oil until they are crispy. Add them to the soup not more than 10 minutes before serving. Garnish the soup with minced red pepper.

Note: Leftover soup can be chilled and used as an appetizer spread, sandwich spread, or dip for corn chips.

Almost Instant Clear Soup with Fu and Greens

Serves 6

6 to 7 cups water
4″ piece kombu
1 teaspoon salt
2 cups kale, chopped very fine
2 tablespoons natural soy sauce, or to taste
2 pieces flat fu

- Bring the water to a boil with the kombu and salt. Simmer 5 minutes then remove the kombu, reserving it to use in cooking with vegetables, beans, or other seitan dishes.

- Add the kale and simmer about 5 minutes or until just tender but still brightly colored. Add natural soy sauce to taste.

To Serve: Break the 2 pieces of fu into 6 equal parts and place 1 piece into each bowl. Ladle the soup into each bowl, and serve immediately.

Golden Squash Potage

You can even start your day with the sweetness of winter squash. This soup is just as delicious as it is simple to make.

Serves 6

2 links cooked seitan 7, sliced into 1/4″ pieces

1 medium butternut squash, diced into 1″ cubes (makes 6 to 7 cups)
4 cups water
1 teaspoon salt

    1/4 teaspoon allspice
    2 to 3 tablespoons corn or sesame oil
    3 tablespoons minced parsley

- Cut the squash in half and remove the seeds. Peel the squash if it is not organic. Dice it into 1″ cubes, which will make 6 to 7 cups.

- Boil or pressure-cook the squash in the water until tender, about 15 minutes at a medium boil or 5 minutes by pressure cooking. Purée the cooked squash in a food mill, blender or food processor. Return the cooked squash to the cooking pot. Add the salt and allspice. Cover and keep warm over a low heat.

- Pan-fry the seitan slices in the corn oil and set them aside to use as a garnish for the soup.

To Serve: Garnish the soup with 2 or 3 seitan slices and 1 teaspoon parsley. Lay the seitan on top of the soup and sprinkle the parsley over it.

Main Dishes and Casseroles

One cannot think well, love well, sleep well, if one has not dined well.
—Virginia Woolf (1882–1941), *A Room of One's Own*

Seitan Stroganoff

A delight for both weight-watchers and gourmands. Prepare the cooked seitan as much as a few days in advance—it can be refrigerated until you need it. Serve Seitan Stroganoff over broad egg noodles accompanied by a salad of crispy greens, and add a side dish such as Glazed Carrots with Sesame (see page 202). In this way you can prepare an elegant meal quickly.

Serves 6

2 cups seitan 4 or 3, simmered with strong-flavored natural soy sauce broth

1 tablespoon sesame oil
2 cups onions, diced
1 pound mushrooms, quartered or sliced 1/8" to 1/4" thick
2 teaspoons salt
1/2 teaspoon white pepper
3 to 3 1/2 cups water
1 pound tofu
1 tablespoon umeboshi paste
3/4 cup thick starch from preparing seitan
1/2 cup saké or dry white wine
1/4 cup parsley, minced

- Slice the cooked seitan into strips 2″ × ¼″. In a heavy saucepan, heat the oil and lightly brown the onions. Add the mushrooms, salt and pepper, and sauté 8 to 10 minutes. Add the seitan pieces and water and simmer together.

- While the seitan and vegetables are cooking, combine the tofu, umeboshi paste and starch in a blender to achieve the consistency of sour cream.

- Ten minutes before serving add the wine and the tofu mixture to the seitan. Heat thoroughly until the sauce is thick, mixing to keep it smooth. Adjust the seasonings and simmer for 10 minutes. Do not overcook the sauce at this point, or it may separate. Add the parsley, and serve the stroganoff immediately over rice or broad noodles.

Stuffed Red Peppers ────────────────

Red bell peppers are filled with seasoned brown rice, seitan, and vegetables. Using pre-cooked brown rice makes this dish an easy, economical one. If you do not have rice already cooked, prepare some couscous, bulgur, or kasha for a quickly made filling.

Note: See "From The Pantry" for the preparation of couscous, bulgur, and kasha.

Makes 4 large or 6 small peppers

> 2 cups uncooked seitan 4, simmered as directed below, OR
> 2 to 3 cups cooked seitan cutlets, diced (use the cooked seitan of your choice)

For the Broth:

> 1 tablespoon natural soy sauce
> 3 cups water
> 2" piece kombu

For the Filling:

> 1 1/2 cups cooked brown rice (or couscous, bulgur, or kasha)
> 1/2 cup minced onion
> 2 tablespoons sesame oil
> 1 recipe Savory Seasoning Mix
> 1 tablespoon chickpea flour
>
> 4 large or 6 small sweet red peppers
> Paprika for garnish

- If you are using uncooked seitan, prepare the seitan by cutting or breaking it into very small pieces and simmering for 20 minutes in the broth. Remove the pieces of cooked seitan from the broth with a slotted spoon and save any remaining broth for seasoning or sauces.

- Chill the seitan pieces and grind them. Mix in the onion, oil, seasoning mix, and chickpea flour. This should make about 1½ cups of filling.

- Preheat the oven to 350° F.

- Slice the tops off the peppers and remove the seeds and stems. Rinse the peppers inside and outside, then parboil the peppers and their top "rings" for 1 minute. Drain the peppers and refresh them immediately in cold water. Chop the tops very well and mix with the rest of the filling.

- Lightly oil a 9" × 13" baking pan.

- Cut the peppers in half lengthwise and fill them, using enough filling to mound up on the top of each one. Sprinkle a little paprika over the top if desired and bake for about 40 minutes or until the peppers are tender.

Mushroom Lasagne Au Gratin —————————

I have been told that this casserole is "Italian approved," so enjoy! Steamed kale with a tart dressing, or another colorful green salad, can complete this simple meal.

Serves 6 to 8

> 2 cups seitan 11, cooked with Savory Seasoning Mix I (reserve 1 teaspoon seasoning mix to combine with bread crumbs—see below)
>
> 1 pound spinach lasagne, cooked al dente
> 4 cups sliced mushrooms (about 3/4 pound)
> 2 1/2 tablespoons olive oil
> 1 1/2 teaspoons salt
> 2 cloves garlic, crushed and minced
> 2 cups plain soymilk
> 1 1/4 teaspoons water or stock
> 2/3 cup thick starch from making seitan
> 1/2 pound soft tofu
> 2/3 cup dry white wine (optional)
> 2/3 cup whole wheat bread crumbs
> 1 tablespoon paprika
> 1 teaspoon Savory Seasoning Mix I
> 1 tablespoon corn oil

- Preheat the oven to 400° F.

- Slice the seitan into 2″ lengths about ½″ wide. Sauté the mushrooms in the olive oil. Add the salt, garlic, and seitan pieces and cook together for 2 or 3 minutes. Add the soymilk and water or stock. When this is almost boiling, stir in the thick starch and continue stirring as the sauce thickens.

- Crumble the tofu into the sauce, stirring the sauce as it thickens. Add the wine. When the sauce is thick, adjust seasonings and remove from the heat.

- Make alternate layers of the cooked noodles and the sauce in a lightly oiled 9″ × 13″ baking pan. The top layer should be sauce.

- Combine the bread crumbs with the paprika and the seasoning mix and rub the corn oil into this mixture. Sprinkle the crumb mixture evenly over the top of the sauce. Cover with foil. Reduce the oven temperature to 375°F. and bake for 25 minutes. Remove the foil and bake 8 to 10 minutes more to form a light crust on top of the sauce.

Pan-Fried Cutlets with Mushroom Sauce ———————

These cutlets with their richly flavored gravy, may invite you to serve them with mashed potatoes, peas and carrots.

Makes 6 to 9 cutlets

> 2 cups uncooked seitan 1 or 3, to be simmered as thin cutlets, OR
> 6 to 9 thin, cooked seitan cutlets

For the Broth for Cooking Cutlets—use with the uncooked seitan only:

> 6 cups water
> 3″ piece kombu
> 3 tablespoons natural soy sauce
> 2 tablespoons lemon juice
> 1 1/2 tablespoons Aromatic Seasoning Mix
> 2 teaspoons sesame oil

To Dredge the Cutlets:

> *Combine:*
> 1/2 cup chickpea flour
> 1/2 cup corn flour
> 1 tablespoon arrowroot flour OR use
> 1 cup corn flour plus 1 tablespoon unbleached white flour

For the Mushroom Sauce:

> 1 1/2 teaspoons sesame oil allowed for each cutlet
> 10 to 12 mushrooms, sliced very thin
> 1 1/2 to 2 cups broth from cooking cutlets
> 3/4 cup plain soymilk
> 1 tablespoon mirin

- Roll up the uncooked seitan and slice it into 6 to 9 pieces, each ¼″ thick.

- To flatten the uncooked cutlets, make a fist and use the palm or outside edge of your hand to lightly pound the uncooked cutlet slices into a shape twice the area and half the thickness of the original slice. Use a sliding motion as you pound.

- Heat the above broth ingredients to boiling, then reduce heat to very low and add the cutlets one at a time, carefully retaining the shape of each cutlet and laying it flat on top of the broth. Simmer 1½ hours. The cutlets will be fairly firm, so they may be removed from the broth while still hot. Allow the cutlets to cool before proceeding.

- Combine the chickpea flour, corn flour, and arrowroot flour in a pie plate or other flat dish. Dredge both sides of the cutlets in the flour, pressing the flour firmly into the cutlets.

● Heat half the total quantity of oil needed (allowing 1½ teaspoons of oil for each cutlet) in a heavy skillet. Pan-fry the cutlets on both sides until they are golden brown. Add a little more oil to the pan as needed.

● When all the cutlets have been cooked, remove them and set aside. Add a little more oil to the pan if needed to sauté the mushrooms.

● Put the mushrooms into the pan in which the cutlets were cooked. Sauté the mushrooms briefly over a medium-low heat. Add the seasoned broth reserved from cooking the cutlets, and simmer the mushrooms in the broth for a few minutes, until they are tender.

● Make a smooth paste of the remaining flour mixture and the soymilk, and add it to the mushrooms. Continue to stir this sauce until it has thickened. This will be a very light gravy, not too thick. Add the mirin and adjust seasonings to taste.

Sweet and Spicy Stew with Dried Fruits ──────────

This stew is easy to make and very festive. Bring it to your next holiday buffet.

Serves 6

> 3 cups braised seitan "roast" 11, cooked with natural soy sauce-ginger broth
>
> 2/3 cup dried apples
> 1/4 cup raisins
> 2/3 cup dried apricots
> 1 cup water
> 1 cup dry red wine
> 1/2 cup cider vinegar
> 2 shallots, minced
> 1/2 teaspoon cumin
> 2 small or 1 large bay leaf
> 3 tablespoons olive oil
> 3 or 4 carrots, cut into 3/4″ chunks

● Cut the seitan into 1″ cubes.

● Combine the following and heat to boiling: all dried fruits, water, wine, vinegar, shallots, cumin, and bay leaves. Remove from heat immediately, and let the mixture rest so dried fruits will soften.

● Preheat the oven to 400° F.

- In a heavy pan, sauté the cubes of seitan until they are browned and crispy. Add the carrots. Drain the dried fruits, and add them to the seitan and carrots. Cook together 5 minutes over a low heat, then move all to a covered casserole. Add the seasoned juices and cover tightly with foil. Replace the cover on top of the foil. Reduce the oven heat to 350°F. Bake for 1 hour, or until the carrots are tender. Stir once before serving; the small amount of sauce remaining should be thick.

Creamed Corn and Cutlet Casserole ──────────

Dried flint corn is noted for its deep corn flavor. It is the traditional American corn, used for tortillas and cornmeal cereal.

Serves 6

6 to 8 cooked seitan cutlets, 1 or 3

1 egg
3/4 cup cornmeal
1 tablespoon plus 1 teaspoon Spicy Seasoning Mix
1/3 cup sesame oil
3 cups dry flint corn, (cook according to instructions on page 192)
1 1/2 teaspoons salt
1 1/2 cups onion, diced
1 1/2 cups plain soymilk
1/2 cup parsley, minced

- Pat the cooked cutlets with a paper towel to remove excess moisture. Beat the egg lightly with a fork and dip each cutlet into it. Combine the cornmeal and Spicy Seasoning Mix, and dredge each cutlet in this mixture.

- Heat the sesame oil in a heavy skillet and pan-fry the cutlets on both sides until golden. Remove the cutlets and place on paper towels to remove some of the oil.

- Drain the cooked corn and combine 3 cups of it with the salt, onion, hot oil from the frying pan, and soymilk. Process the corn until creamy in a blender or food processor.

- Add the creamed corn mixture to the remaining cooked corn. Fold in the chopped parsley and pour into a lightly oiled pan such as a 9″ × 13″ baking pan.

- Gently press the pan-fried cutlets onto the top of the corn, spacing them an equal distance apart to indicate portions. Cover and bake for 30 to 40 minutes. Remove the cover and bake 10 minutes more.

Apricot-Glazed Seitan "Roast"———————————

This oven-braised seitan is prepared with a glaze of homemade apricot butter.

Serves 6

>4 cups braised seitan "roast" 11, cooked with natural soy sauce-ginger broth

For the Broth to Use for Braising:

>4 cups water
>1" piece ginger, sliced thin
>1/2 cup natural soy sauce
>4" piece kombu, broken into 2 pieces
>1 tablespoon sesame oil
>
>1 recipe Apricot Butter (see page 167)

• Divide the uncooked seitan into 2 or 3 sections and prepare the braised "roast" according to instructions on page 49, using the amounts of water, ginger, natural soy sauce, kombu, and sesame oil listed above. Remove the ginger slices before serving.

• If you are using cooked seitan divide the "roast" into 2 or 3 parts and place them cut side down on a baking sheet. Spread the apricot butter smoothly over the tops of the seitan sections.

• Bake at 350° F. for 10 to 20 minutes, until the glaze has thickened and caramelized somewhat. Serve hot or cold.

Seitan Rolls Braised in Saké Sauce ———————————

This more elaborate dish consists of seitan filled with seasoned leeks and rice. The rolls are steamed to give them a firm shape, then browned, and oven-braised in a seasoned saké sauce.

Serves 4

>2 cups uncooked seitan 2
>
>4 medium leeks, chopped fine (about 4 cups)
>2 tablespoons olive oil
>2 cups sticky cooked rice
>1 teaspoon thyme
>1 teaspoon salt
>2 large garlic cloves, crushed and minced
>1/2 teaspoon allspice

2 teaspoons prepared Dijon mustard
4 tablespoons sesame oil

For the Stock:

1 cup water
4 tablespoons Hearty Seasoning Mix
1 cup sake
1 onion, quartered
2 carrots, cut in large chunks
Arrowroot powder

- Sauté the leeks in the olive oil until they are bright green, but not browned. Combine with the rice, thyme, salt, garlic, and allspice.

- Divide the seitan into quarters and stretch one piece carefully into a rectangle about 8″ × 10″. Spread ½ teaspoon of mustard over it, and evenly distribute one-quarter of the filling mixture over the third of the rectangle closest to you (the 8″ side). Allow about 2″ on each side and 1″ on the front edge to remain empty.

- Fold over the front edge, then the left and the right sides, to enclose the filling. Gently roll the filled area away from you, over and over to the end of the rectangle. Any protruding or bulky side edges should be stretched across the package to opposite sides as you roll, to evenly distribute the wrapping. Tie the filled seitan roll with a length of string long enough to secure the package on all sides, as if you were wrapping a gift.

- Put a vegetable steamer in a pot with 1″ to 1½″ water. Line the vegetable steamer with a damp clean cloth and bring the water to a boil. Carefully place the rolls on the cloth and cover the pot. Any trailing corners of the cloth can be draped up on the pot to get them up out of the way. (See illustration Fig. 12, page 72.)

- Steam for 5 to 10 minutes. Remove the rolls immediately and let them cool. While they are hot they are very fragile, but they will become firmer as they cool.

- Preheat the oven to 400° F.

- In a flameproof baking dish, heat 4 to 6 tablespoons sesame oil. Brown the rolls on all sides until crispy. Add the onion, carrot pieces, seasoned stock, and saké. Cover and simmer for 10 minutes.

- Place the covered pot in the oven and braise the seitan rolls for 10 minutes, then reduce the oven heat to 300° F. Continue to braise for 1 hour, basting occasionally. Use any remaining broth to make a sauce using 1 tablespoon arrowroot dissolved in 1 tablespoon saké. Snip and remove the strings, and serve the sauce over the rolls.

Shepherd's Pie ————————————————————

Mashed potatoes become the crust for this old-fashioned casserole. Use single-serving crockery casseroles or disposable aluminum pie plates for individual pies.

Serves 6—make individual 4½″ pies or one larger casserole.

> 2 cups cooked seitan (about 4 to 5 cutlets, see page 48), diced 3/4″ cubes
>
> 3 medium carrots, diced 1/2″ pieces (about 2 cups)
> 2 celery stalks, diced 1/2″ pieces
> 1 medium onion, diced
> 1 tablespoon sesame oil
> 2 cups plus 2 tablespoons broth from cooking seitan (and 1/4 cup more if not using wine)
> 1/2 teaspoon rosemary
> 2 teaspoons paprika (reserve 1 teaspoon for garnish)
> 1/2 cup thick starch from preparing seitan
> 1/4 cup dry red wine
> 3 to 6 boiled potatoes—mash or whip WITH
> 1/4 to 1/2 cup plain soymilk
> 1/4 to 1/2 teaspoon salt

- Preheat the oven to 400° F.

- Sauté the carrots, celery, and onions in the sesame oil until the onions become translucent.

- Add the seitan broth, rosemary, and 1 teaspoon paprika. Simmer until the vegetables are tender.

- Add the wheat starch and wine and stir constantly until the sauce is thick and glossy. Add the seitan and adjust the seasonings.

- Remove from the stove and cool to room temperature.

Note: To stop now and resume preparation later, cover the potatoes and the stew and refrigerate both until you are ready to assemble the pies.

Make the Pies:
- You can make one large pie as a casserole, use individual crockery casseroles or 4½″ aluminum foil pie plates to make about 6 individual pies. Preparation and assembly are the same for both types.

- Use about ½ cup of the potato mixture for each individual pie. With wet hands, roll the mashed potatoes into a ball. Put into the pie pan and then press the potatoes across the bottom and up the sides of the baking container. Dip a table knife in water and use the flat side of the blade to smooth and shape the edges of the potato "shell" as desired.

- Add the stew into the potato shell.

- If there is any potato left over, it may be used to build up the edges of the shell, or to decorate the top of the stew.

For example: Wet your hands and roll the potato mixture into a cylinder about 1″ in diameter. Make 6 or 8 equally thick slices (or one for each pie). Flatten each one, and place it on the center of the pie. Sprinkle the remaining paprika over the tops of the pies.

- You may also use a pastry bag or cookie press to squeeze a decorative row of potato around the top of each potato shell's edge.

- Bake for 15 to 20 minutes or until the potatoes are slightly browned.

Chili

Makes 4 to 5 quarts—refrigerate, freeze extra, or have a party!

> 3 cups kidney beans
> 4″ piece kombu, broken into small pieces in
> 8 cups water

Additional Ingredients:

> 3 cups cooked seitan 4, ground coarsely or chopped
> 2 links (1/2 recipe) seitan 7, sliced in 1/4″ pieces

1/2 cup olive oil	1 teaspoon cumin
3 cups onion, diced	2 tablespoons chili powder, or to taste
2 cups celery, diced (about 3 stalks)	1 teaspoon basil
1/2 cup miso (mugi or red)	2 teaspoons oregano
28 oz. can ground, peeled tomatoes	1/4 cup parsley, minced
6 oz. can tomato paste	1/2 teaspoon dry mustard
4 cloves garlic, crushed and minced	2 teaspoons paprika

Cook the Beans:
- Soak the beans overnight in water to cover. The next day, drain the beans and boil them in 8 cups of water with the kombu for at least 2 hours, or until tender. Use no salt before the beans are tender. If you do not soak the beans, they may be pressure-cooked with the kombu for 1¼ hours.

- Sauté the coarsely ground seitan in the olive oil for 5 minutes. Add the onions, celery and garlic and sauté a few minutes more, until the onions are translucent. Add the beans and the broth from cooking them. Add the tomatoes and tomato paste, miso, and all other seasonings. Simmer a minimum of 1½ hours. Long, slow cooking makes a better flavor. Stir occasionally.

- About 20 minutes before serving, brown the seitan slices until they are crispy and add them to the chili.

Polenta "Al Forno"

This hearty baked dish is easy to prepare in advance. Golden cornmeal topped with rich tomato sauce help to create a festive mood for an informal meal.

Serves 6

2 cups seitan 4, seasoned with Spicy Seasoning Mix in broth OR
1 1/2 tablespoons Spicy Seasoning Mix added when grinding the seitan

1 1/2 cups cornmeal
1/2 teaspoon salt
4 to 6 cups water
1 medium onion—cut to be ground up
1 1/2 cups prepared Basic Tomato Sauce (see page 168)

Cook the Cornmeal:
- Combine the cornmeal, salt, and 4 cups water in a sauce pan and place on a medium-low heat. Stir constantly. When it begins to thicken and starts to boil, stir in the remaining 2 cups water, adding the water gradually and stirring quickly. Reduce heat to low, and place a flame diffuser under the pot and simmer. Cover for about 40 minutes, stirring and checking the consistency at 10 minute intervals. It should be smooth and thick, but not stiff.

- Turn the cooked polenta out into a lightly oiled baking dish (about 10″ × 10″ × 2″) and refrigerate it or cool it at room temperature ½ hour or more to firm up. Grind the seitan coarsely. If a food processor, meat grinder, or blender are not available, you can use the large holes of a hand-held grater. Add the Spicy Seasoning Mix to the ground seitan and onions.

- Heat the tomato sauce and add the ground seitan and onion mixture to it. Cover and simmer for 10 minutes.

- Preheat the oven to 375° F. Spread the tomato sauce evenly over the top of the polenta. Cover with foil and bake for ½ hour. Remove the cover, and continue to bake 15 minutes more. Longer baking may be needed if the polenta was refrigerated.

Note: This dish may be prepared in advance by keeping the sauce and polenta separate until just before baking time.

Tricolor Pilaf

Tasty and colorful, this combination of whole grain rice and juicy vegetable bits is a natural for family meals.

Serves 4 to 6

    1 cup uncooked seitan (your choice of seitan type)

    1 1/2 cups long grain brown rice
    3 1/4 to 3 1/2 cups boiling water
    1 teaspoon sesame or olive oil
    1 cup carrots, diced (1 medium-large carrot)
    1/4 teaspoon salt
    2 teaspoons natural soy sauce
    Oil for deep-frying
    1 cup corn kernels, removed from cob
    1 cup freshly shelled, or frozen green peas

Additional Suggested Vegetables:

    Celery, diced
    Green pepper, diced
    Sweet red pepper, diced
    Parsley, minced—add just before serving
    Winter squash, diced 3/4" cubes

- Rinse the rice, and place it in a strainer to drain. Bring the water to a boil in a saucepan. In a heavy pot, heat the sesame oil and sauté the carrots slowly for about 5 minutes. Add the rice and continue to sauté, stirring steadily over a medium heat, until the rice is fairly dry and a light golden-brown color. Add the boiling water, salt, and soy sauce. Cover and bring to a boil over high heat. Reduce heat to simmer and place a flame diffuser under the pot. Simmer 50 to 60 minutes until the rice is fluffy and tender.

- Heat the oil. Break off tiny pieces of the seitan before dropping them into the oil (see Instructions for Deep-Frying). Drain the pieces of seitan on paper towels, then place them in a colander and pour boiling water over them to remove excess oil.

- Steam the corn kernels and peas in a separate saucepan. When the rice has finished cooking, add the corn, peas, and seitan pieces and mix gently. Serve immediately.

Seitan Stew Provençale

An elegant stew, this is a whole meal in itself. Accent the stew with crusty sourdough bread and a very simple green salad with vinaigrette dressing.

Serves 6

2 cups uncooked seitan 1, cut into 1"
  cubes and cooked as for Simmered
  Cubes seasoned with Hearty
  Seasoning Mix

1/2 cup whole wheat pastry flour
1/2 teaspoon black pepper
1/2 teaspoon allspice
1 tablespoon paprika
1 teaspoon salt
2 tablespoons olive oil
3 garlic cloves, crushed and minced
1 large or 2 medium onions, diced
3 celery stalks, cut into large chunks

2 carrots, cut into 1/4" rounds
1 medium turnip, OR
3" piece daikon radish, cut into 1/2"
  cubes
4 to 5 cups water

6 to 8 plum tomatoes, 1" cubes or
  quartered if very small
3/4 cup dry red wine
2 bay leaves
1 cup thick starch from preparing seitan
4 tablespoons natural soy sauce
1/4 cup minced fresh parsley

• Combine the pastry flour, pepper, allspice, paprika, and salt. Coat each piece of seitan with this mixture. In a heavy covered pot, brown the seasoned seitan in the olive oil.

• Add the garlic and onion, celery, carrot, and turnip. Add 4 cups boiling water and cover. When the broth comes to a boil, lower the heat and add the tomato pieces, wine, and bay leaves. Simmer until the carrots are tender.

• Mix the thick starch with the natural soy sauce, and add it to the stew. Heat through, stirring until thick. Adjust the seasonings. Simmer 15 to 20 minutes, adding a little more water as needed. Add the parsley just before serving.

Pastichio—Greek-Style Macaroni Casserole

Long macaroni is customarily used for this adaptation of a traditional Greek dish, but other varieties of pasta will work well if that type is not available.

Serves 6

2 cups cooked seitan (any type), ground coarsely

1 pound long macaroni or other pasta
3 tablespoons olive or sesame oil
1 1/2 tablespoons natural soy sauce

For the Sauce:

1 1/2 tablespoons kuzu
1 to 1 1/2 cups water
1 1/2 cups plain soymilk
1 tablespoon tahini

3/4 teaspoon salt
1/2 teaspoon cinnamon
1 cup bread crumbs

• Preheat the oven to 400° F.

• Cook, drain, and rinse the pasta.

• Brown the coarsely ground seitan in the oil, adding natural soy sauce after 3 to 4 minutes. Combine with the pasta, and set aside.

Prepare the Sauce:
• Dissolve the kuzu in ½ cup of the water. In a saucepan, combine the soymilk with the remaining ½ cup water, tahini, salt, and cinnamon. Mix well and heat, almost to boiling. Add the kuzu mixture and stir constantly until thick. Add up to ½ cup more water if needed, and adjust the seasonings.

• Oil a baking dish and layer half of the pasta-seitan mixture in the bottom. Pour half the sauce over it. Layer the remaining pasta and sauce. The top layer should be sauce. Top with a layer of bread crumbs. Cover with foil and bake 15 minutes. Remove the foil and bake 15 minutes more to create a golden crust.

Baked Vermicelli with "Pepperoni Seitan" —————

This thin pasta is accented with spicy seitan and a very light tomato sauce.

Serves 6

1 cup seitan 7, prepared as "pepperoni seitan"

1 to 1 1/2 pounds vermicelli pasta, cooked al dente
1 tablespoon olive oil
1 onion
2 celery stalks
2 cloves garlic, crushed and minced
28 oz. can whole, peeled Italian tomatoes
1/2 teaspoon salt or to taste
1 teaspoon basil

• Oil a baking dish, 2" or 3" high, and put in half of the cooked noodles.

• Slice the cooked seitan rolls crosswise in ⅛" slices.
• Heat the olive oil and briefly sauté the onion, celery, and garlic.

• Drain the tomatoes and reserve the juice. Chop the tomatoes and add them with their juice to the sautéed vegetables. Add the salt and basil and simmer for ½ hour.

- Preheat the oven to 400° F.

- Pour half the sauce over the noodles in the baking dish and add a layer of half the seitan slices. Repeat with the remaining noodles, sauce and seitan.

- Cover with foil and bake 20 minutes. Remove the foil and bake for 5 to 10 minutes.

Seitan Kebabs

Cook these seitan and vegetable kebabs under the broiler or over a charcoal fire. Present a variety of vegetables and let the guests assemble their own kebabs.

Serves 6 to 8

> 2 to 3 cups cooked seitan 1 or 3, seasoned with strong-flavored natural soy sauce broth or Aromatic Seasoning Broth
>
> 1 cup Barbecue Sauce IV or other favorite marinade (see page 166)
> Assorted vegetables, choose enough for 3 pieces each for each skewer:
>   mushrooms—use whole, skewer lengthwise
>   red or green bell peppers—cut in chunks
>   zucchini—1 1/2" rounds, skewer crosswise
>   cherry tomatoes—skewer lengthwise
>   pearl onions—skewer lengthwise
> 8 long metal skewers

- Cut the seitan into 32 cubes and marinate them in the barbecue sauce for 30 to 60 minutes, turning them occasionally to coat all sides.

- If the seitan is cooked shortly before marinating, it may be marinated in the barbecue sauce while it is still hot or warm. However, the seitan cubes should be chilled and firm before skewering.

- Wash the vegetables and pat them dry. Put them on the skewers alternately with the seitan pieces, allowing about 4 pieces of seitan for each of the 8 skewers. Brush the barbecue sauce over all the skewered vegetables and marinate them for 15 minutes.

- To cook the kebabs, lay the skewers across a baking pan or put foil on the rack under them to catch any falling juices from the seitan and vegetables. Broil about 6" from the flame for about 8 minutes, turning and basting with more sauce after 4 to 5 minutes.

Casserole with Mashed Potatoes and Seitan "Pepperoni" —

This hearty casserole is seasoned with a hint of mustard. You can assemble it ahead of time and refrigerate it until you need it.

Serves 6

> 1 piece "seitan pepperoni," sliced into 1/4" pieces
>
> 8 medium potatoes, boiled
> 1/2 cup plain soymilk
> 1/2 to 3/4 teaspoon salt
> 2 tablespoons Dijon-style prepared mustard
> 1/4 to 1/2 cup cornmeal
> 2 teaspoons natural soy sauce
> 2 tablespoons corn oil
> 1 teaspoon paprika, as garnish
> 10 to 12 olives, as garnish

- Preheat the oven to 375° F.

- Mash or whip the boiled potatoes with the soymilk, salt, and mustard. Remove the string from the seitan and slice the seitan into $\frac{1}{4}''$ thick rounds.

- Generously oil a small casserole ($9'' \times 9'' \times 2''$) and dust the inside with the cornmeal.

- Arrange half of the seitan slices, flat side down, on top of the cornmeal. Spread the potatoes evenly over them without disturbing the slices. Push the remaining slices into the potatoes at an angle so they are half buried.

- Mix the natural soy sauce and corn oil well with a fork and sprinkle this sauce over the surface of the potatoes. Scatter the olives over the top, and sprinkle with the paprika.

- Bake, covered, for 45 minutes. Remove the cover and bake for 5 to 10 minutes more to brown the top slightly.

Old-Fashioned Stew in White Sauce over Egg Noodles —

Chickpea flour is a tasty addition to the creamy white sauce in this stew.

Serves 6 to 8

> 6 precooked seitan cutlets, (made from 2 cups seitan 1, cooked with Savory Seasoning Mix I)
>
> 15 to 20 small white boiling onions

1 large carrot, cut into 1/4" thick rounds
2 celery stalks, cut into 1/2" slices
1 teaspoon salt
1 cup seasoned broth, from cooking seitan (or other)
1 cup chickpea flour
1/4 cup thick starch from preparing seitan, OR
2 tablespoons kuzu dissolved in 2 tablespoons water or broth
2 cups frozen or fresh shelled peas
1 to 2 pounds flat egg noodles or fettucine, cooked al dente

- Place the onions, carrots, and celery in a heavy covered pot and add water to 1" below the top of the vegetables. Bring to a boil, then reduce heat and simmer until the carrots and onions are tender, about 15 minutes. Add the salt.

- Meanwhile, use 2 forks to pull the cutlets apart into irregularly shaped pieces about $\frac{1}{2}'' \times 1\frac{1}{2}''$.

- Combine some seasoned broth with the chickpea flour to make a loose paste, and add it to the vegetables, continuing to stir slowly until it thickens. If more thickness is needed, use the seitan starch or kuzu and water mixture.

- Ten minutes before serving, add the seitan pieces and the peas to the stew. Adjust the seasonings.

- Serve over hot noodles.

Yeasted Pizza Dough ━━━━━━━━━━━━━━━━━━━━

To be used with "Deep-Dish Neapolitan Vegetable Pie."

1 1/2 tablespoons dry yeast
1 cup warm water
1 tablespoon barley malt syrup
2 cups unbleached white flour
1 cup whole wheat flour
1 tablespoon olive or sesame oil
2 teaspoons salt

- Dissolve the yeast in $\frac{1}{2}$ cup warm water. Put the remaining $\frac{1}{2}$ cup water and the barley malt syrup into a warm mixing bowl and add the dissolved yeast.

- Combine the flours and then sprinkle them over the water $\frac{1}{2}$ cup at a time, mixing constantly. When the dough becomes too thick to mix with a spoon or paddle, turn it out on a smooth, lightly floured surface and begin to knead it. Continue kneading for 5 to 10 minutes, adding flour a little at a time to prevent the dough from sticking to the work surface.

- Wash the bowl and oil it with the olive or sesame oil. Return the kneaded dough to the bowl and turn it over and over so the surface of the dough is oiled. Cover the bowl with a damp cloth and set it in a warm place to rise for 1 to 2 hours or until doubled in bulk.

- Sprinkle the salt over the top of the risen dough. Punch the dough down and knead it briefly. Roll out the dough as indicated in the directions for "Deep-Dish Neapolitan Vegetable Pie." Before rolling out the dough, sprinkle the work surface with cornmeal to prevent the dough from sticking.

Deep-Dish Neapolitan Vegetable Pie

Feel free to add your favorite pizza toppings in this hearty vegetable pizza.

Serves 6

seitan—choose one or more of the following varieties of seitan:
  2 pieces "seitan pepperoni" cut into 1/4" pieces
  1 to 2 cups cooked seitan cutlets, sliced or cubed
  spicy patties made from 2 cups ground seitan

1/2 cup cornmeal
1 recipe Basic Yeasted Pizza Dough
2 1/2 cups Basic Tomato Sauce

Additional Ingredients:

1 cup sliced mushrooms
1 cup tiny broccoli flowerets, blanched and drained well
2 tablespoons capers
1 green pepper—remove seeds and sliced into thin half-rounds
1/2 pound firm tofu, mixed with 1 teaspoon tahini
1 teaspoon oregano
1/2 teaspoon salt

- Lightly oil a 9" × 13" baking dish and dust it with cornmeal. Roll out the prepared pizza dough to a rectangle ¼" thick, and use it to line the baking dish with the dough extending up the sides of the dish and forming an edge all around. Flatten, flute, or otherwise shape the edge as you like.

- Allow the dough to rise 1½ to 2 hours before filling.

- Preheat the oven to 375° F.

- Sprinkle a little cornmeal over the dough before adding the filling. Spread 1½ cups of the tomato sauce evenly over the risen dough in the pan, spreading the sauce up the sides of the dough as well. Layer the seitan, mushrooms, broccoli, and capers, and add the remaining 1 cup of sauce.

• Crumble or mash the tofu and mix it with the tahini, oregano, and salt. Distribute it evenly over the top.

• Use up the crust trimmings by briefly baking them as crackers.

• Bake the pie 20 to 30 minutes.

Fennie's Dutch Casserole

Our friend Fennie adapted this old family recipe to include seitan.

Serves 5

> 6 to 9 seitan cutlets, cooked with medium to strong flavored natural soy sauce broth seasoning
>
> 4 to 5 medium to large potatoes, boiled with the skins on with 1 teaspoon salt
> 1/2 cup plain soymilk
> 3 cups sauerkraut
> 1 teaspoon corn oil
> 1 teaspoon natural soy sauce

• Preheat the oven to 350° F.

• Drain the boiled potatoes and mash them with the salt and soymilk. Drain the sauerkraut and squeeze it gently.

• Oil a deep, covered baking dish and pack ⅔ of the mashed potatoes all around the interior, about ½″ to ¾″ thick. Lay the sauerkraut over the potatoes, pressing it lightly into the potatoes.

• Place the seitan cutlets over the sauerkraut, setting aside a few pieces to use as decorations for the top of the casserole. If they are more than ½″ thick, slice them in half to reduce the thickness. Fill in the area over the seitan with the rest of the mashed potatoes, smoothing the potatoes over the top. Place the reserved seitan cutlets on top of the potatoes. Mix the corn oil and natural soy sauce together and drizzle it over the top of the seitan and potatoes.

Note: If the top of the potatoes will be in contact with the inside of the casserole cover, the inside of the cover should be oiled for easier removal. Bake 1 hour covered, then remove the cover and bake 10 minutes more to lightly brown the surface.

Country-Style Pot Pies

Make the filling in advance to simplify your preparations.

Makes 8, 4½″ individual pot pies—perfect for luncheon or lunchbox.

For the Filling:

3 cups cooked seitan 1 or 3, cubed

3 tablespoons sesame or olive oil
2 cups onions, diced 1/2″ pieces
3 celery stalks, diced 1/2″ pieces
2 cups carrots, diced 1/2″ pieces
1 1/2 to 2 cups water
1 bay leaf
1/2 teaspoon thyme

1/2 teaspoon black pepper (or to taste)
5 tablespoons starch from preparing seitan
1 tablespoon mirin
4 tablespoons (1/4 cup) natural soy sauce
2 cups fresh shelled or frozen green peas
1 cup fresh or frozen corn kernels

For the Dough:

2 cups whole wheat pastry flour
2 cups unbleached white flour
1/2 teaspoon salt
2 teaspoons baking powder
3/4 cup corn oil
3/4 to 1 cup water
1 egg (for glaze)

8 sheets wax paper, each 16″ to 18″ long

Prepare the Filling:
• Heat the oil and sauté the onions, celery, and carrots until the onions are somewhat translucent. Add the seitan cubes and sauté 5 minutes more. Add the water and seasonings and bring to a boil.

• Reduce heat to medium and add the wheat starch, stirring constantly until the sauce is thick. Add the mirin and natural soy sauce to taste. Remove the stew from the heat and add in the peas and corn.

Note: The stew may be prepared in advance and saved (refrigerated) at this point. Use it in the pies within the next 12 hours, removing it from the refrigerator when you begin to prepare the pie dough.

• Preheat the oven to 375° F.

Prepare the Dough:
• Combine all the dry ingredients and blend them well with a fork. Add the corn oil all at once, and use the fork to mix it into the flour forming pea-size balls. Add

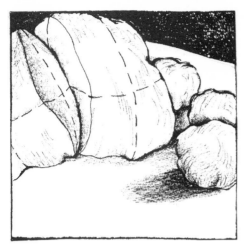

Fig. 13   Divide the dough and form it into balls.

Fig. 14   Place the dough between layers of wax paper, and flatten it with the palm of your hand.

Fig. 15   Roll out the dough between the layers of wax paper.

Fig. 16   Line the pie pan with the dough, and peel away the wax paper.

Fig. 17   Trim the edges of the dough.

Fig. 18   Country Pot Pies.

¾ cup water and use the fork to mix it in with a circular, bottom-to-top, lifting motion. If the dough seems too dry and "short," add up to ¼ cup more water 1 tablespoon at a time as you mix until the dough is more elastic and soft but not wet or sticky. Mix the dough gently. All the flour should pull away from the sides of the bowl as the dough form a ball.

- Cover the dough and set it aside for 3 to 5 minutes.

- Divide the dough ball into 2 halves and use a knife to cut each of these into 8 equal pieces. These 16 sections of dough will each be formed into a ball the size of a golf ball, to be rolled into the top and bottom crusts of all 8 individual pies. Set the sections of dough aside and cover with a slightly damp towel.

Roll the Dough and Fill the Pies:
- Use one 4½" pie pan and 2 sections of dough for each pie. Use 1 sheet of wax paper for each 2 pies. Use more wax paper if needed.

- Fold the sheet of wax paper in half. Open it like a book and place one of the balls of dough on the center of the right-hand side. Lay the other leaf of paper over it, and press slightly with the palm of your hand to slightly flatten the dough. Turn over and repeat.

- Return the paper to side one and begin to roll from the center out, forming a circle. Do this in all directions, then turn the "package" over and repeat on side two. Before rolling on the second side, lift the wax paper by the corner and reposition it, releasing any wrinkles over the dough.

- Turn the "package" back to side one again, releasing any wrinkles in the paper and finish rolling out the dough into a circle at least 6" in diameter.

- Open the wax paper and lay the dough over the pie pan, peeling away the wax paper. Gently press the dough evenly down into the pie pan.

- Fill the pie using ½ cup filling.

- Prepare the second circle of pie dough as for the bottom crust, and lay the top crust over the filled pie. Moisten the edges of the two crusts and press them together. Trim the crusts to extend ½" away from the pie pan. Pinch, flute, or press the edges together with a fork to create a decorative edge.

- Make 4 to 5, 1" slashes in the top crust or use leftover trimmings to decorate the top crust. Roll out dough pieces and cut them with a cookie-cutter or knife. To attach the shapes to the crust, use water to moisten the top crust where the shapes will be placed, and gently press the shapes on.

- Beat the egg with a fork, and paint it all over the top crusts.

• Bake for ½ hour and place on a rack to cool.

Creamy Fettucine with Crispy Seitan Strips ———————

This is a one-pot skillet casserole, creamy and mildly seasoned.

Serves 4

>   1 cup uncooked seitan 4, made into 4 cutlets, use Baked Cutlets method
>   of cooking
>
>   1 pound green (spinach) fettucine
>   1 teaspoon kuzu
>   1 1/3 cups water
>   1 tablespoon tahini
>   1 teaspoon natural soy sauce
>   1/4 teaspoon salt
>   1/2 teaspoon basil
>   1 clove garlic, crushed and minced
>   3/4 cup plain soymilk
>   Parsley, minced for garnish

• Cook the fettucine al dente. Drain and rinse thoroughly under cold water. Cut up the baked seitan cutlets into strips 2″ × ¼″.

• Dissolve the kuzu in the water. Add the tahini to it and mix with a fork until smooth. Add the natural soy sauce, salt, basil, garlic and soymilk.

• Heat a heavy skillet and brush it lightly with oil. Add the cooked noodles and heat them thoroughly, turning frequently to prevent burning.

• Add the seasoned liquid mixture to the noodles and mix gently so the sauce will coat them evenly. Lower the heat when bubbles appear. The sauce should look milky. Cover the pan, reduce the heat, and simmer for 10 minutes.

• Remove the cover and turn the noodles over carefully as the sauce thickens. Correct the seasoning and mix the noodles occasionally. Allow the sauce to simmer to the desired consistency. Add more water, ½ cup at a time, as needed for a thinner sauce. Adjust the seasonings.

• Just before serving, add the seitan strips and gently mix them through the noodles, reserving a few strips to use for garnish.

• Garnish with minced parsley and the remaining seitan strips.

Aunt Ruth's "Turkey" with Couscous Stuffing ─────

Don't wait until Thanksgiving to enjoy Aunt Ruth's inspiration. The marinated seitan is stretched and rolled, then filled with couscous. Bake and baste for a dark and delicious treat.

Serves 4

> 2 cups uncooked seitan 1, 4, or 3

For the Marinade:

> 3/4 cup natural soy sauce
> 3/4 cup saké, OR
> 3/4 cup dry red wine
> 1 tablespoon grated ginger, OR
> 2 cloves garlic, crushed and miced

- Combine the natural soy sauce, saké or wine, ginger or garlic, and knead it into the uncooked seitan. Cover and refrigerate overnight. Drain before further use, reserving the marinade. (See below.)

Couscous Stuffing ─────

To fill Aunt Ruth's "Turkey."

> 1 1/2 cups couscous
> 3 cups water
> 1/2 cup sweet red bell pepper, diced
> 1/4 to 1/2 cup walnuts, chopped
> 1/4 cup parsley, minced
> 1/2 teaspoon thyme
> 1/2 teaspoon salt

- Soak the couscous in the water for 2 to 4 hours, or until all the water has been absorbed. Combine the soaked couscous with the remaining ingredients and use as directed below to fill the "turkey."

Assemble the "Turkey" and Stuffing:
- Preheat the oven to 375° F.

- After the seitan has been marinated overnight, drain it and save the marinade to use for basting. Prepare the stuffing. Line a bread loaf pan (metal ones are easiest to work with) with aluminum foil and oil the foil.

- Roll the seitan into an 18″ square, ¼″ thick. Roll it quickly and firmly in all directions. The seitan will tend to spring back to it's original shape, so keep rolling

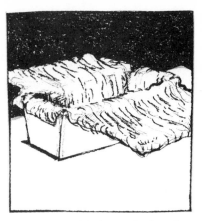

Fig. 19 Roll out the uncooked seitan.

Fig. 20 Lay the sheet of seitan into a bread pan which has been lined with foil, then oiled.

Fig. 21 Fill with the prepared stuffing.

Fig. 22 Lift and stretch the uncooked seitan, tucking it in on the opposite side.

Fig. 23 Invert the finished loaf, remove the pan, and peel away the foil.

Fig. 24 Slices of Aunt Ruth's "Turkey."

until it is the size you want. Having an extra pair of hands is helpful, but one agile cook can do it alone.

• Quickly transfer the seitan to the foil-lined loaf pan. Hold one hand on top of the seitan to keep its shape, and use the other hand to loosely pack the stuffing into the loaf.

• Stretch one side of the seitan over the top of the filling and tuck it in on the opposite side. Baste the surface with marinade, then stretch the seitan from the other side up and over. Be sure to stretch the seitan as it is pulled from one side to the other.

• Make a few short cuts with the point of a sharp knife and baste with plenty of marinade. Bake the loaf for about one hour, basting every 15 to 20 minutes with the marinade. Remove the loaf from the oven when the top is brown and crusty and no longer feels sticky.

• After about 5 minutes, invert the loaf onto a rack and lift off the baking pan. Let the loaf cool 15 minutes or more, and carefully peel the foil away. Place the loaf right side up on a platter, slice, and serve with Chunky Mushroom Gravy (see page 196).

Spanish Rice

Dress up your precooked rice with this combination of zesty seitan and old world seasonings.

Serves 6

1 piece seitan 7, cut into 1/8" thick rounds

3 tablespoons olive oil
1 medium onion, diced 1/2" pieces
3 garlic cloves, crushed and minced
3 celery stalks, diced 1/2" pieces
6 cups cooked long or short grain brown rice
1/2 teaspoon oregano
1 teaspoon basil
28 oz. can whole, peeled tomatoes
2 tablespoons natural soy sauce, or to taste

• Use a medium-high flame to lightly brown the onions and garlic in the olive oil. Add the celery and seitan rounds, and sauté together until the celery is tender.

• Add the rice, oregano, and basil, and fry on a high heat until the rice is a little crispy. Use your spatula to break up any clumps of rice so the grains are separated.

- Add the tomatoes and the natural soy sauce to taste, cover and simmer for
  15 minutes, stirring occasionally.

Side Dishes

*The discovery of a new dish does more for human happiness than
the discovery of a new star.*—Brillat-Savarin (1755–1826),
Physiologie du Gout

Cutlets Braised in Peanut Sauce

**Take about 30 minutes to prepare this exotic variation of simmered cutlets. Make your
salad or steamed greens while the cutlets are simmering.**

Serves 3 to 6

> 6 cooked seitan cutlets, made from 2 cups 2, 1, 4, or 3 seitan cooked in natural
> soy sauce broth
>
> 1 cup water
> 1 teaspoon Aromatic Seasoning Mix
> 2 tablespoons mirin
> 2 tablespoons peanut butter
> 2 tablespoons white miso
> 3 drops to 1/4 teaspoon Chinese Hot Pepper Oil
> 2 scallions, chopped fine

• Combine ½ cup water, the Aromatic Seasoning Mix, and the mirin in a large (10″)
heavy skillet. Add the cutlets and cover. Simmer for 5 to 10 minutes while
preparing a creamy paste of the peanut butter, miso, ½ cup water, and hot pepper
oil.

• Remove the cutlets and add the peanut butter mixture to the broth, distributing
it evenly in the broth. Return the cutlets to the skillet. Cover the pan and simmer
the cutlets in the peanut sauce for 10 minutes, then turn them over and simmer for
10 minutes more. Add in the scallions and simmer, uncovered, until most of the
liquid from the sauce has evaporated.

• Cutlets in Peanut Sauce is best when served hot.

Filled Noodle Nests ———————————————————

This dish is fun to prepare and good for a family meal or casual entertaining. You can cook the noodles a day ahead, and keep them covered in the refrigerator. This way they will stay quite dry and will be more crispy when deep-fried.

Serves 6

> 2 cups cooked seitan 11, cooked with Savory Seasoning Mix I (or other cooked seitan of your choice)
>
> 8 oz. whole wheat spaghetti or linguini—cook al dente and chill
> Oil for deep-frying
> 2 1/2 tablespoons arrowroot
> 1/4 cup water
> 2 tablespoons natural soy sauce
> 1 tablespoon mirin
> 1 teaspoon grated ginger root
> 1 tablespoon sesame oil
> 1/2 pound snow peas
> 8 oz. can sliced water chestnuts
> 1 1/2 cups water or stock

• Cut the seitan into thin strips ½″ wide, 2″ long, and ⅛″ thick. Hold about ½ cup of cooked noodles together firmly with long chopsticks or tongs. Immerse the noodles in the hot oil and hold them against the sides of the pot to help form the shape of a nest. Release the noodles after about one minute, when the shape is set, and turn them over. Remove the noodle nest from the oil when it is golden and crispy. Drain thoroughly on paper towels.

• Dissolve the arrowroot in ¼ cup water. Add natural soy sauce, mirin, and grated ginger.

• Heat 1 tablespoon sesame oil and quickly stir-fry the seitan. When the seitan is crispy on the outside, add the snow peas and water chestnuts. Stir-fry all together to heat through. Add the arrowroot mixture and 1½ cups water, stirring well. The sauce is done when it is translucent. Arrange the noodle nests on a platter, or on individual plates, and spoon the sauce over them.

• Serve immediately.

Red-Simmered "Roast" ———————————————

Have this on hand to accompany Filled Noodle Nests (above)—it has the delicate sweetness of star anise and mirin coupled with an undercurrent of garlic and hot pepper oil. Serve it hot or cold, in chunks or sliced very thin.

Serves 6

1 recipe seitan "roast" 11, cooked with natural soy sauce broth seasoning

3 tablespoons sesame oil
2 cloves garlic
3 tablespoons natural soy sauce
3 tablespoons mirin
8 cloves Chinese star anise (one clove is one section of a "star" of anise)
2 tablespoons rice syrup
1/4 teaspoon Chinese Hot Pepper oil
2 cups water
2 scallions, slivered to use as garnish

• Cut the seitan "roast" into cubes, 1½″ to 2½″ on a side.

• Heat the sesame oil in a heavy pot with a cover. Add the seitan pieces to the oil and brown until crispy on all sides. Add the remaining ingredients and lower the heat. Cover and simmer for two hours, turning the pieces over every 20 minutes. The remaining broth can be reduced by simmering uncovered for a few minutes more. Serve the reduced broth as a sauce with the seitan pieces.

• Serve warm or cold, and garnish with scallion slivers.

Note: Chinese star anise may be purchased at Oriental markets, some natural food stores, and some supermarkets.

Baked Sauerkraut with Spicy Seitan Patties and Apples ——

Hot sauerkraut is accompanied by spicy seitan patties and a hint of apple.

Makes 12 patties, 1½″ in diameter

serves 6

2 cups cooked seitan 3, prepared simmered with natural soy sauce broth

4 cups (one 32 oz. jar) sauerkraut—naturally fermented type
2 cups water
2 tablespoons whole wheat pastry flour
1/4 cup chickpea flour
1 1/2 teaspoons Spicy Seasoning Mix
3 tablespoons sesame oil
1 tart apple (Granny Smith)

• Drain the sauerkraut and squeeze it gently to remove excess brine. Place it in a bowl and cover with 2 cups of fresh water. Soak the sauerkraut for about 15 minutes to remove some of the salt. Save the soaking water.

- While the sauerkraut is soaking, grind the seitan in a blender or food processor. Add the pastry flour, chickpea flour, seasoning, and mix very well. Form the mixture into 12 small patties and pan-fry them in the heated sesame oil until they are browned and very firm.

- Preheat the oven to 300° F.

- Grate the apple, leaving the skin on if you wish. Drain and squeeze the sauerkraut firmly, then mix it with the apple. Put the mixture into a well-oiled, covered casserole, burying the seitan patties in the sauerkraut mixture.

- Pour ½ cup of the soaking water over the top. Cover and bake for 45 to 60 minutes or until heated through.

Barbecue Robai Cutlets

Just making Robai is an experience in itself. The transformation from uncooked seitan to huge golden puffs is one which never loses its fascination. These cutlets are a little soft and chewy.

Serves 4, each serving is 2 pieces

> 2 cups uncooked seitan (see page 60)
>
> 4 tablespoons sweet rice flour
> Oil for deep-frying
> 2 cups water
> 4 teaspoons natural soy sauce
> 1" piece fresh ginger root, cut into 1/8" slices
> 1/4 cup Hickory Barbecue Sauce III (see page 166)

- Divide the uncooked seitan into 4 equal sections of ½ cup each. Knead into each section 1 tablespoon sweet rice flour, and continue to follow the instructions for making Robai as indicated on page 60.

- Bring the water, natural soy sauce, and ginger slices to a boil, and add cooked Robai cutlets. Reduce the heat and simmer for 3 to 5 minutes. Remove and place it on a plate to cool. The cutlets may be refrigerated to chill.

Note: Stop here to save for later completion of the dish.

- When the cutlets are cool, divide each in half, and place them on a cookie sheet. Spread about 1 tablespoon Barbecue Sauce over the top of each one, and broil for 2 to 5 minutes, or until the sauce is dry. Watch carefully during broiling.

Piroshki

These turnovers are great for lunchboxes or luncheons. In fact, they are good just about any time. You can vary the filling if you wish by using leftover grains or vegetables. Or, try a fruit pie filling for a memorable dessert. Make the filling ahead of time to simplify your preparation.

Makes 8 turnovers

For the Filling:

> 2 cups cooked seitan 3, ground with
> 1 cup diced onion
>
> 1 1/2 teaspoons Savory Seasoning Mix I
> 1 tablespoon dried parsley flakes
> 1 teaspoon oregano
> 2 teaspoons paprika

For the Dough:

> 1 cup whole wheat pastry flour
> 1 cup unbleached white flour
> 1/2 teaspoon celery seed
> 1/4 teaspoon salt
> 1 teaspoon baking powder
> 6 tablespoons corn oil
> 1/2 cup plus 1 tablespoon water
>
> 1 small egg
> 1/2 teaspoon natural soy sauce

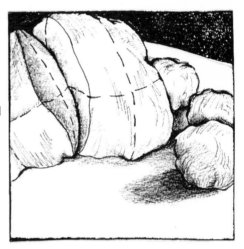

Fig. 25 Divide the dough and form it into balls.

Fig. 26 Place the dough between layers of wax paper, and flatten it with the palm of your hand.

Fig. 27   Roll out the dough between layers of wax paper.

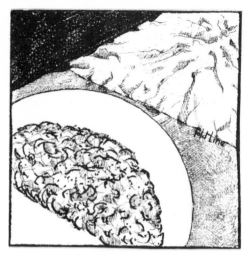

Fig. 28   Place the filling on half of the rolled-out dough nearest the fold line of the wax paper.

Fig. 29   Fold "empty" side of the dough over the filling by picking up the edges of the wax paper.

Fig. 30   Piroshki (seitan turnovers).

Make the Filling:
• Combine all filling ingredients.

Make the Dough:
• Mix all the dry ingredients and pour the oil into the center. Mix with a fork or pastry blender, using a circular chopping motion so the flour and oil will form pea-size balls. Add the water and mix quickly but lightly to make a semi-soft, flexible dough.

Form the Turnovers:

- Preheat the oven to 350° F. Cut 4 or more pieces of wax paper, each 16″ long. Each piece can be used for rolling out 2 to 4 balls of dough. (See illustrations.)

- Divide the dough into 8 equal sections and cover with a damp, not wet, paper or cloth towel. Fold the sheets of wax paper in half, like a book.

- Roll one section of the dough into a ball. Open the wax paper, and place the ball of dough in the center of the bottom layer of paper. Replace the wax paper "cover" over the dough, and press down gently with the palm of your hand flattening the dough to ½″ thick. Roll the dough into a circle about ⅛″ thick. Turn the entire package over. The piece of paper which is now on top will be wrinkled, so lift it up and reposition it to release any deep winkles formed by the rolling. Roll the dough into a circle about 6″ in diameter.

- Turn the entire paper package over again, back to side one, and lift up the now-wrinkled wax paper. Place 3 tablespoons of filling on the half of the dough closest to the centerline of the paper. Moisten ½″ all around the edges of the dough with a finger dipped in water. Lift up the free edge of the paper beneath the dough, and fold it over to cover the filling, lining up the edges of the dough to form a semi-circle.

- Peel back the wax paper and gently press the edges of the dough together to seal them.

- Trim off about ¼″ from the edge of the turnover to make a smooth edge. Flute the edge or compress it with a damp fork, as desired.

- Combine all the trimmings and roll them out to be made into decorative shapes with a knife or cookie cutter. Moisten the backs of the shapes with a little water, and place them on the surface of the turnover.

- Beat the egg and natural soy sauce lightly with a fork and apply it with a pastry brush to paint the surface of the turnover, thoroughly covering all edges of the decorations. Bake 25 minutes. Cool the turnovers on a rack or serve them hot.

- These are great for luncheons or lunch boxes.

Filled Crepes with Orange-Shallot Sauce ━━━━━━━━━

Serve these crepes as a side dish, or as an appetizer for a more formal meal. This three-part recipe may seem complex, but you can make the filling a day ahead if necessary. The crepes may also be made before they are filled and baked. The "Savory Seasoning Mix" helps to lend this dish its unique flavor, but if you prefer to omit it you may do so, and use seitan which has only been seasoned with the natural soy sauce broth in which it was cooked.

Makes 16 filled crepes

Serves 8

1 recipe Basic Crepes see page 191 (makes 16 crepes)

Filling for Crepes:

4 cups or 6 cutlets cooked seitan 1 or 3

16 mushrooms
1/2 medium onion
3 tablespoons Savory Seasoning Mix I
1 cup minced parsley
2 teaspoons mirin

- Use a food processor, blender, meat grinder or hand grater to grind the seitan, mushrooms, and onion. Turn out into a mixing bowl and add the seasoning mix, parsley, and mirin. Mix well. Use about 2½ to 3 tablespoons to fill each crepe as follows:

- Place 2½ to 3 tablespoons filling across the lower third of the crepe, forming a rectangle about 6″ wide and 1″ deep. Pick up the near edge of the crepe, and lift it over the filling to cover, tucking it in on the other side of the filling. Continue to roll the crepe into a tight cylinder. Place it seam side down in a lightly oiled baking dish. Continue for all crepes, placing each one next to the others as they are filled and rolled.

- Preheat the oven to 350° F.

- Brush 1 teaspoon sauce evenly over the top of each crepe. Keep the rest of the sauce hot until serving time. Cover the crepes and bake them for about 20 minutes or until heated through.

- To serve, spoon about 2 teaspoons of the heated sauce (below) onto individual plates, and place the hot crepes on the sauce. Garnish with very thin slivers of orange peel.

Orange-Shallot Sauce for Filled Crepes ━━━━━━━━

Makes about 2 cups sauce

2 tablespoons kuzu
1 1/4 cups water
2 tablespoons plus 2 teaspoons natural soy sauce
2 tablespoons mirin
1 tablespoon olive oil
1 shallot, minced

1/4 cup dry white wine
3 tablespoons fresh-squeezed orange juice

• Dissolve the kuzu in ¼ cup of the water. Add the remaining 1 cup water, the natural soy sauce, and the mirin to the kuzu mixture. Stir constantly over a medium heat until the liquid becomes translucent and thick. Reduce to the lowest heat to keep warm, stirring occasionally.

• Heat the olive oil and sauté the minced shallot for a few minutes over a medium heat. Do not brown the shallot. Add the white wine and simmer with the sauce until the volume is reduced by about ⅓.

• Add the orange juice and simmer for 3 to 4 minutes. Add to the kuzu mixture, stirring to mix well. Keep hot until serving time.

Sweet and Sour Chinese Vegetables and Seitan Cubes———

Succulent batter-coated seitan cubes are accented by the snow peas and other Chinese vegetables. The key to a successful stir-fried vegetable dish is organization—have everything precut and placed in separate bowls arranged in their order of cooking. This dish is at its best when served immediately.

Serves 6

The Vegetables:

2 cups cubed, cooked seitan 1, 2, or 3 (cooked in strong soy sauce broth)
Oil for deep-frying

2 teaspoons sesame oil
1/2 teaspoon salt
8 stalks (or one head) bok choy
1/2 pound snow peas
1/2 pound mung bean sprouts
8 oz. can sliced water chestnuts
8 oz. can bamboo shoots
Canned straw mushrooms (optional)
Canned baby corn (optional)

For the Sauce:

1 cup water
2 tablespoons natural soy sauce
1/4 teaspoon Chinese hot pepper oil
3 tablespoons barley malt or rice syrup (or to taste)
3 tablespoons rice vinegar or cider vinegar (or to taste)
1/3 thick starch from preparing seitan, OR
2 tablespoons kuzu, dissolved in a little water

122

For the Batter:

    3/4 cup whole wheat pastry flour
    2 tablespoons arrowroot powder
    1/2 teaspoon baking powder
    1/2 teaspoon salt
    3/4 cup water
    2 tablespoons arrowroot powder to use for dredging seitan piece

Prepare the Vegetables:
- Separate the white stems of the bok choy from the greens. Slice the bok choy stem in half lengthwise, then crosswise at 1½″ intervals. Layer the greens into one or two piles, and slice lengthwise into strips 1″ wide, then crosswise every 1½″.

- Trim the snow peas, removing any stiff "thread" from the outer edge. Rinse and drain the bean sprouts. Drain any canned vegetables being used. The baby corn cobs may be sliced in half lengthwise.

Make-the Batter:
- Combine all the dry ingredients and mix well with a fork. Add water and mix well. Set the batter aside for 5 minutes before using. (Make the batter then heat the oil, by which time the batter is ready to use.)

Deep-fry the Seitan Cubes:
- Prepare 5 or 6 pieces of seitan at one time.

- Pat the seitan cubes dry with a paper towel. Use the 2 tablespoons arrowroot to dredge all the pieces of seitan on each side, then dip them into the batter. Deep-fry the seitan until crispy and golden. Remove and drain on a few layers of paper towel.

- Set the seitan cubes aside, to be added to the vegetables just before serving.

Prepare the Sauce:
- Combine all sauce ingredients and mix well. If the sauce was set aside for more than 5 minutes, mix well just before using.

Cook the Vegetables:
- Heat a wok or skillet and add the sesame oil. Put in the white bok choy stems and stir-fry until they begin to soften slightly. Add the greens and sprinkle the salt over them. Continue to stir-fry a minute or so more, then add the snow peas; after a minute or two add the bean sprouts and corn, mushrooms, or any other Chinese vegetables. Do not overcook the vegetables—they should be brightly colored and a little crunchy.

- When all the vegetables are hot, mix the sauce once more to a uniform consistency and add it to the hot vegetables. Mix the sauce rapidly through the vegetables so it will not become lumpy. Do this by scooping from the bottom of the pan up and over, with a spatula or broad, flat spoon. Add the seitan pieces and heat thoroughly.

• Adjust the seasonings. If a stronger sweet and sour taste is needed, add 2 table-spoons (or to taste) more of both the sweetener and the vinegar, mixing them together before adding to the vegetables.

Vegetarian Sausage Links or Hot Dogs ────────

One of our 11-year-old neighbors kept asking for more. They are tasty and easy to make—you can form them into any length you like, and serve them right from the pot, broiled, or cut up and used in soups, casseroles, or salads.

Makes 8 to 12 sausages, 4″ to 6″ long

2 cups uncooked seitan (1, 4, or 3 preferred)

1 yard good quality cheesecloth, cut in half
1/2 cup oil
String—thin and very strong

For the Broth:

3 1/2 tablespoons Spicy Seasoning Mix
3 garlic cloves, cut in irregular chunks
2 tablespoons natural soy sauce
2 tablespoons barley malt or rice syrup
8 cups water
3″ piece kombu

• Divide the seitan into two equal pieces and form each piece into a long cylinder about ¾″ thick.

• Dip the cheesecloth into the oil, and saturate it thoroughly. Remove the excess oil by pulling the cheesecloth between the thumb and index fingers of one hand. Open the cheesecloth flat on the work surface.

• If the seitan is more than ¾″ thick, slice it in half lengthwise. Lay the two long pieces end to end in the center of the open cheesecloth, arranging the seitan so it is a uniform thickness throughout. Fold the bottom 4″ to 6″ of cheesecloth over to enclose the seitan, then roll, beginning at the edge closest to you, until you come to the end of the cheesecloth piece.

• Tie the strings very tightly at each end of the entire length of seitan, making the ties close to the seitan. Make very tight ties to form the sausages every 4″ to 6″

Fig. 31 Saturate the cheesecloth with oil, then squeeze the excess oil back into the bowl.

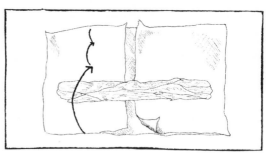

Fig. 32 Open the cheesecloth, and lay the uncooked seitan on top of it. Roll up to form a cylinder.

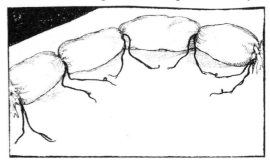

Fig. 33 Tie tightly at intervals to form pieces the size you need.

down the length of the seitan making the pieces as long or short as you like. Cut the string ½″ from the knot.

- Combine all seasonings and the barley malt syrup with the water and kombu, and bring to a boil. Reduce the heat and add the two long pieces of cheesecloth-wrapped seitan links. Simmer the seitan for about one hour. Remove it from the broth for about ½ hour or until the pieces are cool enough to handle. Untie or cut them apart and unwrap them. Return the seitan to the broth to simmer, uncovered, for about 1¼ hours more, turning often until the broth is almost gone.

- The total cooking time is about 2¼ hours.

To Serve: Serve whole as "hot dogs," or slice and deep-fry or broil. Seitan prepared this way is a welcome addition to soups, salads, and casseroles.

Onion-Caraway Balls with Sauerkraut ─────────

The salt content of sauerkraut may vary greatly from one type to another. If your sauerkraut is very salty, soak it for about 15 minutes in cold water, then drain and squeeze it before cooking.

Serves 4 to 6

2 cups uncooked seitan 1 or 2

2 tablespoons natural soy sauce
1/2 to 3/4 cup onion, diced very fine or grated coarsely
1 teaspoon caraway seeds
Oil for deep-frying
2 cups sauerkraut
1 1/4 cups water—or a little more, as needed

- Run hot water over the uncooked seitan to soften it. Place the seitan on the work surface and pat, pound and stretch it out to ½″ thick. Sprinkle the natural soy sauce, the onion, and the caraway seeds evenly over the seitan. Fold the seitan over in half and let it rest for a few minutes. Puncture any air holes with a skewer or sharp pointed knife.

- Knead the onions and seeds into the seitan by repeatedly folding the seitan over and pressing down firmly. Pull, stretch, and twist the seitan as much as is necessary to work the onion pieces well into the seitan. Some of the onion pieces may fall out, but most of them should stick into the seitan. Let the seitan rest again for a few minutes, then roll it up into a cylinder. Again, puncture any air holes.

- Cut the seitan into 2″ chunks, and roll each chunk "into itself."

- Heat the oil. Cut off 1″ pieces of the seitan, and add them to the hot oil one at a time. Using a pair of chopsticks or other implements, try to keep the balls submerged for the first 10 seconds of cooking time so they can expand and cook more thoroughly on the inside. Turn them over when the underside appears to be golden around the edges. If you wait too long, they will not stay turned over but will immediately roll back to the first side, and therefore will not cook evenly.

- Remove the balls from the oil when they are golden; do not let the onions burn. Drain well on paper towels.

- Heat the sauerkraut and water thoroughly in a saucepan. Add the onion balls and mix them lightly throughout the sauerkraut. Cover and heat through for about 20 minutes, mixing occasionally.

Seitan Cubes in Garlic Sauce

Serve over rice or noodles, or with a loaf of hearty whole-grain bread and fresh greens.

Serves 4 to 6

2 cups cooked seitan cubes—use seitan 2, simmered in Savory Seasoning
  Mix I or II
Oil for deep-frying

2 cups water
2 carrots, cut in half lengthwise, then 1" pieces
3 celery stalks, cut crosswise into 1" pieces
4 garlic cloves
1 teaspoon olive or sesame oil
2 teaspoons umeboshi paste
3/4 cup plain soymilk
6 tablespoons thick starch from preparing seitan
1/4 cup water
2 teaspoons natural soy sauce
1/4 cup chopped parsley

• Chill the seitan cubes and pat them to remove any remaining broth. Deep-fry until the outside is crisp, then remove them to drain on paper towels.

• Bring the 2 cups of water to a boil and add the carrots and celery. Reduce the heat and cover. Simmer for 10 minutes, or until the carrots are tender.

• Crush and mince the garlic and make it into a paste with the olive or sesame oil, adding the oil a little at a time. Mix in the umeboshi paste and then the soymilk, blending well until smooth. Add the garlic sauce to the vegetables. Add the seitan pieces to the sauce.

• Mix in the starch, stirring constantly until the mixture has thickened. Add the natural soy sauce, and ¼ cup water if the sauce is too thick. Add the parsley and simmer for an additional 15 to 20 minutes.

Carrots and Daikon with Fu Rings

Use Fu to add another dimension to the sweetness of juicy carrots and daikon.

Serves 6

5 large or 10 small commercially-prepared fu rings

Warm water to cover fu, for soaking
4 to 5 medium carrots, cut into 1/2" rounds
8" daikon radish, cut in 1/2" rounds
1/2" water
1 teaspoon natural soy sauce
2 scallions, cut 2" lengths

• Soak the dried fu rings in warm water to cover for 5 to 10 minutes. Squeeze them gently. If you have used large rings, cut them in thirds.

• Add the carrots and daikon to ½" boiling water and cover. When the water comes to a boil again, reduce the heat to medium-low and simmer for about 10 minutes.

Uncover and simmer until the water has reduced to $\frac{1}{4}''$. Add the fu, natural soy sauce, and scallions. Continue to simmer uncovered for 5 minutes, stirring occasionally until all the water is gone.

Baked Buttercup Treasure Chest ——————————

Use the baked squash itself as a serving bowl, and enjoy the treasures it contains.

Serves 6

> 1 1/2 to 2 cups cooked seitan cutlets or cubes (use 1, 4 or 3, cooked in natural soy sauce broth)
>
> 1 medium buttercup squash (choose one with a flat bottom)
> 2 teaspoons minced parsley
> 1 medium onion, diced 1/2" pieces
> 1/4 cup seasoned stock (from cooking the seitan)

• Preheat the oven to 375° F.

• Scrub the squash and cut the top off to create a lid about 1" thick. Scoop out the seeds and discard them, or save them for roasting or planting. Scoop out some of the squash from inside the cover so the squash will hold more filling.

• Cut the seitan into $\frac{3}{4}''$ cubes if it was not cut into cubes before cooking. Using a small knife and a metal spoon, carefully trim away the inner walls of the squash to about $\frac{1}{4}''$ thick. Chop this scooped-out squash very well and place it in a bowl with the parsley, onion, and seitan.

• Add the seasoned stock to the squash and seitan mixture, and use the mixture to fill the hollowed-out squash. Replace the cover, matching the vertical lines of the squash and the lid to their original position.

• Secure the cover by tying a cotton string or cord around the entire squash. Bake the squash at 375° F for 45 to 60 minutes, or until a fork can easily penetrate the side of the squash. The squash should feel tender when squeezed gently.

Note: For advance preparation, assemble the entire stuffed squash, and refrigerate it for up to 8 hours before baking. Additional baking time may be needed when using a chilled squash.

Old-Fashioned Hickory Baked Beans ——————————

Bring a pot of baked beans to your next picnic or pot luck event—but make an extra one to have at home.

Serves 6

> 2 cups navy beans—soak with the kombu for 8 hours or overnight in 6 cups
> water

Note: If you don't have time to soak the beans overnight, boil them with the kombu and simmer 5 to 10 minutes. Remove from the heat and soak for 2 to 3 hours before mixing with the other ingredients and baking.

> 3″ piece kombu, broken up into 1/4″ pieces
> 3 tablespoons barley malt syrup
> 1/4 cup tomato paste
> 2 tablespoons sesame oil
> 1/4 cup miso (red or mugi) made into a paste with 1/2 cup water
> 1 1/2 teaspoons dry mustard
> 2 cups onions, diced 1/2″ pieces
> 2 cups seitan 4, cooked in strong natural soy sauce broth

• Using a blender, *suribachi* (a serrated bowl used with a pestle), or rubber spatula and bowl, combine the following until smooth: barley malt syrup, tomato paste, sesame oil, miso, and mustard. Add this mixture to the beans and their soaking water. Add the onions.

• Heat oven to 300° F.

• Use a narrow-necked stoneware bean pot or other heavy, ovenproof pot with a tight-fitting cover. Fill the pot ¾ full with the bean mixture. Cover tightly and bake for 3 hours, checking periodically to make sure that the beans do not dry out. Add a little water if necessary. (A wide-necked pot will allow more rapid evaporation.)

• Raise the heat to 375° F.

• Cut the seitan into strips 1½″ × ¼″ and pan-fry the seitan until it is crispy. Add the seitan to the pot when the beans are tender. Bake an additional ½ hour after adding seitan pieces.

Curried Seitan Cubes ━━━━━━━━━━━━━━━━━━

Attractively served on a bed of shredded lettuce, this dish is garnished with raisins and roasted peanuts.

Serves 6

> 2 cups cooked seitan cutlets, cut into 1″ cubes
>
> Oil for deep-frying
> 1 1/2 cups water

2" piece kombu
1/2 cup raisins
3 tablespoons arrowroot or kuzu
1 tablespoon curry powder
1/4 cup water
1 tablespoon mirin
1 tablespoon natural soy sauce
1/2 head lettuce, shredded
1/2 cup roasted peanuts

- Deep-fry the seitan cubes until they are crispy.

- Heat 1½ cups water with the kombu and boil for 2 minutes. Remove the kombu, add the raisins, and lower the heat.

- Combine the arrowroot or kuzu with the curry powder and dissolve them in ¼ cup water. Add the mirin and natural soy sauce to the stock, and stir in the arrowroot mixture. Continue to stir until the sauce becomes thick and glossy. Add the seitan pieces and heat through, but do not overcook the sauce or it may become watery.

- Arrange the shredded lettuce on a platter and pour the seitan with sauce over it. Garnish with the roasted peanuts and serve immediately.

Enchiladas

These easy-to-make filled tortillas are baked in a cream sauce. Complete the meal with Black Bean Soup and early spring greens.

Makes 6

2 cups cooked seitan 4, ground

1 cup Tomato Sauce
3/4 teaspoon chili powder, OR
1/2 teaspoon cumin plus 1/4 teaspoon cayenne
6 soft corn tortillas
1/2 cup Little Cream Sauce (see page 169)

- Combine the ground seitan, tomato sauce, and seasonings. Place 2 heaping table-spoons of the seitan mixture in the center of a tortilla. Fold the sides over, and place seam side down in a well-oiled 10″ × 10″ baking dish. Spoon 1 tablespoon of the Little Cream Sauce over each roll. Cover and bake for 25 minutes.

Broiled Breaded Seitan Cutlets

Simple and straightforward, these basic breaded cutlets can be served alone, with a sauce, or as a part of a more elaborate dish (see Seitan Cutlets Romano, below).

Serves 6

> 7 to 10 cooked seitan 1 cutlets, cooked with Aromatic Seasoning Mix broth
>
> 1 egg
> 1/2 cup plain soymilk
> 1 1/2 cups cornmeal
> 4 teaspoons Aromatic Seasoning Mix
> 2 tablespoons nutritional yeast

- Combine the egg and soymilk. In a separate bowl combine the cornmeal, seasoning mix, and nutritional yeast. Dip each cutlet into the egg mixture, then into the seasoned cornmeal. Press the cutlets firmly into the cornmeal so both sides are well coated. Place the cutlets on an oiled cookie sheet and broil, 6″ below the fire, for 5 to 7 minutes. Turn and broil for 3 to 5 minutes on the second side.

- Use in Seitan Cutlets Romano (below), or serve with the sauce of your choice.

Seitan Cutlets Romano

A more elaborate version of Broiled Breaded Seitan Cutlets (above).

Serves 6 to 8 as a side dish, serves 4 as a main dish

> 1 recipe Broiled Breaded Seitan Cutlets
>
> 1/2 pound tofu
> 1 tablespoon umeboshi paste
> 1 tablespoon tahini
> 2 1/2 cups Basic Tomato Sauce

- Preheat the oven to 350° F.

- Prepare the seitan cutlets as directed. Use a fork to mash the tofu and mix it with the umeboshi paste and tahini. Place them in a shallow baking dish and cover with the tomato sauce, then crumble the tofu mixture over the top.

- Bake uncovered for 20 minutes.

Garden Vegetables with Seitan Strips

If you don't care for beet greens, use 2 or 3 leaves of Swiss chard or kale. This is a good way to use a little bit of uncooked seitan (½ cup) that you may have remaining from another dish.

Serves 6

1/2 cup uncooked seitan (your choice)

3 tablespoons sesame oil
1 medium onion, sliced 1/8″ rounds
1 medium beet, with greens, sliced 1/8″ half-rounds—cut greens into 1/4″
    pieces
1 carrot, sliced 1/8″ ovals
2 cups zucchini sliced, 1/4″ ovals or rounds
2 cups Chinese cabbage, diced 1″ pieces
3/4 cups water
1 tablespoon natural soy sauce or to taste

- Cut the seitan into strips $2'' \times \frac{1}{2}'' \times \frac{1}{8}''$ thick. Heat the oil in a heavy pan with a cover. Pan-fry the seitan strips, turning them as necessary until crispy and golden.

- Layer the vegetables over the seitan strips in the order given. Add $\frac{1}{2}$ cup water and cover. Simmer for 10 minutes, then uncover and season with the natural soy sauce. If necessary, add a little more water to prevent sticking. Cover and continue to cook 5 minutes, or until the greens are tender.

Barbecued Baked Cutlets

Serves 4

2 cups uncooked seitan 4
1 recipe Barbecue Sauce I

- Preheat the oven to 400° F.

- Cut the seitan into 8 slices, each $\frac{1}{2}''$ thick. Place them on a lightly oiled cookie sheet, and bake for 10 minutes. Turn them over, lightly oiling the cookie sheet under each one before replacing it. Bake 15 minutes more, then add the cutlets to the Barbecue Sauce.

- Heat the cutlets in Barbecue Sauce I for $\frac{1}{2}$ hour. Remove the cutlets and put them into a shallow baking dish ($8'' \times 8'' \times 2''$) and pour the rest of the sauce over them. Bake the cutlets for 15 minutes, uncovered, then turn them to evenly distribute the sauce. Bake for a few minutes more until the sauce thickens on the cutlets.

Savory Stuffed Tomatoes

Try to get fresh basil to complement the other seasonings in these generously stuffed tomatoes.

Serves 6

6 medium tomatoes, about 3″ diameter

For the Filling:

2 cups cooked seitan 4, ground

1 tablespoon Savory Seasoning Mix I or II
2 tablespoons whole wheat pastry flour
6 tablespoons chickpea flour
2 teaspoons olive or sesame oil
1 garlic clove, crushed and minced
1/4 cup parsley, minced
1/2 teaspoon fresh basil
1 to 2 tablespoons arrowroot or kuzu (use to make a sauce)

- Preheat the oven to 400° F.

- Combine all the filling ingredients, except the arrowroot or kuzu. Slice ¼″ to ½″ off the top of each tomato and scoop it out with a metal spoon. Place all of the scooped-out tomato centers in a strainer and remove the juice by pressing it against the walls of the strainer with the back of the spoon. Save the juice for sauce (below).

- Chop the pressed tomato and add it to the rest of the filling. Generously fill the tomato shells, heaping the filling up on top.

- Place the stuffed tomatoes on a cookie sheet and bake for ½ hour or until the tomatoes are tender but not split.

- *Sauce:*   Use the reserved tomato juice in soup stocks, sauces, other seitan dishes, or make the following quick sauce: dissolve a little arrowroot in the reserved tomato juice. Heat, stirring until thick, and season with a little natural soy sauce.

- Serve while hot and top with the tomato juice sauce or serve plain, garnished with a sprig of parsley or watercress.

Pan-Fried Cutlets with Onion Rings

Having precooked cutlets ready to use makes it easy to prepare this dish in about 20 minutes.

Serves 6

8 to 12 cooked seitan cutlets, seasoned with "Hearty Seasoning Mix"

2 tablespoons sesame oil for each 4 cutlets used
2 medium onions—sliced into 1/4″ rounds and separated into rings
2 tablespoons minced parsley

- Heat the oil and pan-fry the cutlets on a medium heat, turning the cutlets over when they are browned. When the second side is browned, turn them back to the first side and add the onion.

- Cover tightly, reduce the heat and cook for about 10 minutes or until the onions have softened. Mix the cutlets and onions carefully. Cover again and continue to let the onions and cutlets cook together until the onions are translucent and lightly browned. Turn them occasionally to prevent burning.

- Sprinkle parsley over all, and serve the cutlets arranged on a bed of the onions.

Cutlets Scallop ───────────────

This is a flavorful and tender variation of pounded cutlets.

Serves 4 to 6

6 to 8 thin pounded cutlets, cooked with Aromatic Seasoning Mix in broth

Note: See Pounded Cutlets, page 49

1 cup plain soymilk
1/4 cup mirin
3 tablespoons sesame oil
5 tablespoons flour
1 tablespoon Aromatic Seasoning Mix
1 tablespoon natural soy sauce
1/4 cup parsley, minced

- Soak the cooked cutlets in ¾ cup soymilk for 20 minutes. Combine the flour and seasoning mix and dredge the cutlets in the seasoned flour on one side only. Heat the sesame oil and pan-fry the cutlets, floured side first, until slightly crispy. Shake the pan occasionally so the cutlets won't stick. Turn the cutlets over and cook the other side for a few minutes, shaking the pan as before.

- Remove the cutlets and reduce the heat to low. Make a sauce in the pan by adding the rest of the seasoned flour to the oil in the pan. Stir the flour briskly to absorb any remaining oil, then add the rest of the soymilk and natural soy sauce, mirin and the parsley. Stir the sauce until it is thick, and serve it over the cutlets.

Easy Szechuan-Style Sweet and Sour Cubes ───────

The natural light sweetness of pineapple and rice syrup combine with rice vinegar and hot pepper oil to add zest to crispy seitan cubes, deep-fried without batter.

Serves 4 to 6

>2 cups braised seitan "Roast" 11 (or other seitan of your choice), cut into
> 1" cubes
>
>Oil for deep-frying
>1 can unsweetened pineapple chunks with juice
>2 tablespoons arrowroot flour
>1/4 cup water
>1/2 teaspoon natural soy sauce
>A few drops Chinese Hot Pepper Oil or tabasco (or to taste)
>2 teaspoons rice vinegar or cider vinegar
>2 teaspoons rice syrup or barley malt syrup
>2 scallions, cut into 2" lengths

- Deep-fry the seitan cubes until crispy. Drain the pineapple and add enough water to the juice to make $1\frac{1}{2}$ cups. Heat the juice and pineapple chunks together. Dissolve the arrowroot in $\frac{1}{4}$ cup water and add the natural soy sauce, hot pepper oil, vinegar, and syrup. Stir the arrowroot mixture and add it to the hot pineapple liquid, stirring the sauce until it is thick and clear. Adjust the seasonings. Add the seitan cubes and scallions and heat thoroughly, but do not overcook or the sauce may become watery.

Stir-Fried Seitan Strips with Romaine ─────────

In this quick stir-fry the only vegetable to cut is a head of lettuce. A very light sweet and sour glaze adds to this simple and delicious preparation.

Serves 4 to 6

>4 cooked seitan cutlets, seasoned in natural soy sauce
>
>1 tablespoon kuzu
>1/4 cup water
>1 teaspoon natural soy sauce
>1 tablespoon barley malt syrup
>1 tablespoon brown rice vinegar
>2 tablespoons sesame oil
>1 large head romaine lettuce—6 to 8 cups when cut, but it shrinks!

- Cut the lettuce in half lengthwise and slice each half crosswise into $\frac{1}{2}$" strips.

- Slice the cutlets into strips $\frac{1}{4}$" wide. Dissolve the kuzu in $\frac{1}{2}$ cup water. Add the natural soy sauce, barley malt syrup, and rice vinegar to the kuzu.

- Heat the oil in a large frying pan or wok, and stir-fry the cutlet strips until they are slightly crispy. Add the lettuce and stir-fry quickly, until the lettuce wilts. Add the sauce, continuing to turn the greens and seitan slices so they are evenly coated. Remove from the heat when the sauce is thick and glossy.

Home-Style Stew

In this hearty stew, juicy chunks of seitan are surrounded by sweet vegetables in a rich-tasting, low calorie gravy.

Serves 6

> 6 cooked seitan cutlets, cut into quarters or sixths and deep-fried with batter (see page 58).

For the Batter:

> 3 medium carrots, cut into 1/4" rounds
> 5 celery stalks, cross-cut 1" long
> 2 cups seasoned stock, reserved from cooking cutlets
> 3/4 cup plain soymilk
> 3 tablespoons arrowroot flour, OR
> 1/4 cup thick starch from preparing seitan
> 2 scallions, cross-cut 1" long
> Natural soy sauce to taste

Make the Batter:
- Cook the seitan cutlet pieces according to Instructions for Deep-Frying Using Batter on page 58.

- Layer the carrots and celery in a heavy pot with a tight fitting lid. Add the broth, cover the pot and bring to a boil. Simmer for about 10 to 15 minutes or until the carrots are tender.

- In a small bowl, stir the soymilk little by little into the arrowroot or thick starch until the flour is dissolved. Add this mixture to the vegetables and stir gently until thick and glossy.

- Add the natural soy sauce to taste. Carefully mix in the seitan pieces and scallions. Cover and simmer 5 to 8 minutes to heat through.

Five-Spice Seitan with Green Beans and Sesame Seeds

Star anise, fennel, cinnamon bark, cloves and Szechuan peppercorns are the components of Chinese 5-Spice Powder. This seasoning is used in Chinese cooking to flavor braised meats, in dips for chicken and seafood, and in glazes and syrups for other main dishes and fruit desserts. Here, Chinese 5-Spice Powder adds a complementary flavor to seitan, sesame seeds, and green beans.

Serves 4 to 6

> 1 cup uncooked seitan 4
>
> 2 tablespoons toasted sesame seeds
> 2 pounds green beans
> 3 tablespoons sesame oil
> 1/4 teaspoon salt
> 2/3 cup water
> 1 tablespoon natural soy sauce
> 1 tablespoon mirin
> 1 teaspoon Chinese 5-Spice Powder

- Lay the seitan on a work surface and stretch it out to flatten it a bit. Sprinkle the sesame seeds over the surface of the seitan and roll up the seitan, kneading the seeds into it. Set it aside on a small plate.

- Wash the green beans and snip off the stem end, leaving the beans whole.

- Slice the seitan into ¼″ slices, and cut each slice into ½″ wide strips. Heat the sesame oil in a heavy skillet and add the seitan piece by piece. Sauté over a medium heat until golden, turning when crispy.

- Add the green beans and sprinkle the salt over them. Add the water to the vegetables and seitan and cover the pan. Continue to cook over a medium heat for 5 to 8 minutes or until the beans are bright green and tender.

- Combine the natural soy sauce, mirin, and Chinese 5-Spice Powder with enough water to make ¼ cup total. Pour this mixture evenly over the green beans and seitan, stir briefly, and cook uncovered until no more liquid remains.

Baked Seitan and Vegetables in Dill Sauce ———————————

Serves 6 to 8

> 4 cups braised seitan "Roast" 11 (or other cooked seitan of your choice)
>
> 2 medium onions, diced
> 3 small or 2 large carrots, sliced 1/2″ rounds or ovals
> 3 teaspoons sesame oil
> 2 tablespoons whole wheat pastry flour
> 1/4 teaspoon salt
> 1 cup water
> 3/4 cup plain soymilk
> 1 tablespoon fresh dill, chopped very fine
> 1/4 teaspoon black pepper

For the Sauce:

> 1 tablespoon mirin
> 1 tablespoon fresh dill, chopped very fine
> 1/4 teaspoon salt
> 2 tablespoons chickpea flour
> 1/2 cup plain soymilk

Note: Total amounts needed for divided ingredients are:

> 1/2 teaspoon salt
> 1 1/4 cups plain soymilk
> 2 tablespoons fresh dill, minced

- Preheat the oven to 350° F.

- Cut the seitan into 1″ cubes. Using a flameproof casserole, sauté the onions, carrots, and seitan cubes for 3 to 5 minutes over a medium flame. Sprinkle the pastry flour and ¼ teaspoon salt over the surface and continue to sauté for a few minutes, stirring frequently.

- Add the water, ¾ cup soymilk, 1 tablespoon dill, and the pepper and stir occasionally for about 5 minutes while it begins to thicken.

- Cover the casserole and bake for 45 minutes to 1 hour, until the carrots are tender.

- Remove to the top of the stove, on a low heat. Add the mirin, 1 tablespoon dill, and ¼ teaspoon salt. Make a loose, smooth paste of the chickpea flour and ½ cup soymilk and add it to the stew, stirring constantly until thick. Simmer 10 to 15 minutes more. Serve hot.

Whole Onions Filled with Seitan and Sauerkraut ——————

A new addition to the family of stuffed onions—for sauerkraut fans.

Serves 6

> 1 1/2 cups seitan (your choice)
>
> 6 medium onions, about 3″ to 4″ in diameter
> 3/4 cup sauerkraut, squeezed and chopped into 1/2″ lengths
> 1/2 cup dry bread crumbs
> 1/4 teaspoon black pepper
> 1/4 cup water or stock
> 2 teaspoons natural soy sauce
>
> 1 recipe Little Cream Sauce (see page 169)

- Preheat the oven to 375° F.

- Peel the onions and remove the tops. Use a metal spoon to scoop out the center of the onion, leaving a shell a little less than ¼″ thick. Set aside the onion centers to be used in the filling.

- Parboil the onion shells for 30 to 45 seconds, remove with a slotted spoon and chill.

- Grind the seitan coarsely.

- Chop the onion pulp fine and combine it with the ground seitan, sauerkraut, bread crumbs, and pepper. Spoon the filling into the onion shells, filling to about ¼″ above the top edge.

- Lightly oil a baking dish and put the water and natural soy sauce in it. Stand the filled onions in the water and natural soy sauce, packing any remaining filling around them to help support them.

- Cover with foil and bake for 40 to 50 minutes or until the onions are tender. Check at 25 minutes and add a little more water or stock to the pan if needed. When the onions are tender, remove the foil and bake 5 minutes more.

To serve: Top with the hot cream sauce, or spoon a small amount onto each individual plate and place the baked onion on it. Garnish with a sprig of watercress or parsley.

Spring Rolls

A happy addition to your Chinese meals. For added flavor, use *wasabi* (powdered Japanese horseradish) or hot mustard sauce as a condiment!

Makes 12 to 15 rolls, 2″ × 4″

2 cups cooked seitan 1 or 3, cooked in strongly seasoned natural soy sauce broth

3 cups Chinese or napa cabbage, shredded (about 1/3 head)
1 clove garlic, crushed and minced
3 tablespoons arrowroot flour
1 pound square egg roll wrappers
Oil for deep-frying

Additional Filling Ingredients—Use as few or as many as you like:

Dried shrimp, soaked 1 hour and cut into small pieces
Fresh white fish, cut into small pieces
Shredded cabbage (blanched)
Broccoli flowerets (blanched)

Celery, cut thin (blanched)
Carrots, cut thin (blanched)
Mushrooms, chopped

Note 1:   It is important that all filling ingredients be as cool and dry as possible before mixing.

Note 2:   Have ready 2 cookie sheets—one to hold the wrapped, uncooked Spring Rolls, and one with 3 layers of paper towels to absorb excess oil from cooking. You will also need a small bowl containing 1 tablespoon arrowroot mixed with 3 tablespoons water.

• Squeeze the seitan gently and pat it dry. Shred the cabbage into pieces no longer than ¾″. Combine the seitan, cabbage, and garlic. Sprinkle 2 tablespoons of arrowroot over the mixture and mix to coat the seitan and cabbage.

• Place an egg roll wrapper with one corner pointing toward you. Place about 2 tablespoons filling near one corner of the wrapper. Roll the corner over the filling and tuck the point under. Fold the sides in. Paint the last corner with the arrowroot mixture and roll up tightly to seal. The roll should be about 2″ in diameter. Place the sealed rolls on the cookie sheet, sealed side down. Continue until all the rolls are ready for frying.

• While you are rolling the spring rolls, begin to heat the oil for cooking. Deep-fry the rolls until they are golden and their wrappers are bubbly. You may have to hold the rolls in position on the second side, as they sometimes turn back over to the first side if they are not restrained. Because of this, do not try to cook more than two at a time. Try to time the cooking so you always have one in the pot— this will keep the oil at a more even temperature as well as help you to manage cooking the rolls.

• Remove the spring rolls from the oil when they are crispy and golden all around. Stand the cooked rolls at a 45° vertical angle to drain on the paper towels.

• Serve while hot with Mustard Sauce or wasabi mixed with a little water to the desired consistency. Natural soy sauce or a sweet-and-sour sauce may also be served as condiments with Spring Rolls.

Pouches II

This elaborate preparation is more involved, but we think it's worth the work. Individual rolls are filled with ground seitan, winter squash, or your own invention!

Makes 12 to 14 filled pouches—serves 4 to 6 as a side dish, or serve as an appetizer.

2 cups uncooked seitan 4, cut into 12 to 14 slices, 1/4″ thick

2 teaspoons Aromatic Seasoning Mix
1 package *kampyo* (dried gourd strips)
Oil for deep-frying
1/2 cup corn flour

For the Filling:

1 cup baked seitan 4 (or the seitan of your choice), ground

1 tablespoon natural soy sauce
1 tablespoon sesame oil
2 tablespoons chickpea flour

Alternate Filling:

1 cup raw winter squash, buttercup or butternut—grated
2 to 4 tablespoons chickpea flour
2 to 4 tablespoons whole wheat pastry flour

For the Broth:

3 cups water
2 tablespoons natural soy sauce
1/4 to 1/2 teaspoon (or to taste) Aromatic Seasoning Mix

- Place the gourd strips (*kampyo*) in water to cover. Soak them for 5 to 10 minutes until they are flexible but not too soft. Remove them and squeeze to extract excess water. Set aside—they will be used to tie up the rolls.

- Heat the oil for deep-frying. Combine the corn flour and seasoning in a flat dish such as a pie plate. Roll the seitan into a cylinder 2″ or 3″ in diameter, and cut it into slices ¼″ thick.

- Stretch each slice to 3″ × 4″ and dredge both sides in the corn flour mixture, pressing the seasoned flour well into the surface of the seitan.

Deep-fry the Seitan:
- Slide a piece of seitan gently into the hot oil. With a fork or chopstick in each hand, hold the piece of seitan under the oil and keep stretching it gently, holding the edges firmly so they don't roll up. The seitan will puff up in all directions. When it appears to have reached its limit and is crispy and golden (but watch the heat—don't let it burn) turn it over and continue to cook it on side two. Remove it from the oil and allow the seitan to drain well on 4 or 5 layers of paper towels.

- After each piece is cooked but before it deflates, use a sharp pointed knife to slice it in half through the side edge. Leave a small area (about 1″) connected at one side as a hinge. Do not fill the seitan until all the pieces are cooked and sliced.

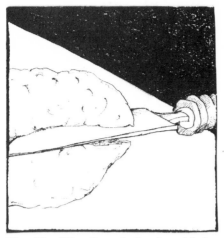

Fig. 34 Slice through the deep-fried seitan, leaving a 1″ space connected, as a hinge.

Fig. 35 Open the cut seitan and lay flat.

Fig. 36 Place the filling on the seitan and roll it up.

Fig. 37 Tie kampyo strips around the filled seitan roll.

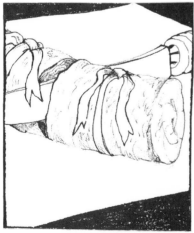

Fig. 38 Slice cooked seitan rolls halfway between the ties.

Fig. 39 Serve the seitan rolls with a sauce.

Make the Filling: Grind the seitan and combine it with the oil and seasonings, make another filling of your choice.

Fill the Pouches:
- Spread out the sliced, deep-fried seitan. Layer 1 tablespoon of filling over the half of it nearest to you, and begin to roll the seitan away from you, folding the left and right sides in as you roll.

- Lay one roll on one soaked kampyo strip, and lie the strip in a knot on top of the roll.

- If a roll is more than 2½" long, tie two or three kampyo strips evenly spaced over the length of the roll. Just before serving, these longer rolls will be cut between the ties, making 2 or 3 pieces of equal length. The knot should appear in the center of each piece whether or not it has been cut.

Cook the Filled Pouches: Bring the broth ingredients to a boil then reduce to very low. Add the pouches and simmer uncovered for 20 minutes, turning occasionally in the broth. Carefully remove the rolls from the broth and set them aside to cool to room temperature.

Note: Stop here and refrigerate the cooked rolls if you want to bake and serve them later.

- Preheat the oven to 400° F.

- Bake the pouches on a cookie sheet for 10 to 15 minutes.

To Serve: Cut the pouches which are longer than 2½" midway between each tie, to make smaller pieces of equal size (see above). Place the pouches on a platter. Use any remaining broth as a sauce, on or beneath the rolls.

Burgers

Easy and delicious, a natural "quarter-pounder" with no fat and lots of flavor!

Makes 4 large quarter pound burgers or 6 medium-size burgers

2 cups cooked seitan, ground and tightly packed

6 tablespoons chickpea flour
3 to 6 tablespoons whole wheat pastry flour
1/2 teaspoon garlic granules or garlic powder
1 tablespoon parsley flakes
1 tablespoon paprika
1/4 teaspoon salt
Sesame oil for pan-frying
Natural soy sauce to sprinkle on top

Note: The garlic, parsley, paprika, and salt may be replaced by your choice of other seasonings, to taste.

- Mix all the burger ingredients together and form into patties. The burgers were originally made 4″ × ½″ thick, but if that is too large or you need more, make them smaller.

- Heat a heavy skillet and coat the surface generously with sesame oil. Pan-fry the burgers over a medium heat about 8 to 10 minutes on each side. Keep the heat low enough so they will heat thoroughly but not burn.

- Before turning the burgers over, sprinkle a little natural soy sauce on the surface of each one. Use your spatula to spread it evenly over the surface. After the second side is done, sprinkle a little natural soy sauce on it, and turn it back to side one for about 5 seconds.

- Serve with barbecue sauce, mustard, or any other favorite burger condiment.

Carrots in Blankets

Use one of the very stretchable types of seitan to wrap around the carrots.

Serves 4 to 6 as a side dish—also can be used as an appetizer.

> 1 cup uncooked seitan 4, 2, or 7
>
> 3 carrots, cut into pieces approximately 2″ long × 3/4″ thick
> 2 cups seasoned stock (seasoning of your choice)
> Watercress for garnish
> Some toothpicks

- Pound and stretch the seitan until it is ¼″ thick. Cut the seitan into strips 1″ wide.

- Carefully stretch each strip until it is very thin. Wrap each thin seitan strip very snugly around a piece of carrot, and secure the end with a toothpick.

- Simmer in the stock for 20 minutes, or until carrots are tender. Turn the carrots frequently to allow the seasoning to penetrate the seitan.

- Garnish with watercress.

Variations: For the carrots, you may substitute:
Parsnips
Burdock—before using burdock, it should be simmered for at least 20 minutes, or pressure-cooked for 5 minutes.

Filled Turnip Cups

This reminds me of my grandmother's creamed turnips.

Makes 4

2 cooked seitan cutlets

4 medium turnips—they should be very crisp and fresh
1/2 cup parsley, minced
1/4 cup plain soymilk
1/2 teaspoon salt
1/4 teaspoon pepper
1/4 cup dry bread crumbs
1 recipe Little Cream Sauce (see page 169), OR
1 cup of your favorite cream sauce

- Preheat the oven to 375° F.

- Scrub the turnips well, and remove the tails and the top ½″ of the turnips.

- With a metal spoon scoop out the inside of the turnip until the walls are about ⅛″ thick, and no more than ¼″ thick. They should all be about the same thickness to ensure equal cooking time.

- Set aside the scooped-out turnips pulp to use in the filling.

- Trim the top edges straight, or make decorative scallop or zigzag edging.

- Immerse the turnip shells in boiling water and cook for 5 to 8 minutes until they are tender but still retain their shape. Refresh in cold water, then drain and pat them dry.

- Cut the seitan into tiny pieces.

- Combine the turnip pulp in a blender or food processor with the parsley, soymilk, salt and pepper.

- Put the turnip mixture in a bowl, and mix in the seitan pieces and bread crumbs. Fill the turnips with this mixture, heaping into a small mound on the top.

- Place the filled turnips in an oiled baking dish and pour 1 tablespoon of the sauce over each one. Sprinkle with paprika, and bake 30 to 40 minutes.

To Serve: Pour 2 tablespoons sauce over each turnip cup, or spoon the sauce onto a plate and set the turnip cup on the sauce. Garnish with a sprig of watercress or parsley.

Seitan and Green Beans Baked in Mustard Sauce ——————

Juicy golden chunks of batter-fried seitan are paired with fresh green beans in a tangy mustard sauce.

Serves 4 to 6

> 2 cups cooked seitan, your choice of seitan type
> Oil for deep-frying

For the Batter: Makes about 1¼ cups.

> 1/2 cup whole wheat pastry flour
> 1/4 cup corn flour
> 1 tablespoon arrowroot flour
> 1/2 teaspoon salt
> 1/2 cup plus 2 tablespoons water
>
> 1 pound green beans, sliced crosswise in half, then in half lengthwise
> 1 recipe (1 1/2 cups) Mustard Sauce

Make the Batter:

- Mix all the dry ingredients together, then add the water. Mix well, and refrigerate for 10 to 30 minutes. If necessary, add more water before using the batter. It should be a dense coating for the seitan, but should not be too thick.

- While the batter is "chilling," parboil the green beans and prepare the mustard sauce.

- Cut the seitan in ¾″ cubes. Preheat the oven to 350° F.

- Heat the oil. Coat the seitan cubes with the batter above (or other favorite thick batter). Deep-fry the seitan and blot on paper towels.

- Arrange the green beans and batter-fried seitan cubes in a baking dish, with the seitan cubes on top of the beans.

- Pour the mustard sauce over the cubes and beans. Cover and bake for 15 to 20 minutes, then uncover and bake for 5 to 10 minutes more.

Salads

Oh, herbaceous treat!
Back to the world he'd turn his fleeting soul,
And plunge his fingers in the salad bowl;
Serenely full the epicure would say,
"Fate cannot harm me,—I have dined today."
—Sydney Smith (1771–1845), *A Receipt for a Salad*

Watercress and White Mushroom Salad with Golden Seitan Strips

In this salad, parboiled watercress and white mushrooms are combined with golden seitan strips and a tangy umeboshi dressing.

Serves 6

> 1/2 cup uncooked seitan 4
>
> Oil for deep-frying
> 5 quarts boiling water
> 2 large or 3 small bunches watercress
> 1/2 pound white mushrooms, cut into 1/8" slices
> 1/4 cup creamy umeboshi dressing

- Cut the seitan into thin strips and deep-fry according to instructions for deep-frying. Place the fried seitan strips in a colander. Pour boiling water over them 3 times, using about 1 quart of water each time, and tossing the seitan pieces in the colander after each rinsing. This will remove some of the excess oil. Squeeze the seitan gently, and cut into 2" lengths.

- Immerse the watercress in boiling water, one bunch at a time, for ½ minute each. Remove the watercress and plunge it immediately into cold water. Squeeze firmly and cut into 2" pieces.

- Place the sliced mushrooms in a colander and pour 2 quarts of boiling water over them. Toss, then wait ½ minute before pouring cold water over them. Drain the mushrooms well.

- Combine the vegetables and seitan and toss them lightly with the dressing. This salad may be prepared ahead of time. Do not add the dressing to the vegetables until just before serving. For best results, the dressing and vegetables should be at room temperature before combining.

Green Bean and Walnut Salad ────────

Have some seitan available to use in this salad of cooked vegetables, marinated onions, and walnuts.

Serves 6

>   1 1/2 cups braised seitan "Roast" 11, (or other cooked seitan of your
>   choice) cut into slices 1/2" × 1 1/2"
>
>   3/4 cup walnuts
>   1/2 red onion, sliced very thin
>   1/4 to 1/2 cup Creamy Umeboshi Dressing
>   1 1/2 pounds green beans, trimmed and cut in thirds

- To roast the walnuts, place them in a dry frying pan over medium heat for about 5 minutes, stirring constantly.

- Marinate the onion slices and the walnuts in the umeboshi dressing for 15 minutes, while the green beans are cooking.

- Steam the green beans until they are just tender but still retain their bright green color. Place them in a colander and plunge into cold water to stop cooking and keep the color bright. Drain the green beans and pat them dry, or lay them on a cloth towel to dry.

- Add the green beans and half the seitan strips to the dressing, and toss lightly. Arrange the salad on a platter with the remaining seitan strips on top.

Fu with Dandelion Greens ────────

Parboiled greens and seasoned, toasted fu make a nutritious and tasty springtime salad.

Serves 4

>   6 large dried fu rings
>
>   2 teaspoons dark sesame oil
>   2 teaspoons natural soy sauce
>   Dandelion greens, to equal a bunch about 6" × 3"
>   2 quarts boiling water
>   2 tablespoons lemon juice
>   1/4 teaspoon salt

- Combine the oil and natural soy sauce and brush some of the mixture over each piece of the fu. Place the fu on a cookie sheet and toast, 6″ below the broiler, for 1 to 2 minutes. Cut the toasted fu with a bread knife or break into 1″ pieces.

- Immerse the washed dandelion greens in 2 quarts boiling water until they are tender but still a bright green color. Plunge them immediately into a bowl of very cold water. After 5 minutes, remove and drain the greens. Squeeze them and cut into 1″ pieces.

- In a mixing bowl, combine the lemon juice and salt. Add the greens, toasted fu, and the lemon juice and toss lightly.

Variation: Add chopped dill or other favorite herbs to the oil/soy sauce mixture.

Savory Seitan Salad ——————————————————

Marinated seitan, baked in a sauce then chilled, is the foundation for this hearty, richly flavored salad.

Serves 6

>   2 cups uncooked seitan 4

For the Marinade:

>   1 tablespoon sesame oil
>   3 tablespoons Savory Seasoning Mix II
>   2 cups water
>   2 tablespoons wine vinegar

To be Baked with the Seitan:

>   1 cup plain soymilk
>   1 teaspoon tahini
>   1 teaspoon umeboshi paste
>   2 tablespoons saké

Vegetables:

>   4 radishes, sliced into thin rounds
>   1/2 red onion, sliced into thin crosswise rounds
>   1/4 cup pitted ripe black olives, sliced crosswise
>   Boston or Bibb lettuce—use as a serving base for the salad

For the Dressing:

>   1/2 cup prepared mayonnaise
>   2 tablespoons reserved marinade

- Combine all the marinade ingredients and heat to boiling. Slice the uncooked seitan into cutlets $\frac{1}{8}$" thick. Arrange them in a 9" × 13" baking dish, and pour the hot marinade over them. Marinate for 2 hours, basting the seitan slices and turning them over occasionally.

- Preheat the oven to 350° F.

- Drain the marinade from the seitan slices and refrigerate it for later use. Combine the soymilk, tahini, umeboshi paste and saké. Keep the seitan in the flat baking dish and spread the slices with the soymilk mixture.

- Bake for 20 to 30 minutes, turning the seitan over after 15 minutes. Remove the seitan and chill it. Use 2 forks to pull the chilled cutlets apart into smaller, irregularly shaped pieces.

- Lightly mix the mayonnaise and marinade to make a dressing, and combine it with the seitan and vegetables.

- Serve on a bed of Boston or Bibb lettuce.

Two-bean Salad with Hickory Slices —————————

Crispy green beans and marinated white beans keep good company with hickory-flavored seitan.

Serves 4 to 6

> 1 cup navy beans—soaked overnight in water to cover
> 3 cups water
> 1 1/2" piece kombu

For the Dressing: Make the dressing at least $\frac{1}{2}$ hour before using, to allow the flavors to blend. Refrigerate to store.

> 2 garlic cloves, crushed and minced
> 2 tablespoons olive or sesame oil
> 1 tablespoon plus 2 teaspoons umeboshi paste
> 2 teaspoons prepared Dijon-style mustard
> 1/2 teaspoon celery seed
> 3 tablespoons brown rice vinegar or apple cider vinegar
> 2 tablespoons water
> 1/2 cup parsley, minced

The Seitan and Vegetables:

> 1 cup cooked seitan cutlets 1, 2 or 3, cut into strips 1 1/2" × 1/4"
>
> 1 1/2 cups green beans, cut into 1 1/2" lengths
> 1/4 to 1/2 medium red onion, diced

Hickory Broth:

> 2 teaspoons red or mugi miso
> 2 teaspoons natural soy sauce
> 2 teaspoons Hickory Smoke Liquid
> 1/4 cup water
> 1/2 teaspoon sesame oil
> 1 garlic clove, crushed and minced
> 1/2 teaspoon brown rice vinegar or apple cider vinegar

Cook the Beans by one of the following methods:
- Drain the soaked beans and bring to a boil, with the kombu, in 3 cups fresh water. Cover and cook at a low boil for 1 to 1½ hours or until tender. Add water as necessary during cooking.

- Beans may be pressure-cooked 20 to 40 minutes. Bring the pressure down by placing the pot under cold running water. Simmer, partially covered, to finish cooking. Do not add salt to the beans until they are tender.

Make the Dressing:
- Combine the garlic and umeboshi paste. Add the oil slowly, mixing continuously so the oil and umeboshi paste are well blended. Add the celery seed, mustard, and vinegar and blend until smooth. Mix in the parsley and let the dressing rest at least 5 minutes to allow the flavors to blend.

- Add the onions to the salad dressing. Drain the cooked beans and add them while hot to the salad dressing. If the beans were cooked in advance, heat them before adding to the dressing to marinate. Mix the dressing into the beans and onions and refrigerate until chilled. Mix occasionally because the dressing gradually sinks to the bottom of the bowl.

- In a sauce pan, bring all the ingredients for the broth to a boil. Cook the seitan in the broth over a medium-high heat for about 5 to 8 minutes, stirring frequently until all the broth is absorbed. Put the seitan on a plate, cover and refrigerate.

- Steam the green beans for 5 to 8 minutes or until just tender and bright green. Refresh them in cold water, drain and dry on a cloth towel. Cover and refrigerate.

- When the marinated navy beans are cool, add the seitan pieces and half the green beans. Put the bean salad on a serving platter and arrange the remaining green beans around the edges of the salad.

Wild Rice Salad

An elegant main course salad garnished with mirin-flavored tangerines, Wild Rice Salad is welcome year 'round.

152

Serves 6

2 cups cooked seitan cutlets or cubes, seasoned with Savory Seasoning Broth I

3/4 cup raisins
1/2 cup water
2 cups cooked wild rice
2 cups cooked long grain brown rice
1/2 red onion, minced (about 1/4 cup.)
2 celery stalks, diced (about 1 1/2 cups)
4 red radishes, sliced thin rounds
2 tangerines, peeled and sectioned
1/4 cup mirin

Note: The cooked seitan is to be broiled before it is combined with other salad ingredients.

For the Dressing: Makes about 1 cup.

2 tablespoons toasted sesame oil
1 teaspoon cinnamon
4 to 5 tablespoons natural soy sauce
6 tablespoons fresh orange juice
5 tablespoons fresh lemon juice

Make the Dressing: Whisk the oil, cinnamon, and natural soy sauce together until they are well blended. Continue to whisk while adding the juices 1 tablespoon at a time until the dressing is well blended.

Assemble the Salad:
• Boil the raisins, covered, for 2 to 3 minutes in ½ cup water. Keep covered and set aside so the raisins can cool and absorb the water.

• Cut the cooked seitan into ¾″ cubes and arrange them on a cookie sheet. Broil 3″ below the flame, for 4 to 6 minutes, turning the pieces over after 2 or 3 minutes. Remove and allow to cool.

• Simmer the tangerine sections in the mirin for 2 to 3 minutes. Chill them and use as a garnish.

• Combine all the salad ingredients with the dressing and mix lightly. Serve on a bed of Boston or leaf lettuce.

• Garnish with the mirin-flavored tangerine sections.

Carrot Greens and Cabbage Salad with Sesame

This salad is especially (but not only) for people with gardens full of carrot greens. A dressing of white miso and toasted sesame seeds complements the fresh greens.

Serves 6

 1/2 cup uncooked seitan 4 (or other uncooked seitan of your choice)

 Oil for deep-frying
 4 quarts boiling water
 6 carrots with greens—use greens only
 1/4 head cabbage—core and shred very fine
 6 tablespoons toasted sesame seeds (white seeds look better in this dish)
 2 teaspoons white miso, diluted to a smooth thin paste
 2 teaspoons natural soy sauce

• Form the uncooked seitan into a cylinder and slice it into very thin cutlet-like slices. Deep-fry these slices until they are golden and crispy. Drain the cutlets on paper towels, then put them into a colander and pour the boiling water over them to remove some of the surface oil. Squeeze them gently and slice into thin strips, 1″ to 1½″ long.

• Wash the carrot greens very well and remove the tough bare stems. Boil the greens in 2 quarts rapidly boiling water for about 5 minutes, then plunge them immediately into a bowl of cold water. Soak the greens for 10 minutes. Then squeeze them and fill the bowl with fresh cold water and soak them 10 minutes more. Discard the water and squeeze the greens firmly. You will now have a firmly packed cylinder of carrot greens. Cut it crosswise into 2″ lengths.

• Parboil the cabbage—its color should be clear, bright green and white.

• In a *suribachi* or mortar and pestle, grind the sesame seeds with the miso or natural soy sauce. Combine all the greens with the seitan strips, and toss lightly with the miso (or natural soy sauce)/sesame dressing.

Chinese Pasta Salad

Flecks of dark green kale, golden seitan strips, and fragrant shiitake mushrooms add color and texture to tartly-seasoned Chinese rice noodles.

Serves 6

 1/2 cup uncooked seitan 4 (or other uncooked seitan of your choice)

 17 oz. package Chinese rice noodles
 2 cups kale, chopped very fine
 2 shiitake mushrooms, fresh or dried
 Oil for deep-frying
 3 to 4 quarts boiling water
 1/4 to 1/2 cup Creamy Umeboshi Dressing

For Seasoning the Seitan:

> 2 tablespoons water
> 2 tablespoons natural soy sauce
> 2 slices fresh ginger, 1/8" thick

• Cook the noodles about 3 minutes, or just until tender. Drain immediately. Cook the kale in boiling water for 3 minutes; remove it and plunge it immediately into cold water. Drain and squeeze to remove excess water.

• If using dried mushrooms, soak them in ½ cup warm water for 10 to 20 minutes or until they are tender. No "woody" or dried areas should be visible when they are cut. Slice the mushrooms into ⅛" strips. If fresh mushrooms are used, omit the soaking.

• Cut the uncooked seitan into slices ⅛" thick and deep-fry them. Drain on paper towels, then place the fried seitan cutlets into a colander and pour the boiling water over them to remove excess oil. Squeeze them firmly and cut them into ¼" slices.

• Cook the mushrooms and seitan strips in the natural soy sauce-ginger "seasoning" broth (above) for about 5 minutes, stirring frequently. Remove the ginger slices and add the cooked mushrooms and seitan to the noodles. Add the kale and the dressing and toss lightly.

Broccoli Rabe Salad with Tiny Croquettes

Tender broccoli rabe is the heart of this steamed salad garnished with golden croquettes and seasoned with soy sauce, ginger, and rice vinegar.

Serves 6

For the Dressing:

> 2 tablespoons brown rice vinegar
> 2 teaspoons natural soy sauce
> 1/2 teaspoon ginger root juice (finely grate 1" piece fresh ginger and squeeze it to extract the juice)

For the Croquettes:

> 1/2 cup cooked seitan—your choice of seitan
>
> 1/2 cup cooked brown rice (rice should be more soft than dry)
> 1 teaspoon Hearty Seasoning Mix
> 1 teaspoon arrowroot flour
> Oil for deep-frying
>
> 1 1/2 pounds fresh broccoli rabe

Make the Dressing: Combine the dressing ingredients.

Make the Croquettes: Grind the seitan in a blender or food processor. Combine with the rice, seasoning mix and arrowroot. Form the mixture into small balls, using about 1 teaspoon seitan mixture for each ball. Deep-fry the balls until they are golden brown and crispy. Drain on paper towels.

Assemble the Salad: Boil the broccoli rabe for 5 minutes or until tender but still bright green. Plunge immediately into cold water, then drain. Squeeze the greens gently to remove excess water. Cut crosswise into 1½" lengths, and separate the pieces. Combine the vinegar, natural soy sauce and ginger root juice to make the salad dressing. Add the dressing to the vegetables and seitan and toss lightly.

Seitan and Escarole Salad with Anchovy-Tarragon Vinaigrette

The bright green of curly fresh escarole is accented by the black olives and nori and the light-colored seitan dumplings, then topped with a zesty anchovy-tarragon dressing.

Serves 6

1/2 cup uncooked seitan—your choice of seitan

2 cups water
2" piece kombu

For the Dressing:

8 anchovy fillets
2 tablespoons lemon juice
1 teaspoon dry mustard powder
2 tablespoons sesame oil
1/2 cup plus 2 tablespoons olive oil
2 tablespoons brown rice vinegar
1 1/2 teaspoons tarragon
2 garlic cloves, crushed

For the Salad:

1/2 cup red onion, sliced crosswise into thin rounds
1/2 teaspoon lemon peel (yellow part only), minced very fine
1 sheet nori sea vegetable
1 large head escarole or chicory
1/4 cup black olives (oil-cured preferred)

• Bring the water and kombu to a boil and add the seitan, breaking off tiny pieces from the main piece and dropping them into the water one by one. Cook the dumplings for 10 to 20 minutes.

Make the Dressing:
- Use a fork to mash the anchovies and mix them with the lemon juice. Add the olive oil and vinegar alternately, one teaspoon of each at a time, mixing constantly with a fork or whisk.

- Add the tarragon and the crushed cloves of garlic and store the dressing in a covered jar for at least 20 minutes before using to allow the flavors to blend. Any dressing remaining may be refrigerated for future use.

- Place ¾ cup of the salad dressing in a bowl with the onion slices and minced lemon peel. Drain the seitan and add it while hot to the dressing. Refrigerate to marinate until chilled, stirring occasionally.

- Toast the sheet of nori by holding it in one hand and passing it back and forth above the hot burner. Tear the nori into irregular bite-size pieces. Wash and dry the escarole and break it into bite-size pieces.

- Just before serving, add the escarole to the marinated seitan and onions, and toss lightly. Add more dressing to taste if necessary. Garnish with the olives and nori.

Hearty Seitan "Roast" Salad with New Red Potatoes ———

Tender red potatoes are accented by strips of marinated, broiled seitan.

Serves 6

For the Marinade:

> 1 1/2 cups cooked seitan 11 (or other cooked seitan of your choice), seasoned with natural soy sauce broth
>
> 4 tablespoons olive oil
> 3 tablespoons cider vinegar
> 2 1/2 tablespoons natural soy sauce

Salad Vegetables:

> 1/2 teaspoon paprika
> 6 medium red potatoes
> 1/4 cup chopped parsley
> 1/2 cup grated carrot—to be used as garnish

For the Dressing:

> Marinade remaining from seitan
> 2 or 3 garlic cloves, crushed and minced
> 2 scallions, chopped very fine
> 1/2 teaspoon prepared Dijon-style mustard
> 1 tablespoon cider vinegar

- Combine all marinade ingredients.

- Cut the seitan into 2″ cubes and marinate for 45 minutes to 1 hour, turning the cubes over in the marinade every 10 or 15 minutes. Remove the seitan from the marinade, gently pressing each piece against the side of the container to remove excess marinade.

- Slice the seitan into wide, flat slices ⅛″ thick or less and arrange them on a cookie sheet. Sprinkle lightly with the paprika and broil, 6″ below the broiler flame, for about 3 minutes. Turn over and repeat.

- Cut the potatoes in large cubes, leaving the skins on. Boil gently in lightly salted water until they are tender.

- To make the dressing, combine all the dressing ingredients in a large bowl. Add the potatoes while they are still hot. Chill for 15 minutes then add the broiled seitan pieces and the parsley.

- Serve chilled or at room temperature on a bed of Boston or Bibb lettuce. Garnish with the grated carrot.

Mediterranean Vegetable Medley ———————————

Steamed, marinated vegetables with seitan dumplings become a filling summertime salad.

Serves 6

2 cups uncooked seitan 4.

For the Broth:

2 leeks
2 carrots
3 quarts water
4″ piece kombu
4 tablespoons Savory Seasoning Mix I

For the Marinade:

3 to 4 tablespoons olive oil
1/2 cup lemon juice
2 tablespoons natural soy sauce
1 tablespoon capers
1/2 teaspoon oregano
3 teaspoons tarragon
1/2 lemon—grate rind coarsely

Salad Vegetables:

> 1/2 red onion, cut crosswise into thin rounds
> 1 sweet red pepper, diced
> 1 zucchini, cut into rounds 1/8" or less

- Cut the leeks in half lengthwise. They may be a little sandy, so wash them well under running water. Cut the leeks into ¼" crosswise slices. Cut the carrots into ¼" rounds.

- Bring the broth to a boil then reduce the heat and add the seitan, breaking off small pieces and adding to the broth one by one. Simmer, partially covered, for 45 minutes to 1 hour. Remove the seitan and vegetables with a slotted spoon, reserving any remaining broth for use in a soup stock or sauce, or for cooking grains or pasta.

- Combine the ingredients for the marinade, and add all remaining vegetables and the cooked seitan and vegetables. Chill the mixture, stirring occasionally. Adjust the seasonings.

Large-Shell Macaroni Salad with Walnut and Pimiento Dressing ———————————————

Serves 6 to 8

> 2 cups cooked seitan, seasoned with natural soy sauce broth—tightly packed 1/2" cubes
>
> 12 oz. package large-shell macaroni or spiral macaroni
> 1/2 cup dulse
> 2 pounds green beans
> 1 cup onion, minced very fine

For the Dressing:

> 1/2 cup walnuts
> 3 tablespoons olive oil
> 4 tablespoons brown rice vinegar
> 1 teaspoon tarragon
> 1/4 cup pimiento strips, 1/4" × 1"
> 1/2 teaspoon salt
> 1/2 cup fresh orange juice

- Cook the pasta al dente, then slowly pour into a colander to drain. Place the colander into a large bowl or pot, and fill it with cold water. Keeping the macaroni in the cold water, change the water to keep it cold, so the noodles retain their shape. The shells are very large and fragile when freshly cooked. When they are firm, drain them, cover and refrigerate.

- Rinse and clean the dulse removing any small shells or sand. Shred or cut it very fine, and set it aside.

- Steam the green beans until they are bright green and tender, then plunge them into cold water to stop the cooking. Drain the beans and lay them on a towel to dry. Cut into 2″ lengths.

Make the Dressing:
- Heat the walnuts for 5 minutes in a heavy skillet over medium-low heat, stirring constantly. Place the walnuts on the work surface and crush them with a rolling pin while they are still hot, leaving some larger pieces of about ½″ in diameter. Transfer the walnuts to a small mixing bowl, and use a fork to mix the oil in little by little. Blend in the vinegar, and then the remaining dressing ingredients.

- 1 to 1½ hours before serving combine the dressing with the chilled pasta, vegetables, and the cooked seitan cubes. Occasionally mix gently to allow the flavors to blend.

Confetti Rice Salad ———————————————

Cooked brown rice is combined with summer vegetables and seitan for a light but filling summer meal.

Serves 4 to 8

1 to 2 cooked seitan cutlets, cooked with your choice of seasoning

6 cups cooked short grain or long grain brown rice
2 to 4 tablespoons natural soy sauce
2 to 3 tablespoons lemon juice
1/2 to 1 teaspoon *wasabi* powder
1 cup sweet red bell pepper, diced 1/2″ pieces
2 medium cucumbers, diced 1/2″ to 3/4″ pieces
2 scallions, sliced very thin
1 small yellow summer squash, cut into thin matchsticks (for garnish)

For the Dressing:

2 1/2 tablespoons umeboshi paste
1 cup plain soymilk
4 teaspoons sesame or safflower oil
1 teaspoon brown rice vinegar

- Cut the seitan into strips ½″ wide and put them on top of the rice.

- Combine the natural soy sauce, lemon juice, and wasabi powder. Pour this mixture over the rice and seitan and mix it in well. Be careful not to break up the seitan. If the rice is hot, allow it to cool before proceeding.

Make the Dressing: Thin the umeboshi paste by adding the soymilk to it little by little. Mix well. Add the oil a little at a time while mixing with a fork or whisk. Add the rice vinegar and mix well. Refrigerate the dressing and shake well before using.

Assemble the salad:
- Combine all the other vegetables with the rice mixture and add the dressing. You may want to save some of the dressing to use over the squash matchsticks.

- Place the salad on curly green leaf lettuce or other bright, crisp greens. Garnish with the summer squash matchsticks and top with the remaining dressing.

Winter Salad with Radishes

Leafy Chinese cabbage, salted then compressed under a weight, is lightly seasoned with a little olive oil and lemon juice.

Serves 4 to 6

> 1 cup braised seitan "roast" 11 (or other cooked seitan of your choice), cooked with seasoning as desired
>
> 1/2 medium head of Chinese or napa cabbage—shred into thin strips 2" long
> 1 tablespoon salt
> 6 red radishes, preferable with leaves
> 2 scallions, sliced into 2" × 1/8" strips
> 1 tablespoon olive oil
> 1 lemon—use juice, (about 2 tablespoons or to taste)

- Slice the seitan into thin strips 2" long and ¼" wide. Place the shredded cabbage into a large mixing bowl and sprinkle the salt over it. Mix well with your hands, thoroughly but not roughly rubbing the salt into the cabbage.

- Slice the radishes and their leaves very thin and mix lightly into the cabbage, separating the radish slices. Mix in the scallions the same way.

- Press the vegetables for 2 to 4 hours using one of the following methods:

1. Use a salad press, available at many Oriental food stores. Put the vegetables in it and tighten the pressure down as far as possible. Check at 15 minute intervals to increase the pressure if possible.

2. Use a deep bowl. Select a plate or saucer which will fit into the container, covering the surface of the vegetables to be pressed. For a weight, use a clean covered jar filled with water or beans, or a heavy, well-scrubbed rock.

- With either method, the cabbage should be pressed to about half of its original volume. Any liquid rising to the top should be discarded.

- After pressing, remove the vegetables and drain them. Place them on a platter or serving bowl. Mix in the olive oil, and lemon juice to taste, and garnish with the slices of seitan.

Spring Salad with New Potatoes and Snow Peas ──────────

Crispy strips of seitan accent this springtime potato salad.

Serves 6

> 2 cups uncooked seitan 4 (or other uncooked seitan of your choice)
>
> Oil for deep-frying
> 1 red onion, sliced into very thin half-rounds
> 1 celery stalk, sliced 1/8" slices
> 3/4 cup Mustard Dressing
> 18 to 20 new red potatoes, about 2" in diameter. (If small red potatoes are unavailable, use fewer, larger potatoes cut into 2" cubes.)
> 1/2 pound snow peas
> 3 quarts boiling water

- Cut the uncooked seitan into ¼" slices. Cut each of these slices into very thin strips. Deep-fry according to instructions for deep-frying (see page 56), and drain the seitan on paper towels. Place the pieces in a colander and pour the boiling water over them to remove excess oil.

- Marinate the onions and celery with the mustard dressing in a large bowl.

- Peel away a narrow strip from around the centers of the whole potatoes, to prevent bursting. Gently boil the potatoes in lightly salted water until they are tender. Drain the potatoes, and cut them in half.

Prepare the Snow Peas:
- Remove the stem and its attached "string" and rinse the snow peas in a colander. Heat 4 quarts of boiling water, and pour it over the snow peas in 3 or 4 stages, shaking the colander to rotate the peas after each application of water. Wait for 1 or 2 minutes, then refresh the peas in cold water. Drain, cover, and refrigerate.

- Mix the potatoes and seitan strips carefully with the marinating vegetables. Marinate together ½ hour or more before serving. To serve, carefully mix in the snow peas, or arrange them around the salad on a platter.

Flint Corn Salad

This is a main course salad using whole kernels of dried corn which are cooked before being added to the salad. The result is a colorful combination of golden corn, bright kale, and accents of red pepper.

Serves 6 or more

>1 cup uncooked seitan (use uncooked seitan type of your choice)
>Oil for deep-frying

For the Dressing:

>1 large or 2 small garlic cloves
>2 1/2 tablespoons olive oil
>1 1/2 tablespoons umeboshi paste
>2 tablespoons cider vinegar
>1 teaspoon tarragon
>1/4 cup plus 2 tablespoons plain soymilk
>2 tablespoons water

For the Salad:

>4 1/2 cups cooked flint corn (whole kernels of dried corn)—Use 1 1/2 cups
>   uncooked flint corn—see directions in "From The Pantry", page 192.
>2 cups kale, cut into small pieces
>2 radishes, sliced into 1/8" rounds
>1 sweet red pepper
>1 cucumber, sliced 1/8" to 1/4" thick
>1/2 cup celery, diced

For the Broth:

>3/4 cup water
>2 teaspoons natural soy sauce
>1 slice fresh ginger root, 1/8" thick
>Toasted nori strips, as a garnish

Make the Dressing:

• Combine all dressing ingredients in a blender, or cook the flint corn according to the directions on page 192, using half of all amounts given there. Drain the corn and pour the dressing over the hot corn to marinate. Chill the corn, mixing occasionally.

• Steam or parboil the kale until it is bright green and tender. Drain the kale, then refresh it in cold water. Cover it and chill separately. Add all the remaining vegetables to the corn and marinate them together for at least ½ hour.

- Cut up or break the seitan into tiny pieces and deep-fry them until they are crispy and golden. Drain the seitan on paper towels. Place the seitan pieces in a strainer or colander in the sink, and pour very hot or boiling water over the pieces to remove excess oil. Press the seitan gently against the walls of the colander to remove the water.

- Combine and heat the ingredients for the broth, and add the seitan pieces. Reduce the heat to simmer, and cook uncovered until all the broth is absorbed by the seitan. Chill the seitan and cut it into bite-size pieces if necessary before adding it to the rest of the salad.

To Serve: Place the salad in a flat bowl or on a platter, and surround it with the kale. Garnish with squares or strips of toasted nori sea vegetable (see page 203).

Sauces, Dressings, and Marinades

Appetite is the best sauce.
—French Proverb

Mustard Sauce

Makes about 1½ cups

> 1 tablespoon arrowroot powder or kuzu starch
> 3/4 cup water
> 1/2 cup prepared Dijon-style mustard
> 2 1/2 teaspoons brown rice vinegar
> 2 tablespoons rice syrup
> 1 teaspoon natural soy sauce

- Dissolve the arrowroot or kuzu in a little water. Combine it in a small saucepan with the remaining water and the mustard, vinegar, sweetener, and natural soy sauce. Heat all together, stirring constantly until the sauce is thick and glossy.

- Use with deep-fried seitan cubes as a dip, or as a spread for Hickory Bits Bread.

Barbecue Sauce I

Makes about 2¼ cups

> 2 cups water
> 2" piece kombu
> 1 recipe Spicy Seasoning Mix
> 2 tablespoons barley malt syrup
> 1 tablespoon natural soy sauce
> 2 tablespoons sesame, safflower, or olive oil

- Combine all ingredients and bring to a boil. Simmer 10 minutes. Use as a marinade before broiling seitan cutlets.

Barbecue Sauce II—Mild ―――――――――――――――

Makes 1¼ cups

       1 cup stock left from cooking cutlets
       3 tablespoons tomato paste
       2 tablespoons brown rice or cider vinegar
       2 teaspoons barley malt syrup

• Combine all the ingredients over a low heat and simmer for 15 minutes. Spread on each cutlet and broil 6″ below the fire.

Barbecue Sauce III—Hickory ―――――――――――――

Makes 1½ cups

       1 1/2 tablespoons mugi or red miso
       4 tablespoons tomato paste
       2 tablespoons Liquid Hickory Smoke
       2 tablespoons barley malt syrup
       2 1/2 tablespoons cider vinegar
       1 tablespoon olive oil
       1/2 medium onion, minced
       2 garlic cloves, crushed and minced

• Simmer all ingredients together 5 to 8 minutes. Serve in one of the following ways:
1. Refrigerate covered for use in salad dressings, sauces, marinades, or on sandwiches
2. Spread on thin slices of seitan "roast" 11 and then broil.
3. Use in sandwiches.

Barbecue Sauce IV ――――――――――――――――――

Use this sauce for kebabs, salad dressings, sauces, marinades, or as a "ketchup" for burgers, cutlets, or "corn doggies."

Makes about 1 cup

       1/4 cup red or mugi miso
       1/4 cup tomato paste
       1/4 cup grated onion (about 1/2 medium onion)
       2 garlic cloves, crushed and minced well
       2 tablespoons olive oil
       1/4 cup cider vinegar
       1/4 cup barley malt syrup
       1/4 teaspoon dry mustard
       1/4 teaspoon allspice

- Combine the miso, tomato paste and grated onion, mixing thoroughly. Mix in the garlic and olive oil, then the cider vinegar. Add the barley malt syrup, mixing vigorously. Blend in the mustard and allspice.

- Cover the sauce and set it aside at room temperature for ½ hour allowing the flavors to blend.

Apricot Butter

Makes 1¾ to 2 cups

> 1 medium orange—use grated rind
> 1 medium lemon—use grated rind
> 1 cup unsulphured dried apricots
> 3 cups water
> Pinch salt
> 1/4 teaspoon cinnamon
> 3 tablespoons rice syrup

- Grate the orange and lemon rinds on the large holes of a hand grater. Simmer the dried apricots, covered, in 3 cups water with the salt, cinnamon, and grated citrus rinds. Cook the apricots for about ½ hour, or until they are very tender. Puree in a blender or food mill. Mix the rice syrup into the pureed apricots.

- If this is to be cooked further in another recipe, stop here.

- If the apricot butter is to be used as a spread, in a dessert, or as a condiment, then simmer the puree for 5 to 8 minutes. Keep refrigerated.

Red Chiles Marengo

> 3 oz. dried red chiles
> 3 cups boiling water
> 8 cloves garlic
> 1/4 teaspoon cumin powder
> 1/4 teaspoon oregano
> 1/4 to 1/2 cup powder miso

- Break open the chiles and remove the seeds, but keep the orange seams. Cover with boiling water and soak until soft, at least ½ hour. The water will then be a dark red color.

- Remove the chiles and save the soaking water. Puree the chiles with garlic in a blender, adding enough soaking water to make a paste consistency. Add cumin, oregano, and the miso to taste, and blend again.

- Simmer the mixture for 10 minutes.

- Use as an appetizer dip with chips, raw vegetables, or seitan dishes, or serve Red Chiles Marengo as a condiment.

- Red Chiles Marengo keeps well in the refrigerator when covered, and can be used as a seasoning in stews, soups, and casseroles, as a condiment to accompany beans or tacos, or in a marinade for tofu, fish, or seitan, prior to grilling.

Basic Tomato Sauce

Thick and robust, this sauce can be made lighter by adding vegetable broth. Adjust the seasonings accordingly.

Makes 4 quarts—freezes well

> 1/2 cup olive oil
> 4 cups diced onions
> 6 garlic cloves, crushed
> 4 cups celery, diced
> 2 teaspoons salt
> 2 cups water
> 2 tablespoons oregano
> 2 tablespoons basil
> 1/4 teaspoon allspice
> 6 oz. (one small can) tomato paste
> 2, 35 oz. cans whole peeled tomatoes, including juice
> 2, 28 oz. cans ground, peeled tomatoes
> 4 tablespoons diluted miso
> 2 teaspoon barley malt syrup

- Heat the olive oil and sauté the onions and garlic together until they are lightly browned. Add celery, salt, and the water and simmer 5 minutes. Add seasonings, the tomatoes, miso, and barley malt syrup. Simmer for 1 hour partially covered, and 2 hours uncovered. Stir occasionally.

Mediterranean Marinade

Serve this marinade at room temperature for fullest flavor.

Makes about ¾ cup

> 1/4 cup olive oil
> 1/2 cup lemon juice
> 2 tablespoons natural soy sauce
> 1/2 teaspoon oregano
> 1/2 teaspoon salt
> 3 teaspoons tarragon

1/2 lemon rind, grated
1 tablespoon capers

• Heat all the ingredients together to just below the boiling point. Pour this dressing over vegetables or seitan while the dressing is still hot. Rinse and add the capers. Toss all together to coat lightly, and refrigerate 2 hours.

Teriyaki Marinade

Makes 1 cup

1/2 cup natural soy sauce
3 tablespoons mirin
2 tablespoons rice syrup
1 tablespoon brown rice vinegar or cider vinegar
1 tablespoon paprika

• Combine all ingredients together.

• Marinate simmered seitan cutlets for 10 minutes on each side. Place the cutlets on a cookie sheet and broil, 3 to 4 inches below the flame, for 3 to 4 minutes on each side. Turn the cutlets over twice, basting as needed with remaining marinade.

Thick Marinade with Miso

Makes almost 1½ cups

2 tablespoons red miso (more to taste)
1/2 cup water
1 tablespoon dark sesame oil
2 tablespoons brown rice vinegar
1 tablespoon mirin
1 tablespoon barley malt syrup

• Mix the miso and water into a paste, adding the water to the miso ¼ cup at a time. Add the remaining ingredients one by one, mixing well after each addition.

Little Cream Sauce

Serves 4—over turnip cups, cutlets, or vegetables.

Makes about 1 cup

1 tablespoon kuzu
1 cup plain soymilk

1 1/2 teaspoons tahini
3 teaspoons *ume-su* (umeboshi vinegar)

• Dissolve the kuzu in ¼ cup soymilk, then mix well with the rest of the soymilk, the tahini, and the ume-su. Stir constantly over a medium heat until thick and creamy. Other seasonings may be added to taste.

Quick Gravy Using Seitan Broth

Makes 1¼ cups

1 tablespoon kuzu, arrowroot, or thick starch from making seitan
1/2 cup water (use 1/4 cup if using seitan starch)
1 tablespoon whole wheat pastry flour
1/4 cup seitan cooking broth or other seasoned stock
1/2 cup plain soymilk
1 teaspoon natural soy sauce, or to taste

• Dissolve the kuzu or arrowroot in ¼ cup of the water. Add the pastry flour and mix until smooth. In a sauce pan, heat the rest of the water and all the remaining ingredients. When they have boiled briefly, reduce the heat and stir in the kuzu mixture. Continue to stir over a low heat until the sauce is thick and creamy. Simmer about 5 to 8 minutes and adjust the seasonings.

Easy Garden Vegetable Sauce for Pasta

Serves 6 as a main dish with pasta

4 to 6 collard greens (leaves with stems)
8 cups water
4" piece kombu
1/4 teaspoon salt
2 cups celery, diced
1 1/2 cups carrots, diced
3/4 cup plain soymilk
2 tablespoons natural soy sauce
2 tablespoons tahini
3/4 cup thick starch from making seitan (see pages 36–37)

• Separate the collard greens from the stems. Cut the stems crosswise into ¼" pieces. Stack the greens, and cut them lengthwise then crosswise in ½" strips each way.

• Bring the water, kombu and salt to a boil. Reduce the heat slightly and add the celery, carrots, and the collard greens and stems. Cover and cook over a medium heat until the vegetables are tender.

- Remove the large piece of kombu, and cut it into ½″ squares. Return the cut kombu to the vegetables.

- Combine the soymilk, natural soy sauce, tahini, and seitan starch to make a thick paste. Add this mixture to the vegetable broth, stirring constantly until the sauce has thickened. Simmer for 10 to 15 minutes. Adjust the seasonings.

Creamy Umeboshi Dressing

Vary the flavor of this easy creamy dressing by adding your favorite herbs.

Makes 1 cup

> 2 1/2 tablespoons umeboshi paste
> 1 cup plain soymilk
> 4 teaspoons sesame or safflower oil
> 1 teaspoon brown rice vinegar

- Thin the umeboshi paste by adding the soymilk to it little by little. Mix well. Add the oil a little at a time while mixing with a fork or whisk. Add the rice vinegar and mix well.

- Refrigerate. Shake well before using.

Miso-Lemon Dressing

Makes 1 cup

> 1/4 cup white (or other) miso, diluted in:
> 1/2 cup water
> Juice of 1 to 2 lemons, to taste

- Combine these ingredients for use with cooked dark green vegetables, or salads. Miso-Lemon Dressing may also be used for basting broiled fish.

Basic Vinaigrette

Makes 2 cups

> 1 teaspoon salt
> 1 teaspoon dry mustard powder
> 1 cup olive oil
> 1/4 cup brown rice or cider vinegar

    1/2 cup sesame oil
    1/4 cup lemon juice
    4 cloves garlic, crushed

• Combine, then beat the following with a fork or whisk until smooth: salt, dry mustard, ¼ cup olive oil, rice vinegar. Add the sesame oil, and mix well again. Continuing to whisk, slowly add the lemon juice and the remaining olive oil. While slowly adding these ingredients.

• Add the garlic and set the dressing aside in a covered jar for several hours to blend the flavors. Any dressing remaining may be refrigerated for future use.

Anchovy-Tarragon Vinaigrette ——————

Makes 2 cups

    16 anchovy fillets
    1/4 cup lemon juice
    2 teaspoons dry mustard powder
    1/4 cup sesame oil
    1 1/4 cups olive oil
    1/4 cup brown rice vinegar
    3 teaspoons tarragon
    4 cloves garlic, crushed

• Use a fork to mash the anchovies and mix them with the lemon juice. Add the mustard and sesame oil and mix well. Add the olive oil and vinegar alternately, one teaspoon of each at a time, mixing constantly with a fork or whisk.

• Add the tarragon and the cloves of garlic and store the dressing in a jar to blend the flavors before using. Any dressing remaining may be refrigerated for future use.

Sweet and Sour Dressing ——————

Makes 1¼ cups

    1 cup plain soymilk
    2 tablespoons rice syrup
    2 teaspoons umeboshi paste
    2 teaspoons sesame or safflower oil
    1/4 cup lemon juice
    1/2 teaspoon celery seed (optional)

• Mix all ingredients together until smooth. This dressing is very well suited to cole slaw or Waldorf salad.

Creamy Chive Dressing

Makes 1 cup

> 1/2 cup plain soymilk
> 1 tablespoon white miso
> 1 tablespoon umeboshi paste
> 4 teaspoons tahini
> 1/4 cup water
> 2 tablespoons lemon juice, or to taste
> 1/4 cup chives finely chopped (fresh chives preferred)

- Add the soymilk to the miso and umeboshi a little at a time, mixing until smooth. Add the tahini and mix well. Add the water and lemon juice to taste, then mix in the chives.

- Shake before using.

Spicy Miso-Orange Dressing

Makes 1¼ cups

> 1/4 cup miso
> 1 cup orange juice (preferably fresh squeezed)
> 1 teaspoon tabasco sauce or Chinese Hot Pepper Oil
> 4 teaspoons sesame or safflower oil

- Dilute the miso by gradually adding the orange juice and mixing well with a fork or spoon. Add the seasoning and blend in thoroughly. Mix in the oil little by little.

- Shake before using.

Tamari-Lemon Dressing with Tarragon

Makes 1½ cups

> 1 cup lemon juice
> 1/2 cup natural soy sauce
> 2 teaspoons sesame or safflower oil
> 4 teaspoons tarragon
> 1 clove garlic, crushed

- Combine all the ingredients. Set the dressing aside for 15 to 20 minutes to allow the flavors to blend. This dressing also makes a good marinade or basting sauce for broiled fish.

Creamy French Dressing ———————————

Makes about 1 cup

> 1/4 cup prepared mayonnaise
> 1/4 cup Barbecue Sauce IV (see page 166)
> 1/3 cup water

• Blend all the ingredients together and refrigerate in a covered jar. Shake well before using.

Mustard Dressing ——————————————

Makes ¾ cup

> 1 garlic clove, crushed and minced
> 2 tablespoons umeboshi paste
> 2 1/2 tablespoons olive oil
> 2 teaspoons prepared Dijon-style mustard
> 1/4 cup brown rice vinegar
> 1/4 cup apple juice

• Put the minced garlic into a bowl and use the back of a spoon to combine the umeboshi paste with it. Add the oil 1 teaspoon at a time, mixing constantly. Add the mustard, then add the vinegar and apple juice gradually. Use a whisk to whip the dressing until it is thick and creamy.

Ume-Orange Dressing ——————————————

Makes about ¾ cup

> 2/3 cup orange juice (preferably fresh squeezed)
> 2 tablespoons *ume-su* (umeboshi vinegar)
> 1 tablespoon olive oil or toasted sesame oil
> 1 teaspoon grated orange rind

• Combine all ingredients together in a covered jar and shake well to mix. Refrigerate.

Condiments

Plain cooking cannot be trusted to plain cooks.
—Countess Morphy

Nori Sprinkles and Spirals

To be served as crumbled "sprinkles" or simply as baked sliced "spirals," these seitan and nori rolls are tasty and easy to make.

> 1 cup uncooked seitan 3 (or other type of your choice)
>
> Natural soy sauce
> 2 sheets nori sea vegetable

- Preheat the oven to 375° F.

- Toast the nori by passing it back and forth, 3″ to 5″ above the open flame or heating element of the stove, until the color changes from purple-black to green-black.

- Dampen your work surface, and stretch out the uncooked seitan into a rectangle the size of the 2 nori sheets. With the nori on top, press the nori sheets into the seitan and begin to make a tight roll, starting at the edge closest to you and rolling away. Slice the roll into pieces ¼″ thick. Place these slices on a lightly oiled baking sheet. Drop 2 or 3 drops of natural soy sauce on each slice and spread it over the surface.

- Bake for 10 minutes. When the slices are cool, serve them as an appetizer with a tofu dip or cut them smaller and grind in a food processor or blender with a few more drops of natural soy sauce.

Savory Seitan Spread with Miso

Use as a condiment for hot rice or noodles, or as a spread for crackers and sandwiches.

Makes about 1 cup

1 cup cooked seitan—grind, grate, or chop very fine

1 1/2 teaspoons sesame oil
2 cloves garlic, crushed and minced
1 1/2 teaspoons fresh ginger root, grated (use about 1" piece ginger)
2 scallions, cut very fine
1/8 teaspoon (2 or 3 drops) Chinese Hot Pepper Oil or Tabasco Sauce
2 tablespoons red miso
1/4 cup water
1 tablespoon mirin

• Heat the oil and sauté the ground seitan and garlic for about 3 minutes. Add the ginger, scallion and hot pepper oil.

• Make a smooth paste of the miso with ¼ cup water and add it to the seitan mixture. Add the mirin and simmer until bubbles appear, stirring occasionally. Remove from the stove and cool. Serve at room temperature.

Hickory Strips ————————————————

A highly seasoned topping for hot rice or noodles.

1 cup cooked seitan 2, cut in thin strips

Oil for deep-frying
1 cup water
1 tablespoon Spicy Seasoning Mix
1 tablespoon natural soy sauce
1 tablespoon Liquid Hickory Smoke
1 tablespoon barley malt syrup
1/4 cup scallions, finely chopped

• Heat the oil and deep-fry the seitan strips according to instructions for deep-frying. (see page 56)

• Bring the water to boil, and add all remaining ingredients except the scallions. Reduce the heat and simmer the deep-fried strips in the broth for ½ hour, then return the heat to high until all the broth is absorbed. Chill the cooked seitan strips to make them firmer.

To Serve: Cut the strips crosswise in very small pieces and combine with the finely chopped scallions. Use as a topping for hot rice, barley, or noodles.

Seasoned Seitan "Bits" ————————————

Use as a garnish for hot grains and noodles, or salads.

Makes about ¾ cup

3/4 cup cooked seitan (your choice of seitan)

1/2 teaspoon garlic, crushed and minced
1/2 teaspoon oregano
1 teaspoon paprika
1 tablespoon chickpea flour
2 teaspoons natural soy sauce
Oil for deep-frying

Note: You may substitute any other combination of seasonings (of your own creation or from this book) for the garlic, oregano, paprika, and natural soy sauce.

• Grind the cooked seitan and combine it with all the remaining ingredients.

• Heat 2″ to 3″ of oil for deep-frying and carefully drop in the seitan mixture by teaspoonfuls. It will not hold together well, but will spread out into tiny pieces. When these are crispy (it doesn't take long), remove them with a flat strainer and drain on paper towels.

To Serve: Use as a garnish for hot grains and noodles, or on salads.

Seitan Paté with Ginger, Onion, and White Miso ————

Use as a condiment with hot grains or noodles, as a spread for bread and crackers, or as a dip for raw vegetables.

Makes ¾ to 1 cup

1/2 cup uncooked seitan (your choice of seitan)

Oil for deep-frying
3 quarts boiling water
1″ piece fresh ginger root, peeled and grated
1 tablespoon white miso
5 tablespoons water
1/4 cup onion, diced
1 tablespoon mirin
1/4 cup parsley, minced

• Slice the uncooked seitan into 6 or 7 strips and deep-fry until they are crispy and golden. Drain them on paper towels, then place them in a colander and pour the boiling water over to remove the excess oil. Drain and squeeze the seitan. Grind the seitan in a blender or food processor.

• Peel and grate the ginger. Dilute the miso with 2 tablespoons water and mix to make a smooth paste. Combine the miso and ginger in a saucepan with the onion, mirin, and ground seitan.

• Heat the seitan mixture and add the remaining water. Reduce the heat and add the parsley. Simmer for 5 minutes.

Sandwiches

It has been said that a hungry man is more interested in four sandwiches than four freedoms.—Henry Cabot Lodge, Jr. (1902–)

Hot Barbecued Seitan Sandwich

Makes one sandwich

Seitan "roast" 11, sliced very thin

Barbecue Sauce IV (Hickory) or other of your choice
Whole wheat bread
Alfalfa sprouts

- Spread a layer of sauce on the bread. Layer the thinly-sliced seitan on it, spreading a little sauce over each piece. Allow a generous layer of sauce for the top of the sandwich.

- Place the sandwich on a cookie sheet and broil for a few minutes until the sauce is slightly bubbly and browned. Don't let it burn.

- Cut the sandwich in half and top with alfalfa sprouts. Serve with "Bill's Dills." (See page 197.)

Seitan Sandwich with Tangy Miso-Tahini Sauce

Makes one sandwich

Seitan "roast" 11 or cutlets 1, 3 or 4—thinly sliced

3 tablespoons Tangy Miso-tahini Sauce (below)
2 tablespoons minced red onion
Tomato slices
Alfalfa sprouts

- Spread 1 tablespoon of the sauce on the bread. Arrange thin slices of seitan and tomato over the sauce. Sprinkle the onion over the seitan, and pour about 2 tablespoons or more sauce over the top.

• Broil the sandwich until the seitan is hot and the sauce is bubbly and just beginning to brown. Cut the sandwich in half and top with the alfalfa sprouts.

Tangy Miso-Tahini Sauce

Makes about 1 cup—enough for 4 to 5 sandwiches

      3 tablespoons white miso
      1/2 cup water
      3 tablespoons tahini

      optional additions:
      1/4 cup grated onion
      Fresh chopped chives
      Fresh minced dill
      3 tablespoons lemon juice (or to taste)

• Make a smooth paste of the miso and water. Add the tahini and stir the sauce until it is smooth. Add the onion, chives, dill, or any other ingredients as desired. Add the lemon juice to taste.

Hot Super-Sandwich

Makes 2 sandwiches

      Seitan "Roast" 11, or cutlets, sliced very thin

      1 tablespoon prepared mayonnaise
      2 teaspoons Dijon-style prepared mustard
      1 bulky roll, cut in half (top and bottom), OR
      1 French bread baguette, cut in half (top and bottom)
      Red onion, sliced very thin
      1/4 to 1/2 cup sauerkraut—squeeze before using
      Fresh tomato slices

• Combine the mayonnaise and mustard. Place the bread on a cookie sheet.

• Assemble the following ingredients on each half: $1\frac{1}{2}$ teaspoons mayonnaise mixture, seitan, onion slices, sauerkraut, tomato.

• Broil 6″ below the heat for 5 minutes. Remove to a serving plate and spread half of the remaining sauce over the top of each sandwich.

• Top with sprouts or lettuce.

Tofu Spread with Variations ———————————

Makes 1½ to 2 cups

Combine the following in a blender until creamy:

    1 tablespoon white miso
    1 tablespoon tahini
    1 pound soft or firm tofu
    1 tablespoon umeboshi paste
    1/4 to 1/2 cup water
    1 teaspoon brown rice vinegar

• Add in any of the following ingredients by hand, after the basic mixture is made:

    Minced chives
    Minced parsley
    Paprika
    Chili powder
    Chopped black olives
    Chopped green olives
    Chopped red onion
    Chopped carrots
    Chopped celery
    Chopped cucumbers
    Diced pimientos
    Crushed and minced garlic (sauté with a little olive oil before adding to the
       spread)

Seitan-Tofu Paté ———————————————

Makes about 2 cups, or enough for 6 open sandwiches on bread slices

    1 cup cooked seitan cutlets 1 or 3

    1/2 pound soft tofu
    2 scallions, chopped fine
    1 clove garlic, crushed and minced
    2 teaspoons prepared Dijon-style mustard
    1 1/2 teaspoons umeboshi paste
    3/4 teaspoon natural soy sauce
    2 teaspoons prepared mayonnaise

• Grind the seitan. Mash the tofu with a fork, and add the seitan and all other ingredients as listed. Mix well.

As a Paté: Preheat the oven to 350° F. Put the seitan mixture into a small ovenproof bowl and bake uncovered for 20 minutes. Use hot or cold on crackers, toast, or as a dip for raw vegetables.

For Hot Sandwiches: Spread generously on a slice of bread, place under the broiler for about 3 minutes—watch carefully. Top with lettuce, onions, tomato slices, pickles, or sprouts as desired.

Desserts

Coconut-Lemon Cookies

Crispy on the edges and chewy on the inside, these golden cookies are really a "giant" treat.

Makes 30 to 33 cookies, 3″ to 4″ in diameter

> 2 cups whole wheat pastry flour
> 1 teaspoon baking powder
> 1/2 teaspoon salt
> 1 1/2 cups unsweetened shredded coconut
> 2 lemons—grate rinds on large holes
> 1/4 cup plus 1 tablespoon corn oil
> 1 cup thick starch from preparing seitan
> 1/2 cup plus 2 tablespoons maple syrup
> 1/2 cup barley malt syrup
> 1/4 teaspoon vanilla extract
> 1 1/2 teaspoons lemon extract

- Preheat the oven to 300° F.

- Sift the flour, baking powder and salt together. With a fork, mix in the coconut and lemon rinds. Pour in the corn oil and blend with a fork or pastry blender to form pea-size lumps.

- In a separate bowl combine the starch, syrups, and the lemon and vanilla extracts. Mix well until smooth. Add the syrup mixture to the flour and coconut and mix well to make a wet batter. Let it rest for about 10 minutes.

- Turn your cookie sheets over and oil the underside. Large cookies baked on this side of the cookie sheet are easier to remove and will bake more evenly. Drop by tablespoons, 2″ apart, making 6 to 8 cookies per sheet.

- Bake for 10 minutes. The edge of each cookie should be golden brown, slightly darker than the rest of the cookie. Remove immediately to a rack to cool. When cool, the cookies will be crispy on the edges and chewy in the center.

Choco-Carob Fudge Sauce ————————————————

Luckily this keeps well in the refrigerator, because you will probably think of a lot of ways to use it.

Makes about 4 cups. Refrigerate.

> 1 cup water
> 3 oz. (3 squares) unsweetened baking chocolate
> 1/2 cup roasted (dark) carob powder
> 1 1/2 cups plain soymilk
> 3/4 cup maple syrup
> 1/4 cup rice syrup
> Pinch salt
> 1/2 cup thick starch from making seitan
> 1 teaspoon vanilla extract

● Use a medium flame to heat the water and chocolate together in a saucepan. Stir occasionally until the chocolate is melted. Set aside to cool.

● Use a whisk or fork to make a smooth, loose paste with the carob powder and half of the soymilk (¾ cup). Add the remaining soymilk, maple and rice syrups, and salt. Add in the chocolate mixture, stirring constantly over a medium-low heat until the sauce is almost boiling. Reduce the heat to low and add the starch. Stir constantly until the sauce has thickened. Add the vanilla and simmer for 10 minutes, stirring frequently. Use hot or cold.

Banana Dream Pudding ————————————————

Just close your eyes and be transported to a tropical isle . . . Banana Dream Pudding may also be used as a pie filling for individual single-shell pies.

Makes 6½ cups, serves 6–8

> 1/3 cup unroasted almonds
> 4 cups boiling water
> 3 1/2 cups clear starch water (see page 215) from making seitan, or water
> 2 to 3 bananas
> 3/4 cup plain soymilk
> Pinch salt
> 1 teaspoon vanilla
> 1/2 cup maple syrup
> 1 cup thick starch from making seitan
> 1/2 cup unsweetened coconut (shredded)

- Blanch the almonds by parboiling them for 2 minutes, then drain them into a colander. Remove the skins by squeezing the wide end of the almond; the nut should then slide through the skin at the pointed end. Put the almonds in a blender or food processor with 2½ cups of the clear starch water and process until creamy. Put this mixture into a sauce pan.

- Process the bananas, the soymilk, and the remaining 1 cup of the clear starch water (or water) in the blender until smooth. Add this mixture to the almond mixture in the saucepan.

- Heat the almond and banana mixture slowly, stirring gently to blend them. Add the salt, vanilla, and maple syrup. Mix the thick starch well so it is smooth, and add it to the rest of the ingredients in the saucepan. Simmer for 20 minutes, stirring frequently until the entire sauce is thick and creamy.

- Use a low to medium heat to toast the coconut until golden and very fragrant in a dry, heavy frying pan. Stir it constantly and shake the pan back and forth periodically.

- Pour the pudding into individual serving bowls or cups, and sprinkle the toasted coconut over the top. Serve warm or chilled.

Chewy Date-Walnut Cookies ━━━━━━━━━━━━━━━

Makes 24 to 30 cookies, 3″ in diameter

> 2 cups walnuts
> 1/4 teaspoon salt
> 1 1/2 teaspoons baking powder
> 3/4 cup chopped dates
> 1/2 cup barley malt syrup
> 1 1/4 cups thick starch from preparing seitan

- Preheat the oven to 350° F.

- Grind the walnuts in a food processor or blender. Put the ground nuts in a mixing bowl and break up any clumps. Carefully sprinkle the salt and baking powder over the top of the nuts and combine them thoroughly. Mix in the date pieces.

- Combine the barley malt syrup with the starch, using a fork to blend them together until smooth. Add the syrup mixture to the nuts and mix well.

- Drop by tablespoons, 2″ apart on a lightly oiled cookie sheet. Bake for 15 to 18 minutes. Remove to a rack to cool.

Almond Essence Whip

Use as a topping for puddings, cakes, fresh fruit or fruit salad, cooked dried fruit, and dessert crepes.

Makes about 3 cups

Prepare by Cooking:

>   3 tablespoons kuzu
>   3 tablespoons thick starch from preparing seitan
>   3/4 cup soymilk
>   1/2 cup maple syrup
>   1 teaspoon vanilla extract
>   3/4 teaspoon almond extract
>   Pinch salt
>   1/4 cup water

Note: Starch from making seitan 1 or 3 is fine to use, but pieces of bran will be evident. If you want a really white-colored topping, use starch from seitan 2 only (made from unbleached white flour).

Prepare in the Blender:

>   1 cup blanched almonds
>   1/4 cup maple syrup
>   1/3 cup soymilk
>   1/4 to 1/2 cup water

- In a saucepan, combine the kuzu, wheat starch, and half of the soymilk stirring to dissolve the kuzu. Add the remaining soymilk and the syrup, vanilla and almond extracts, salt, and water.

- Stir this mixture constantly over a medium heat until it is thick. As the sauce thickens, it will become very stiff. Use a firm, whipping stroke to keep it smooth. Stir vigorously while simmering for 2 to 3 minutes. Remove to a bowl and chill until it is very firm.

- Blanch the almonds in boiling water to cover for 30 seconds. Drain. Remove the skins by holding the wide end of the almond and squeezing. The almond should slide through the skin.

- In a blender, combine the blanched almonds with the other "blender" ingredients and whip until smooth. Break up the chilled syrup-starch mixture into chunks, and add one piece at a time into the almond mixture, continuing to whip at a high speed. Refrigerate.

Divine Fresh Fruit Shake

Use fresh fruit instead of ice cream, and you can create your own flavors.

Makes 1

> 3/4 cup plain soymilk
> 1 tablespoon maple syrup
> 1/4 teaspoon vanilla extract (optional)
> 3 to 4 ice cubes

Choose one or more fresh fruits, such as:

> 1 large apple
> Banana
> Strawberries
> Peaches
> Cantelope

• Combine all together in a blender and enjoy!

Maple-Walnut Custard

Soymilk and eggs combine to make this easy, rich-tasting unbaked custard.

10 servings, ⅔ cups each

> 1 1/2 cups (8 oz.) granulated tapioca
> 3 cups plain soymilk
> 5 cups water
> 1/4 teaspoon salt
> 4 eggs
> 1 teaspoon maple syrup
> 1 teaspoon vanilla extract
> 1/2 to 1 cup shelled walnuts

• Heat the tapioca granules with the soymilk, water, and salt. Bring to a boil, then reduce the heat and simmer 2 or 3 minutes, stirring constantly. Beat the eggs and maple syrup together. Add ⅓ to ½ of the hot tapioca mixture to the eggs, mixing steadily. Add the egg-tapioca mixture back into the remaining tapioca. Simmer 3 to 5 minutes more. Add in the vanilla.

• When the custard has finished cooking, pour it into individual serving bowls, garnish with walnut halves and chill.

188

Variation:

• For a more elaborate dessert, make the custard without walnuts and layer it into wine glasses alternating layers with raspberries, or blueberries, or sliced strawberries. Top with one or more of the chosen berries. Chill until serving time.

Note: The walnuts may be added in various ways: crushed, reserving a few for a garnish, they may be added into the custard. If you want a completely smooth custard with walnuts only on top, use nice-looking walnut halves as garnishes for each individual serving.

Cinnamon-Chestnut Puffs

Chestnut flour makes a sweet, powdered coating for these little deep-fried puffs.

Makes 30, 1″ puffs

    1/2 cup uncooked seitan 1 or 2
    Oil for deep-frying

    3 tablespoons chestnut flour
    2 tablespoons crushed, roasted walnuts
    1 tablespoon maple granules (maple sugar)
    1/2 teaspoon cinnamon

• Deep-fry the seitan according to instructions for deep-frying, pinching off ½ inch pieces of seitan to drop gently into the hot oil. Remove the puffs when they are golden.

• Drain briefly on paper towels.

Note: Pay careful attention to the temperature of the oil, because oil which is too hot will leave the inside of the puffs uncooked. Oil which is too cool will give you "oil-saturated" puffs.

• Mix all the dry ingredients together in a small bowl. As soon as each few puffs have cooked and drained for a few seconds on the paper towels, roll them immediately in the chestnut flour mixture while they are still hot and set them on a plate to cool.

• Serve as an accompaniment to hot or cool tea, or as snacks.

New "Good Old Chocolate Pudding"

For a more elegant dessert, chill this pudding in wine glasses and serve topped with Almond Essence Whip and a toasted almond or a fresh strawberry.

Makes 8—1 cup servings

> 6 cups clear starch water from making seitan
> 2 1/2 cups thick starch from making seitan
> 3/4 cup maple syrup
> 1 1/2 cups plain soymilk
> 7 tablespoons carob powder
> 1 1/2 squares unsweetened bakers' chocolate
> 1/4 teaspoon salt
> 2 teaspoons vanilla

- Put the clear starch water and thick starch into a large saucepan. Stir them well until they are smooth. Add the maple syrup and half of the soymilk (¾ cup).

- Put the carob powder into a small mixing bowl and add the other half (¾ cup) of the soymilk to the carob powder, little by little, mixing until it becomes a smooth paste. Use the large holes on a hand-grater to shave the chocolate into this mixture.

- Add the carob-chocolate mixture to the starch-soymilk mixture in the saucepan and combine them well. Heat over a medium flame, stirring constantly until the sauce begins to thicken.

Note: Too high a heat at this point will result in starchy lumps. Be patient.

- Add the salt and the vanilla. Continue to stir over a moderate heat until the mixture is smooth, shiny, and runs off a spoon in a thick sheet.

- Reduce the heat and simmer, partially covered, for 15 to 20 minutes. Pour into individual cups and chill.

Date-Nut Filled Puffs ━━━━━━━━━━━━━━━━━━

A variation of dessert puffs, this time the uncooked seitan is filled before baking.

Makes 12 filled puffs

> 1 cup uncooked seitan 2

For the Filling: Makes 1 cup

> 1/2 cup walnuts
> 1/2 cup chopped, pitted dates
> 2 tablespoons barley malt syrup
> 1/4 teaspoon vanilla
> Pinch salt
> 3 tablespoons orange juice

• Preheat the oven to 350° F.

• Press the seitan out to ½″ thick, and cut into 12 equal pieces.

Prepare the Filling:
• Crush the walnuts with a rolling pin or coarsely grind in a food processor or blender. Combine all the ingredients in a saucepan over low heat, stirring to prevent sticking. Simmer about 2 to 3 minutes and remove from heat. Cool the filling before using it.

Fill the Puffs:
• Working with one piece at a time, stretch the seitan as much as possible without tearing it. Hold it down with one hand, and place 2 to 3 teaspoons of filling on one-third of the stretched seitan. Fold the other side of the seitan over the filling and press the edges together. Allow the filled seitan pieces to "relax" for a minute, then place them 2″ apart on an oiled cookie sheet.

• Bake the filled puffs for 10 to 15 minutes. Brush the tops with a little maple syrup while they are hot, then place the puffs on a rack to cool.

From the Pantry

*Man is a cooking animal. The beasts have memory, judgement,
and all the faculties and passions of our mind, in a certain
degree; but no beast is a cook.*—James Boswell (1740–1790),
Tour to the Hebrides

The following recipes are presented to help you integrate the seitan recipes into
complete whole-foods menus.

Basic Crepes

**Fill these crepes with ground seitan (see Filled Crepes with Orange-shallot Sauce) or
a dessert filling of your choice.**

Makes 16 to 18 crepes, 8″ in diameter

> 2 cups whole wheat pastry flour
> 1 1/2 cups plain soymilk
> 1 cup water
> 3 eggs
> 2 tablespoons corn oil
> 1 teaspoons salt
> Oil for the pan, as needed

- Combine all liquid and eggs, and beat until smooth. Use a whisk or blender to
  whip all ingredients into a smooth batter. Add the salt and flour, $\frac{1}{4}$ cup at a time,
  while mixing to form a smooth batter.

- Heat a 9″ skillet over a medium heat. Brush a very small amount of oil on the
  surface. Pour in about $\frac{1}{4}$ cup of batter while lifting the pan and moving it around,
  tipping it from side to side to distribute the batter evenly over the surface of the
  pan in a thin layer.

- After 1 to 2 minutes the edges of the crepe should be golden and begin to pull away
  from the sides of the pan. The top of the crepe should be almost dry and slightly
  bubbly. Turn the crepe over and cook it for 1 to 2 minutes on the other side.

- Crepes may be stacked using a sheet of waxed paper between each layer. They
  may be prepared ahead of time and filled at serving time.

Note: When the crepes are cool, the stacks may be wrapped in foil or a plastic freezer bag (with waxed paper separating the crepes) and frozen.

Flint Corn

Flint corn is a traditional American grain, often used in cornmeal, tortillas, and other Southwestern dishes. In this book you will find Flint corn used in casseroles and salads. Cooked flint corn may also be ground into a mash called "masa," from which tortillas are traditionally made. Masa is also a fine base for a creamed corn soup or thick cereal.

Serves 6 to 8

> 3 cups dry flint corn
> 1/2 cup wood ash (must not contain any painted or vanished wood or newspaper)
> 18 cups water

- Pressure-cook the corn and ash with 9 cups of water for 1 hour. Reduce the pressure by placing the pot in the sink and running cold water over the top until all safety valves are in their normal pre-pressure positions. Drain the corn into a colander with large holes. Rinse the corn continuously with water while rubbing it between your plams to loosen the hulls and remove them from the corn kernels. Repeat this until most of the hulls are rinsed away and the corn is a bright yellow color. Watch carefully for any solid particles of burned wood (left from the ash) which must be discarded.

- Return the corn to the pot and add 9 cups of water, or just enough to cover the corn. Pressure-cook once more for 30 to 40 minutes. Reduce the pressure and check the corn for tenderness. If it is not tender, pressure cook for an additional 10 to 15 minutes.

Tofu "Feta Cheese"

A useful non-dairy substitute for feta cheese, this may be used in salads or mixed-vegetable dishes.

> 1 pound firm or soft tofu
> 2 teaspoons umeboshi paste
> 1 teaspoon tahini
> 1 teaspoon brown rice vinegar
> 12" square of good quality cheesecloth

- Mash the tofu with a fork. In a small bowl, combine the umeboshi paste, tahini, and vinegar. Add the umeboshi mixture to the tofu and combine very well.

- Mound the tofu in the center of the square of cheesecloth and bring up the edges and corners. Tie the cheesecloth together close to the tofu, or secure it tightly with a rubber band.

- Bring 1 cup of water to a boil, and immerse the cheesecloth package in it. Reduce the heat and simmer for 15 minutes. Remove the tofu and drain well, then refrigerate to chill thoroughly.

- Open the package when you are ready to use it. Break the tofu up into clumps, and use it like feta cheese in appetizers, salads, or casseroles.

Whole Wheat Bread with Hickory Bits ——————————

Makes a large loaf, great with hot mustard sauce.

> 1 cup braised seitan "roast" 11 or other cooked seitan of your choice, cooked with strongly flavored soy sauce broth
>
> 2 1/2 teaspoons dry yeast
> 1 teaspoon rice syrup or other sweetener
> 1/4 cup water
> 2 eggs—one for dough, one for egg wash
> 1/2 cup warm water
> 1 teaspoon salt
> 1 tablespoon basil
> 2 cups whole wheat flour
> 1 to 1 1/2 cups unbleached white flour
> 2 cups onions, diced
> 1 tablespoon olive oil
> 1/2 to 1 cup cornmeal

For the Marinade:

> 2 tablespoons Liquid Hickory Smoke
> 1 teaspoon Spicy Seasoning Mix
> 1 teaspoon natural soy sauce
> 2 tablespoons water

- Combine the yeast, rice syrup and warm water in a small bowl. Stir to dissolve the yeast, then let it rest about 10 minutes or until it bubbles.

- In a larger mixing bowl, combine 1 lightly beaten egg with the warm water, salt, and basil. Add the yeast mixture and the whole wheat flour. Add 1 cup of the unbleached white flour ¼ cup at a time, mixing well after each addition to form a soft dough.

- Put a little flour on the kneading surface, and turn out the dough onto it. Knead well for 5 to 10 minutes until the dough is smooth and elastic. Use the rest of the white flour as needed to prevent sticking. Place the dough in a clean bowl to which 1 tablespoon olive oil has been added, and roll it around so the surface of the dough has been oiled.

- Cover the bowl tightly with plastic wrap and place it in a warm spot to rise for 1 to 2 hours or until doubled in bulk.

- While the dough is rising, combine the marinade ingredients and marinate the seitan cubes for 1 hour. Remove the seitan and broil for 3 minutes, then turn the pieces over and broil for 2 minutes.

- Sauté the onions in 1 tablespoon olive oil until lightly browned. When the dough has risen, punch it down and add the onions and seitan, kneading them into the dough. If the dough is too sticky to form into a loaf, knead in a little cornmeal.

- Sprinkle some cornmeal on the surface of a cookie sheet. This will prevent the dough from sticking as it bakes, as well as add a toasted corn flavor to the crust. Form a round or oval loaf and place it on the cookie sheet. Cover the dough with a clean, damp cloth towel and let it rise again until double in size, about ½ to 1 hour.

- Preheat oven to 350° F.

- Before baking, beat the remaining egg and brush it over the surface of the loaf. Make 3 diagonal slashes in the top, and sprinkle cornmeal over the top of the loaf.

- Bake 30 to 40 minutes, or until the loaf makes a hollow sound when tapped on the bottom.

Corn Bread

A colorful, delicious, and easy to prepare all-season companion to soups and salads.

Serves 6 to 8

>   3 cups yellow cornmeal
>   1/2 teaspoon salt
>   2 teaspoons baking powder
>   6 tablespoons corn oil
>   1 pound tofu
>   1 egg
>   3 tablespoons maple syrup (more for a sweeter corn bread)
>   1 1/2 cups water

- Thoroughly combine the cornmeal, salt and baking powder with a fork. Add the oil to the dry ingredients, again mixing with a fork to form pea-size lumps.

• In a blender, combine the tofu, egg, syrup, and ½ cup water. Add 1 cup of water to the cornmeal mixture and beat 50 strokes or so to make the batter. Add the tofu mixture to the batter and beat to mix in well. Let the batter rest for 10 minutes.

• Preheat the oven to 375° F.

• Pour the batter into an oiled 9″ × 13″ baking pan and bake for 30 to 35 minutes. Test for doneness. The edges of the corn bread should be slightly browned and pulled away from the sides of the baking pan. The top will be a little cracked. Place the entire pan on a rack to cool, and cover with a clean linen dish towel or other dry cloth.

Note: If a corn bread thicker than 1½″ is needed, use a smaller pan. The baking time will be longer.

Millet

Basic preparation for millet, a grain often used as a main dish, cereal, or in soup.

Serves 4

> 1 cup millet
> 3 cups water
> 1/8 teaspoon salt

• Check through the millet and remove any small twigs or stones that may be present. For a more nutty flavor, toast the millet in a dry skillet for about 10 minutes over a medium-low heat, stirring constantly.

• Bring the water to boiling and add the millet and salt. Reduce the heat and cover the pot, placing a flame diffuser under it. Simmer for 40 minutes, or until all the water is absorbed and the millet appears fluffy. Stir once and cover. Let rest 2 to 3 minutes, then remove from the pot.

To Serve: Serve millet with Miso-Tahini Sauce or another favorite sauce or stew. Leftover millet may be reheated by steaming or pan-frying with vegetables, made into croquettes and deep-fried, or used in a soup or casserole.

Millet "Mashed Potatoes"

When you want a whole grain but you need a dish with a smooth texture, try this creamy millet and cauliflower combination to accompany your cutlets and stews.

Serves 4 to 6

6 cups water
1 1/2 cups millet
1 large head cauliflower, cut into large flowerets
1/2 to 3/4 teaspoon salt

• Bring the water to a boil. Add the millet, the cauliflower, and the salt. Reduce the heat to simmer. Cover the pot and place a flame diffuser under it. Cook for 40 minutes or until the millet and the cauliflower are both tender and all the water has been absorbed.

• Puree the millet/cauliflower mixture in a blender, food processor, or food mill. Serve hot with Chunky Mushroom Gravy (below) or other sauce or stew of your choice.

Variations:
• Millet "Mashed Potatoes" can also be baked in a deep or shallow casserole with a little corn oil and natural soy sauce drizzled over the surface. Sprinkle with paprika and bake about 20 minutes at 350° F.

• Squeeze the Millet "Mashed Potatoes" through a cookie press or pastry bag for a decorative effect.

Chunky Mushroom Gravy

Serve with Millet Mashed Potatoes and cutlets or Aunt Ruth's "Turkey."

Serves 6

2 pounds mushrooms
3 medium onions
1 tablespoon sesame oil
Vinegar
2 to 3 tablespoons arrowroot flour, diluted in 1/4 cup water, OR
1 cup thick starch from preparing seitan
Natural soy sauce
Salt
1/4 cup chopped parsley

• Cut the mushrooms and onions into chunks and sauté in sesame oil until the onions are translucent. Add a dash of vinegar to bring out the flavor of the mushrooms and retain their color.

• Add water to cover ¾ of the vegetables. Bring to a slow boil, and add the arrowroot or wheat starch.

• Simmer for 10 minutes, stirring constantly as the sauce thickens. Season to taste with natural soy sauce and salt.

• Add the chopped parsley just before serving.

Note: If you are using arrowroot, do not overheat the sauce or it may become watery.

Bill's Dills

Thanks to Mary Nowalk of Maplewood Farm, these pickles will make you famous.

>   1 gallon water
>   1/2 cup salt
>   4 to 5 pounds small pickling cucumbers—without wrinkles
>   4 or more fresh garlic cloves
>   2 or more large handfuls fresh dill
>   3 bay leaves

Optional Seasonings:

>   Whole peppercorns
>   Whole mustard seeds
>   Dried red peppers

• Heat the water and salt together to a slow boil. Remove from the heat and set aside to cool to room temperature.

• Wash the vegetables. Arrange all the seasonings to be used in individual bowls or combined as a mix.

• Place the vegetables and seasonings in very clean large glass or crockery containers. Plastic containers, while not ideal, are usable. When filling the containers, layer the seasonings, then vegetables, into the containers so the flavors will penetrate better. Continue to fill the container alternating the layers, to no higher than 6″ from the top. If you have enough dill, put a layer of it on top of everything.

• Pour the cooled salt water over the vegetables to cover. Place a plate inside each container or crock—the plate should fit closely but not tightly, leaving about 1″ between the edge of the plate and the container. Add just enough weight on top to keep the vegetables submerged in the salt water. Vegetables which are exposed to the air will spoil before they can pickle. Pickles should be kept in a cool place, away from direct sunlight. Taste in 4 to 6 days. When the pickles are done, keep them in their brine, cover and refrigerate. Transfer them, with the brine, to smaller jars for more convenient storage.

Note: In hot, humid weather the vegetables will pickle faster, so check their progress after 2 or 3 days. Stronger flavor will develop with additional pickling time.

More Summer Vegetable Pickles ⸺

Use the following vegetables to make pickles following the same procedure as for Bill's Dills.

Onion wedges, 1/2″ to 3/4″
Carrots, cut 1 1/2″ long, then in thin lengthwise slices
Zucchini, cut into 1/4″ rounds
Yellow summer squash, cut into 1/4″ rounds
Celery, cut into 2″ lengths
Cauliflower, cut into small flowerets

Homemade Sauerkraut ⸺

With white winter cabbage, available in the fall, you can make your own sauerkraut. All you need is cabbage, salt, a crock, and a rock. Make enough in pint or quart jars to give as gifts, 4 to 8 weeks later.

4 to 6 pounds white winter cabbage
Sea salt or kosher salt
A crock (or other ceramic or plastic container)
A plate (to fit inside of the container, leaving 1″ space all around)
A rock (or jar filled with water or beans)—at least 3 pounds or heavy enough to keep cabbage submerged under its juice

• Cut or shred the cabbage very fine. Tradition says it should be no thicker than a dime. Mix about $\frac{1}{2}$ cup salt thoroughly into the cabbage, rubbing in well with your hands. The cabbage should feel gritty all over. Do not be afraid to use as much salt as you need, as it will help prevent spoilage as well as insure thorough pickling. If the sauerkraut is too salty for your taste once it is finished, you can soak it briefly to remove some of the salt.

• Put the salted cabbage into the crock and press down very hard. Add the next batch of salted cabbage and press down very hard. Continue to add cabbage, pressing down heavily after each addition. Some water should begin to come out of the cabbage. Continue to push down until the brine covers the cabbage.

• Place the clean plate on top of the cabbage and apply the weight. If you use a rock, be sure it is washed very well. You may want to put it in a plastic bag to keep it from coming in contact with the brine, which will increase in quantity as the cabbage becomes more pickled. The sauerkraut should be under the brine at all times. Lay a clean towel over the top of the crock.

• Sauerkraut is a long-term pickle. It is ready when the cabbage is a translucent yellow color. When the cabbage is still whitish, the pickles may be eaten, but it is not truly "sauerkraut."

- During the pickling process, keep the sauerkraut in a cool, dark place. Temperatures above 72° F. may contribute to spoilage.

- Check the progress of the cabbage after one week. Remove any mould which may accumulate. Remove any discolored cabbage—pink, green, or black spots indicate spoilage. Remove all discolored cabbage, and taste a piece of what seems all right. If it is not slightly salty, mix in more salt, wash the plate, the exposed interior sides of the crock, and the weight, and try again.

- Sauerkraut takes 5 to 8 weeks to pickle completely. When it is ready, pack it tightly in its brine and store in a cool, dark place.

- If the sauerkraut is too salty for your taste, soak it for 15 to 30 minutes in cool, fresh water. Squeeze to remove water.

Pesto

This one is dairy-free and really delicious. Make enough to last through the winter, to enliven any dreary days.

Makes 2½ cups

> 2 cups blanched almonds (remove skins)
> 1/4 cup olive oil
> 5 garlic cloves
> 1/2 to 1 tablespoon salt
> 2 small cans anchovy fillets
> 3/4 to 1 cup water, or enough to make a smooth paste
> 4 cups fresh basil, washed and chopped coarsely to fit into the blender

- To blanch the almonds, place them in boiling water for about 1 minute. Drain in a colander, running cold water over them until they are cool to the touch. To remove the skins, squeeze the wide end of the almond. The nut should slide through the pointed end.

- Use a blender or food processor to puree the almonds with the oil, garlic, salt, anchovies, and about half the water.

- When the almonds are fairly well chopped, blend in the basil a little at a time. Stop the machine as needed to push the basil down into the mixture. Continue until all the basil is used and a paste is made. Add the water as needed to continue mixing. The texture of the ground nuts will be evident.

- Serve the pesto mixed into *hot* linguine or other pasta. The hotter the noodles are, the better the pesto will spread over them. Use 1 to 2 tablespoons per serving, or more to taste.

To Store Pesto: Pesto can be stored tightly covered in the refrigerator for up to a week, depending upon the temperature. Or, put it in small containers in the freezer. To freeze individual servings, put the pesto into ice cube trays and, when frozen, remove the pesto "cubes" and store them all together in a plastic freezer bag. Remove as many as you need at a time. Allow 1 cube for each serving of pasta.

Pasta with Pesto

Make the pasta of your choice, and toss while very hot with pesto (above). Use 1 to 2 tablespoons pesto per serving, adding more to taste.

Couscous

Almost too easy to be true, couscous is the base for many a very quick meal. Couscous is adaptable to just about any type of sauce.

Serves 4

> 2 cups water
> Pinch of sea salt
> 1 cup couscous

- Bring the water to a boil, then add the salt and couscous. Cover, and reduce heat to the lowest possible setting. If you have an electric stove, turn the heat off—the burner will retain enough heat. Put a flame diffuser under the pot and let the couscous steam/simmer for about 15 to 20 minutes.

- Remove the pot from the heat and put the couscous into a serving bowl immediately or it will stick together. Fluff it with a spoon or paddle to separate the grains.

- Serve couscous with the sauce of your choice. Leftover couscous may be reheated with vegetables, or reheated with extra water and a little cinnamon and some raisins.

Sweet and Sour Marinated Beet Salad

Juicy deep red discs of sweet and tart beets will brighten any meal. Covered and refrigerated, these will keep for a few days.

Serves 4 to 6

> 5 medium beets
> 3 to 4 quarts water

1/8 teaspoon salt
2 teaspoons (or to taste) brown rice vinegar or lemon juice
2 teaspoons (or to taste) rice syrup
1/4 cup parsley, minced

- Wash the beets and trim greens down to 1″. Leave the tails on. Be careful not to cut the skin of the beets or you will lose some of the flavor and color.

- Bring to a boil in 3 to 4 quarts water, then simmer the beets until they are tender when a toothpick is inserted.

- Put the cooked beets in a colander and run some cold water over them. As you do this, pull off the stem and tail ends, and the rest of the skin of the beet should slide off easily.

- Slice the cooked, peeled beets into ⅛″ to ¼″ crosscut rounds. Place the sliced beets in a bowl, and sprinkle the salt over them.

- Combine the rice vinegar (or lemon juice) and rice syrup. Pour the dressing over the beets, and mix gently to coat them. Carefully mix in the parsley.

- If you like a stronger sweet and sour taste, add more dressing. Cover the beets and refrigerate. Serve the beet salad alone, or in combination with other salads and appetizers.

Variation: Marinate paper-thin rings of raw onion with the beets.

Sunshine Mint Tea

Very mild and refreshing, with the energy of real sunlight in every glass. Serve mixed with chilled apple juice, or put a slice of apple, orange, lime, or lemon in the bottom of each glass. Frost the empty glasses by placing them in the freezer for a few hours before using them.

Makes one gallon

1 to 2 cups freshly picked mint leaves
1 gallon spring water

- Crush the mint leaves slightly by squeezing, then put them in a one-gallon jar and add the spring water. Cover the jar securely with plastic wrap or aluminum foil, and place it outside in full sunlight. Leave the jar in the sun for the entire day, or as long as possible. The longer it stays in the sun, the stronger the flavor will be.

- Strain the liquid and discard the leaves. Refrigerate the tea and serve as suggested above.

Wakame Sea Vegetable with Onions and White Miso ────

Serves 4 as a side dish

> 10, 4" strips wakame
> 2 cups onion, sliced half-rounds 1/4" thick
> 1 teaspoon light or dark sesame oil
> 2 tablespoons white miso, diluted to a paste in 1/4 cup water
> 1/4 cups water for cooking

• Rinse the wakame strips briefly, then place them in a bowl with water to cover. Soak the wakame for about 10 minutes, or until it is tender but not mushy. The amount of time needed for soaking will depend upon the type of wakame used.

• Remove the wakame from the water and gently squeeze it. Cut it crosswise into $\frac{1}{4}$" strips.

• Slice the onions lengthwise (through the top and bottom) in half, then crosswise into $\frac{1}{4}$" half-rounds. Heat the oil briefly in a saucepan, and add the onions. Sauté over a medium heat until they are translucent.

• Add the wakame to the onions. Add the miso to the wakame and onions and mix thoroughly but carefully to coat the vegetables.

• Add the $\frac{1}{4}$ cup water to the vegetables. Cover, and simmer for about 10 minutes, or until all the water has been absorbed and the vegetables are tender. Add a little more water as needed.

Glazed Carrots with Sesame ───────────

Serves 6

> 8 small to medium carrots, cut into 1/2" crosswise rounds or diagonals
> 2 cups water, or enough to almost cover carrots in cooking pot
> Pinch salt
> 2 to 3 tablespoons rice syrup
> 2 to 3 tablespoons toasted sesame seeds

• Place the carrots, water, and salt in a saucepan and bring to a boil. Cook uncovered until the carrots are tender and the water is almost all evaporated, with about $\frac{1}{8}$" left in the pot.

• Add the rice syrup and toss or mix lightly to coat the carrots. Leaving the pot on a medium-high heat, shake the pot as if you were making "flapjacks," allowing the carrots to move around in the pot so they all will have a turn being on the bottom of the pot, closest to the heat. This is what will create the caramelized, glazed quality. Shake the pot six or seven times in this way, replacing the pot on the high heat for 5 seconds or so between each time.

- Add the sesame seeds and toss with the carrots one or two times more. Remove from the heat and serve.

Steamed Greens—Kale, Collard, and Mustard

> Greens of your choice
> 1″ water in a saucepan
> Pinch salt

- These greens may be prepared in generally the same way, the main variation being the amount of cooking time needed. Kale and collard greens will require approximately the same length of time, while mustard greens need less time. Variations in types of cookware, stoves, and cutting styles make giving a specific cooking time difficult.

Basic Procedure:
- Wash the greens and separate the leaves from the stems. If you want to use the stems, cut them in half lengthwise. Place the uncut leaves and the stems in a covered saucepan with the water and salt. Bring to a boil, then reduce heat to medium and cook until the greens are bright green but tender.

- Remove the greens to a colander and immediately run cold water over them to stop the cooking, or plunge them into a bowlful of very cold water. Cool the greens very quickly because valuable nutrients can be lost if they are left in the water too long.

- Remove the greens from the water and squeeze them firmly to remove the excess water from the vegetables. Place on your work surface and slice or chop as desired. When these vegetables are sliced crosswise, very thinly, they can be served as a delicate garnish or as a very attractive cooked salad.

- Greens prepared in this way are delicious served plain or in salads and soups, or as fillings in "wrapped" or stuffed preparations.

Toasted Nori Strips

- Toasted nori is usually used as a garnish for soups, salads, or vegetable dishes. However there are times when it is incorporated into the preparation of another dish, such as Brown Rice Rolls. To use toasted nori as a garnish, crumble it, break it up into irregular shapes, or use a scissors to cut it into sharply-edged strips or other geometric shapes.

- Choose nori which is very dark and thick. The lighter purple nori, which is usually much thinner, is not as strong and, although it is usable for crumbled nori, will not be strong enough for rolling as required for Brown Rice Rolls.

Basic Preparation: Holding a sheet of nori by one edge, pass it back and forth about 2″ above a medium heat (open burner). You may toast one or both sides of the nori in this way. The color will change from a dark purple or black to a very dark, sometimes iridescent shade of green.

Brown Rice

Slightly sweet and nutty tasting, whole-grain rice comes in many forms, all having their own special characteristics. Any way you cook it, rice can play an important role in your meals, from soups to desserts.

Serves 6

Pressure-cooked Brown Rice;

>   3 cups brown rice
>   5 cups water
>   1/4 teaspoon salt

- Place all ingredients in a pressure cooker. Tighten the lid and bring to pressure according to manufacturer's instructions. When pressure is reached, reduce the heat and place a flame diffuser under the pot.

- Pressure-cook the rice for 45 to 50 minutes using a low heat, just enough to maintain the pressure.

- Remove the pot from the heat and allow the pressure to return to normal. Open the pot and mix the rice with three or four strokes from bottom to top before removing it to a serving bowl.

Note: The grains of properly cooked rice are fully "popped open," slightly separate but just moist enough to stick to each other without being mushy.

Boiled Brown Rice:

>   3 cups brown rice
>   5 1/2 cups water
>   1/4 teaspoon salt

- Bring all ingredients to a boil, reduce heat to low and place a flame diffuser under the pot. Cook at a low boil for 50 to 60 minutes or until all water is absorbed and the grains have burst open.

• Mix the rice with three or four strokes from bottom to top before removing it to a serving bowl.

Brown Rice Rolls (*Norimaki Sushi*) ───────────────

Use precooked rice to make these quick and easy rolls which can go anywhere—from snacks and lunches to elegant buffets.

Makes 1 roll—allow 1 roll per serving

> 1 sheet good-quality nori, toasted (see Toasted Nori Strips)
> 1/2 to 1 teaspoon umeboshi paste per roll
> Umeboshi paste

Choose One or More:

• Thin carrot strips—boil for 5 minutes, then refresh with cold water, drain and pat dry.

• Scallions—use green part only, sliced lengthwise into strips no wider than ⅛".

• Pickles—*takuan* (Japanese daikon pickle), dill, ginger, or other vegetable pickle of your choice.

• Lay the toasted nori on a bamboo mat ("sushi mat"). Wet your hands and press ½ to ¾ cup of rice onto the nori, covering about ¾ of the surface. The rice will be about ⅜" thick. Leave the top ¼ of the nori sheet empty, all the way across.

• Lay your choice of carrots, scallions, and/or thinly sliced pickles across the center of the rice. This will show up as a colorful design in the center of each cut piece of the nori roll.

• Pick up the edge of the bamboo mat closest to you, and begin to roll away from you. When you reach the end of the rice, wet your fingers and lightly moisten the remaining nori. Continue to roll, pressing the mat together as you roll. Place the nori roll seam side down until serving time, when you will cut it into 7 or 8 pieces, each about 1" wide. Use a sharp knife to cut the rolls. The knife should be wiped with a damp sponge after each cut, to prevent it sticking to the next cut piece.

To Serve: Arrange on a platter, or pack in your lunchbox.

Bulgur ──────────────────────────────

Bulgur is a type of wheat that has been partially cooked then dried, making it very quick-cooking.

- In fact, for some dishes it is not necessary to cook it at all, but only to soak it for a few hours. Bulgur may be used in place of couscous when a heartier, whole-grain flavor is needed. It is also appropriate to use in soups, cooked with vegetables, and as a filling in "wrapped" or stuffed preparations. Bulgur is mild-tasting and will accept many types of seasonings. Allow ½ to ¾ cup of uncooked bulgur per serving.

Use 2 cups water for each cup bulgur—the following proportions serve 2:

> 1 cup bulgur
> 2 cups water
> 1/8 to 1/4 teaspoon salt

- *Preparation:* Bring the water and salt to a boil and add the bulgur. Cover and reduce the heat to very low, placing a flame diffuser under the pot. Simmer for about 15 to 20 minutes. Remove from the heat when all the water is absorbed and bulgur is tender.

Kasha

Like bulgur, kasha is just what you need when your cooking time is limited.

Serves 1 or 2

- Because kasha is very hearty, it can accept strong seasonings such as natural soy sauce, white miso, tomato sauce, and herbs and spices like garlic and black pepper. Kasha is generally available in two types, roasted or unroasted, and is available as whole "buckwheat groats" or smaller "kasha grits."

- To complement kasha, cook it with sautéed onions, mushrooms, broccoli, cabbage, or corn. Serve it accompanied by a salad.

- Allow ½ to ¾ cup kasha per serving. Use 2 to 3 cups water for each cup kasha to be cooked, depending upon how separate you want the grains to be. Fried kasha is better when prepared with more separate, fluffy grains (less water) while using kasha as a filling for "wrapped" dishes will require a stickier grain (more water).

> 1 cup kasha
> 2 to 3 cups water
> 1/8 to 1/4 teaspoon salt

- *Preparation:* Bring the water with salt to a boil and add the kasha. Cover, and reduce heat to the lowest possible level. Place a flame diffuser under the pot, and simmer for about 25 minutes. Serve hot, with a sauce, or as filling in wrapped or stuffed preparations. Cooled kasha may also be used as the foundation for a hearty salad.

Arame Sea Vegetable with Natural Soy Sauce ————————

Arame, like most sea vegetables, is very versatile. It is delicious served simply and hot, as follows, or served chilled or at room temperature in a salad, by itself, or with a light or creamy dressing.

Variations: You may want to vary your preparations by adding one or more of the items below:

> Onions—diced
> Carrots—diced
> Cauliflower—small flowerets
> Cooked or uncooked seitan—small pieces
> Uncooked or deep-fried tofu—large or small cubes, or crumbled (uncooked tofu)
> Scallions—add at the end of cooking
> Umeboshi paste—dilute with some water and use instead of natural soy sauce

Basic Arame

Serves 4

> 1 1/2 cups arame
> Water, to cover arame
> 1 teaspoon light or dark sesame oil
> 2 teaspoons natural soy sauce

• Rinse the arame in a strainer, briefly passing it under running water. Put the arame in a bowl, and add fresh water to cover. Soak for about 10 minutes.

• Lift out the arame and squeeze it to remove excess water. Save the soaking water to use for cooking. Lay the arame on the work surface and cut it into ½″ lengths.

• Heat 1 teaspoon oil in a saucepan and add the arame. Sauté for 1 to 2 minutes over a medium heat, stirring occasionally to prevent sticking. Add ¾ cup of the reserved soaking water and bring to a boil. Reduce heat and add the soy sauce.

• Simmer the arame for 30 minutes or until all the water is absorbed and the arame is tender. Adjust the seasoning (add 1 teaspoon more soy sauce if needed).

Special Baked Apples ————————————————

Your family will never tire of baked apples when you use their favorite jam or fruit butter in a delicious syrup to dress up this easy dessert.

Serves 6

> 6 Golden Delicious or Granny Smith apples—or other apples which will keep
> their shape well

3/4 cup jam or fruit butter of your choice—strawberry, apricot, peach, orange
   marmalade, apple butter or apricot butter
1/2 cup maple syrup
Pinch salt
1/2 teaspoon cinnamon
1/4" water in the bottom of the pan

- Preheat the oven to 375° F.

- Wash and core the apples. Score the apples ⅛" to ¼" deep, horizontally around
  the apple about ⅓ of the way down from the top. This will prevent the apples
  from bursting as they bake. Place the apples in a lightly oiled baking pan.

- Combine the jam, maple syrup, and salt. Spoon this mixture into the holes of the
  apples. Put about ¼" water in the pan and sprinkle the cinnamon over the apples
  and into the water.

- Bake the apples 30 minutes, then check to see if they are done by inserting
  a toothpick or skewer. Baste the apples with the water from the pan, which by this
  time should be turning into a syrup. Continue to bake the apples for 30 to 40
  minutes more or until very tender.

- Spoon 2 or 3 spoonfuls of syrup over each apple and serve them hot or cold.

Marinated Cucumbers and Watercress Salad ——————————

**This very simple marinated salad is a fresh-tasting complement to some of the richer
tasting seitan dishes.**

Serves 4

1 large bunch watercress, cut into 2" pieces
2 medium cucumbers, sliced into 1/8" rounds

For the Dressing:

2/3 cup fresh-squeezed orange juice
2 tablespoons *ume-su* (umeboshi vinegar)
1 tablespoon olive oil or dark sesame oil
1 teaspoon grated orange rind

- Combine all dressing ingredients and shake to mix well. Pour it over the watercress
  and cucumbers and marinate for ½ hour, turning the vegetables occasionally in
  the marinade.

Miso-Tahini Sauce or Spread ─────────────

This creamy sauce is also useful as a spread for sandwiches or crackers, and it can even be the base of a salad dressing or seasoned to use as a dip for cooked or raw vegetables. Experiment with using different types of miso to vary the flavor of the sauce.

Makes about 1 cup

> 2 tablespoons white miso
> 3 tablespoons water
> 1/4 cup tahini
> 1/2 cup water

- Make a paste of the miso and 3 tablespoons water.

- Heat the tahini in a saucepan over a low heat. Stir constantly until it is bubbly. Add the water, stirring constantly. Add the miso and simmer for 1 minute, or until the sauce is thick and creamy.

Variation:
- Add any other flavoring ingredients, such as:

> Fresh chives, chopped or snipped
> Onion, finely chopped or grated
> Caraway seeds
> Celery seeds

Kukicha Tea ───────────────

Kukicha is a very mild tasting tea that goes with everything. It can be reheated in the pot, even though the leaves may still be in the pot. Do not boil.

> 1 to 2 cups water
> 1 teaspoon tea per cup of water

Note: The tea leaves may be used again by adding more water.

- Bring 1 or more cups of water to boil. Turn off the heat and add about 1 teaspoon kukicha tea per cup of water. Cover and allow to steep until it is a medium amber color.

210

Basic Bean Cookery

Beans are easy to cook and are a very versatile food. Tonight's hearty bean soup can be frozen or refrigerated for later reheating—traditionally, the flavor of bean soups improves on the second day. You can use it, puréed, as a sandwich spread or seasoned as a dip. Add some pasta to the soup and it becomes something new. Use precooked grains and vegetables with the beans in a casserole.

There are a few guidelines which will add to the success of your bean dishes:

1. To use beans as a side dish, use 2½ to 3 cups of water for each cup of beans.
2. To use beans in a soup, use 4 to 6 cups of water for each cup of beans.
3. To make beans more digestible, soak them overnight in water to cover, then drain them and cook in fresh water.
4. To make beans more digestible, put a 1″ piece of kombu sea vegetable in the pot for each cup of beans being cooked.
5. Never add salt until the beans are tender. (Or they may never become tender.)
6. Long, slow cooking will give you more tender, juicy beans.

Some Approximate Cooking Times:
• Cooking time depends upon the variety and age of the beans, amount of heat and/ or pressure used for cooking, and the quantity of water being used.

Lentils—1 hour boiling, 20 minutes pressure cooking
Split peas—1 hour boiling (do not pressure-cook)
Navy and Lima beans—1 to 1½ hours boiling (do not pressure-cook)
Pinto beans—1½ hours boiling, 45 minutes to 1 hour pressure cooking
Kidney beans—2 to 2½ hours boiling, 1 to 1½ hours pressure cooking
Chickpeas—2 to 3 hours boiling, 1½ to 2 hours pressure cooking

Note: These are a few of the more common beans available in supermarkets, natural food stores, and ethnic markets. Some will take longer to cook than others.

Sample Lunch and Dinner Menus

Enough is as good as a feast.
—John Heywood, 1497 (?)–1580 (?) *Proverbs*

The following menus are intended as examples of how seitan can be used in daily meals as well as in special occasion meals. These menus are not intended for sequential use; that is, Dinner I for Summer would not necessarily be served following Lunch I for Summer.

Recipes for the items preceded by a (•) are found in the Chapter "From the Pantry." (see p. 191) All other recipes appearing in this book are followed by the page on which they appear. I hope you will enjoy experimenting and use the menu suggestions freely.

Summer Lunches and Dinners

LUNCH I.

Chinese Pasta Salad (p. 153)
• Assorted Pickles Made with Summer Vegetables (p. 198)
• Toasted Nori Strips (p. 203)
Fresh Fruit Shake (p. 187)

DINNER I.

Garden Vegetable Soup with Golden Nuggets (p. 75)
Toasted French Bread with
• Miso-tahini Spread (p. 209)
• Marinated Cucumbers and Watercress with (p. 208)
Ume-Orange Dressing (p. 174)
Fresh Melon Slices
• Cool Mint-Sunshine Tea (p. 201)

LUNCH II.

Flint Corn Salad (p. 162)
• Arame Sea Vegetable with Tamari (p. 207)

DINNER II.

• Pasta with Pesto Sauce (p. 200)
Broiled Seitan Kebabs (p. 99)
Fresh Sweet Corn on the Cob
Watercress Salad with Crispy Strips (p. 147)
• Bill's Dills (p. 197)
Banana Dream Pudding

Fall Lunches and Dinners

LUNCH I.

Piroshki (p. 117)
• Steamed Kale (p. 203)
• Special Baked Apples (can be made ahead of time—serve hot or chilled) (p. 207)

DINNER I.

Squash Potage (p. 82)
Pan-Fried Cutlets with Mushroom Sauce
• Millet-Cauliflower "Mashed Potatoes" (p. 195)
Tossed Green Salad and
Tamari-Lemon Dressing with Tarragon (p. 173)
Chewy Coconut Puffs (p. 32)
• Hot Tea (p. 209)

LUNCH II.

Open-Faced Sandwiches
• Homemade Sauerkraut (p. 198)
Fresh Seasonal Fruit—Apples and Pears
• Hot Tea (p. 209)

DINNER II.

Seitan Strognoff (p. 85)
• Brown Rice, or Broad Noodles (p. 204)
Steamed Broccoli Spears with
Miso-Lemon Dressing (p. 171)

• Glazed Carrots with Sesame (p. 202)
Maple-Walnut Custard (Desserts, p. 187)
• Tea or coffee (p. 209)

Winter Lunches and Dinners ━━━━━━━━

LUNCH I.

Pan-Fried Noodles with Seitan and Greens
• Homemade Sauerkraut (p. 198)
Tea or Coffee

DINNER I.

Mushroom Lasagne Au Gratin (p. 87)
Tossed Salad with
Spicy Miso-Orange Dressing (p. 173)
Applesauce
Hot Tea

LUNCH II.

• Hickory Bits Bread with (p. 193)
Mustard Sauce (p. 165)
Winter Salad with Red Radishes—may be made with or without the seitan (p. 162)

DINNER II.

Black Bean Soup (p. 77)
• Corn Bread (p. 194)
• Steamed Greens with (p. 203)
Sweet and Sour Dressing (p. 172)
Chewy Date-Walnut Cookies (p. 185)
Hot Kukicha Tea

Spring Lunches and Dinners ━━━━━━━

LUNCH I.

Large-Shell Macaroni Salad with Pimiento and Walnut Dressing
• Wakame Sea Vegetable with Onions and Miso (p. 202)
Fresh Fruit
Tea

DINNER I.

Creamed Corn and Cutlet Casserole (p. 90)
Steamed Green Beans
  • Arame Sea Vegetable (p. 207)
  • Marinated Beet Salad (p. 200)
Coconut-Lemon Cookies (p. 183)
Hot Kukicha Tea or Coffee

LUNCH II.

Mediterranean Vegetable Medley (p. 157)
  • Brown Rice Nori Rolls (uses precooked Brown Rice) (p. 205)
Fresh Fruit
Cinnamon Chestnut Puffs

DINNER II.

Oven-Braised Stew served over rice (p. 200), pasta (p. 31), or
  • Couscous (p. 200)
  • Assorted Homemade Pickles (onion, cucumber, carrot, celery, etc.)
New "Good Old Chocolate Pudding" (p. 188)

Appendix

I. All About Saving and Using Wheat Starch

The term "starch water" refers to the combination of water, starch, and bran remaining after extracting gluten from wheat flour. This by-product of making seitan can be used in a variety of ways—the nutrient-rich thick starch is an excellent thickening agent suitable for soups, sauces, and desserts. The clear liquid has additional uses, as well.

Refrigerating Thick Starch

After you have poured off the starch water during the seitan-making process, set it aside for at least 2½ hours, then carefully pour the thin, yellow colored water into a separate container. This will be referred to as "clear starch water." (See below for uses for the clear starch water.) What is left in the container is the "thick starch."

To refrigerate the thick starch, add a 2″ layer of fresh water. Cover it and refrigerate. Change the water every two or three days, carefully pouring off the layer of water, and adding fresh water again. To use the thick starch, simply pour off the water, scoop out the amount of thick starch needed, and add another layer of fresh water. Whatever fresh water is accidentally mixed with the thick starch will simply separate out in about an hour.

The reason for adding fresh water instead of leaving the clear starch water on top of the thick starch is that using the clear starch water will allow fermentation to happen much more quickly. (See: Sourdough Starter.)

Saving the Clear Starch Water

You may want to save the clear starch water, which is also useful for such things as:

- Adding to bath water (for infants, children, and adults)
- Watering plants (use a small amount)
- Giving to pets as a small part of their liquid for the day
- Using in soup stocks or sauces

The clear starch water can be refrigerated separately.

Drying the Thick Starch

Another method for conserving the thick starch is to dry it and reconstitute it later with water. With this method, the wheat starch can be used in approximately the same proportions as arrowroot or kuzu.

After separating the thick starch from the water, pour it onto a clean cookie sheet and spread it out so it is even. It should not be more than ⅛″ thick, so use extra cookie sheets if you have a lot of starch. Let it dry away from the general kitchen traffic, in a dry place where there is plenty of air circulating (or it will just get mouldy).

When it is dry to touch, break it up into 2″ pieces to quicken the drying time. When it is really, thoroughly dry (it may take a few days), break it up or pulverize it in a blender, and store in a covered container. If the starch is thoroughly dried, it will not require refrigeration.

Making Sourdough Starter from Starch Water

You can also use the starch water to make a sourdough starter for bread. After the starch water has separated into the thick starch and clear starch water, pour off about ⅔ of the clear starch water and reserve it separately or discard it. Mix the remaining third of the clear starch water back into the thick starch, and pour it all into a glass jar or a clean crock and cover it with a bamboo mat or a clean cloth.

Let this "batter" rest in a warm place (again, with plenty of air circulating) for 2 to 4 days. The warmer and more humid the environment, the faster the fermentation will develop. You may stir it after 10 hours or so, and each 3 hours thereafter, to check the development of the starter. It should have the consistency of a thick batter. When it smells slightly alcoholic and a little sweet, and has plenty of bubbles throughout it, the starter is ready to use in your favorite sourdough bread recipe.

II.   Storing Uncooked Seitan

There will be times when you want to make more seitan than you can use in one meal. Sometimes you will use half a recipe of seitan in one dish that requires cooking at that time, leaving the other half of the seitan uncooked.

What can you do with the uncooked seitan that remains? In addition to cooking, there are three main ways to store the uncooked seitan.

• *Refrigerate:* Place the seitan in a container (use 1 cup of seitan per container), and add water to cover the seitan. Cover the container tightly and refrigerate for up to 1 week. Change the water every 2 days and rinse off the seitan to maintain maximum freshness. When you want to use the seitan, just remove the seitan from the water and rinse it under cold running water, squeezing firmly a few times. Proceed to cook the seitan as you would if you had just made it, in recipes requiring "uncooked seitan."

• *Freeze:* Place the uncooked seitan (one cup at the most, for shorter defrosting time) in a container and add water to cover the seitan. Cover the container and freeze. When you want to use the seitan, remove it from the freezer in the morning and cook the seitan the same evening. Or, remove it from the freezer and keep in the refrigerator if you don't want to use it for another two to five days. (See Refrigerating Seitan.)

• *Freezing Cutlet-size Slices:*   Roll the uncooked seitan into a cylinder and slice it into cutlet-size pieces, about ¼″ thick. Flatten the cutlets with the palm of your hand, and layer them between sheets of plastic wrap. Using about 4 cutlets, make a package of the layered cutlets and wrap the entire package in aluminum foil. Freeze the seitan until you are ready to use it. Allow a few hours for defrosting. Defrosting will take less time if you unwrap the package and separate the layers of seitan. When the seitan is defrosted, it may be cooked as if you had just made it, in recipes requiring "uncooked seitan."

III.   Storing Cooked Seitan

When I prepare seitan for my family, I always make more than enough for just one meal. I usually cook the seitan just to have it available for a variety of uses, although sometimes it is made with a particular dish in mind. But whatever the reason for making it there is always plenty to be used in lunches, casseroles, with vegetables, or to eat just as it is.

Cooked seitan can be stored successfully in both the refrigerator and the freezer, depending upon your needs. As with uncooked seitan, the cooked varieties may be stored in both "bulk" and cutlet forms.

• *Refrigerated in Broth:*   Seitan stored this way, in a closed container, will be usable for up to 10 days, depending upon its salt content and the temperature of your refrigerator. Salt is a preservative, therefore seitan which is very salty will retain its freshness longer. This is one reason why some commercially prepared seitan is very salty. Some commercially prepared seitan is said to have a shelf life of 1 month, however this is at a temperature of 33° F. Most home refrigerators are not that cold, probably averaging a temperature of about 45° F. to 50° F.

If you prefer your seitan to have a milder, less salty flavor—or if you have cooked it in kombu and water only (without natural soy sauce or other salt added)—it may be refrigerated for 3 to 6 days and maybe longer. Both cutlets and larger pieces may be stored this way.

• *Refrigerated Seitan "Roasts":*   Seitan cooked this way will probably last for about 7 to 10 days, depending upon its salt content and the temperature at which it is kept.

• *Freezing in Broth:*   You may use a plastic freezer container or plastic "freezer bags" to store both cutlets and other pieces of seitan in their broth. The seitan should be room temperature before freezing. For quicker defrosting, place the container in or under hot water. When defrosted, it may be used as if it was just freshly made.

• *Freezing Individual Cutlets:*   This may easily be done by wrapping room-temperature cutlets individually in plastic wrap, then individually or in "packages"—groups of 3 to 6 wrapped cutlets covered with aluminum foil. To defrost, simply remove the foil and separate the individually wrapped frozen cutlets. Sometimes they may be cooked while they are still frozen.

• *Freezing Ground Seitan:* Baked, ground seitan may be frozen just as is in plastic containers or freezer bags. Being dry it defrosts very quickly at room temperature. Ground seitan made from simmered cutlets, cubes, or chunks may also be successfully frozen if it is not too wet.

• *Freezing Prepared Dishes:* Certain prepared dishes will adapt very well to freezing, such as some cutlets in sauce, burgers, and seitan "pepperoni."

• *Freezing Deep-fried Seitan:* Deep-fried seitan without batter and Robai may also be frozen in plastic freezer bags.

Most frozen seitan should be defrosted before using, however cutlets which have been frozen individually may be cooked while still frozen if you keep the heat on the low side until the cutlets have defrosted.

IV.   Commonly Encountered Problems and Some Solutions

1.   Why did I get such a low yield of gluten from the flour—wet and stringy, with very separate strands:

You may be using low-gluten flour, or flour that was ground too coarsely. It is also possible that you did not knead the dough enough or allow enough time for the flour to rest in order for the gluten to develop.

Another possibility is that you were too vigorous in your initial rinsing of the dough. Remember, do not squeeze it between your fingers or it may break up instead of sticking together. Other indications of this are:

• The dough breaks up very quickly when starting to rinse it out.
• The dough turns into batter and goes down the drain.

2.   What causes the cooked seitan to have a sticky, gummy texture?

You didn't wash all the starch out of the dough. Some was left still in the seitan, so it had a starchy quality when cooked.

3.   How can I stop the dough from "disintegrating" as I try to knead it in the water to rinse out the starch and bran?

In some cases, this is the fault of the flour. Some flours, although marked as "bread flour," just are not right for making seitan.

On a more personal level, if it seems that the dough is dissolving and no gluten is holding together, it may be that you are a little too rough or impatient with it. Try using a less firm stream of water, and pick up only one handful of dough at a time. Wash it *very gently* under the water until you have enough gluten holding together to be transferred to another bowl. Use pressure rather than pull on the dough, and continue in this way until all the dough has been through this first washing and you have begun to accumulate some gluten.

Carefully wash the gluten you have saved. Use larger handfuls and wash it a little more firmly than the first time. You should be able to feel it holding together more tightly. Transfer the gluten to a colander and proceed as you normally would, washing the entire amount of gluten very vigorously with a stronger stream of water.

V. Nutritional Information

In addition to being an excellent source of protein, seitan is also low in fat and calories. A four-ounce serving of Upcountry Seitan (ingredients: organic whole wheat flour, water, tamari, cooked with kombu, a sea vegetable) contains only

PROTEIN COMPARISON per 100 grams

Food	Cal.	Total Protein (gm.)	trypto-phan (mg.)	threo-nine (mg.)	isoleu-cine (mg.)	leucine (mg.)	lysine (mg.)	methio-nine (mg.)	phenyl-alanine (mg.)	valine (mg.)	histidine (mg.)
Seitan	118	18	230	538	821	1,421	347	347	915	884	316
MDR†		61.5	250	500	700	1,100	800	200	300	800	
% of **MDR** (100 gm. seitan)	N/A	**29**	**92**	**108**	**117**	**129**	**43**	**173**	**305**	**110**	
Fu (dried wheat gluten)	365	28.5	N/A	850	1,300	2,250	550	550	1,450	1,400	500
Whole Wheat Flour	333	13.3	164	383	577	892	365	203	657	616	271
Wheat Berries (hard red spring)	330	14	173	403	607	939	384	214	691	648	286
Soybeans (cooked)	130	11	526	1,504	2,054	2,946	2,414	513	1,889	2,005	911
Tofu	72	7.8	120	370	410	590	570	100	480	430	
Miso* (Barley)	N/A	12.8	160	740	940	1,280	170	630	790		
Chickpeas (raw)	360	20.5	170	739	1,195	1,538	1,434	276	1,012	1,025	559
Egg (2 eggs)	155	12.1	505	596	758	1,066	819	392	686	874	
Chicken (1/6 chicken)	236	27	301	1,113	1,344	1,959	2,193	716	1,046	1,307	
Beef (ground sirloin)	207	32.2	360	1,478	1,550	2,613	2,865	864	1,416	1,614	

† Minimum Daily Requirement   * This is for solid miso in paste form

References: *Nutrients in Food*, The Nutrition Guild, 1984; *Agriculture Handbook No. 8, Composition of Foods*, U.S. Dept. of Agriculture; *Guide To Far East Asian Foods*, 1976; *Japanese Scientific Research Council; The Book of Tofu; The Book of Miso.*

70 calories and a single gram of fat. It supplies between 6 and 10 percent of the U.S.R.D.A. of vitamin C, thiamine, ribolflavin, niacin, and iron.

From the preceding chart comparing protein levels in various foods, it is apparent that not only is there considerable protein available from seitan, but there is also a full range of amino acids. When seitan is cooked with soy sauce, additional lysine is provided, resulting in a full complement of all essential amino acids. While it may not be suitable to depend solely on seitan for your daily protein requirements, truly a large amount can be found in seitan.

In addition, the National Research Council of the National Academy of Sciences recommends that 8 to 9 percent of total caloric intake be from protein. Since there are 4 calories per gram of protein, the 18 grams of protein in 100 grams of seitan provide 61 percent calories of protein. Truly seitan is an excellent source of amino acids and protein.

A laboratory in the Boston area which analyzed the seitan made by Upcountry Seitan in Lenox, MA, confirmed these figures for protein, plus found this seitan to contain:

Protein	20%
Vitamin C	6%
Thiamine	8%
Riboflavin	8%
Niacin	8%
Iron	10%

A four-ounce serving of seitan contains slightly more than 120 calories and a single gram of fat.

A cost analysis done at the end of July, 1985 showed that 1½ pounds of cooked seitan cost $1.28. This analysis comes from the following:

Cost of flour at $0.48 per pound winter wheat
3 cups flour in one pound
$0.16 per cup of flour
8 cups whole wheat flour costs $1.28
8 cups flour becomes 2 to 2½ cups gluten
2 cups gluten equals one pound
After cooking, this increases to between 1½ to 1¾ pounds seitan

This costs $1.28 and can serve (along with other dishes) 4 to 6 people, each person getting a little over ¼ pound seitan. Cooked seitan costs approximately $0.75 per pound.

VI. Questionnaire for Readers ———————

To help us improve the information in this book, we would appreciate your help in completing the following questionnaire. Your help will allow us to improve subsequent editions of this book. You can send your responses to the authors in care of the publisher.

Please give any comments you feel would be useful.

1. What are the names of the recipes you prepared? Were the directions clear?
2. What kind of additional information would you like to see presented for the recipes?
3. How easy/hard was it to make, relative to how it sounded?
4. Would you make them again?
5. Could the dishes be arranged in what you consider an attractive way?
6. Who were they prepared for?
7. Did your guests like what you prepared?
8. What comments did they have?
9. Which brand of flour did you use for your preparations?
10. Other comments.

Name and Address (optional).

VII. About Our Ingredients ———————

We have chosen to use certain foods as ingredients due to their quality, taste, and healthfulness. We would like you to know the reasons for these selections.

Whole Grains: Whole unrefined grains are recommended because of their healthfulness and wholesome nature. Whole wheat and rice are considerably more nourishing than refined grains—they contain the naturally occurring bran which is essential for good health.

Types of Flour Used: We have used many varieties of whole wheat flour and found most of these to be suitable for making the dishes in this cookbook. However, because there is often some inconsistency in the types of flour found in local food stores, we have standardized these recipes using Arrowhead Mills hard red winter wheat. We have also found most of the whole wheat flours available at the supermarket to be suitable for making seitan.

Natural Soy Sauce: Natural soy sauce is preferred over the varieties most often found in supermarkets. Natural soy sauces, such as those from Westbrae, Erewhon, Eden, and Ohsawa America are free from added chemicals and preservatives.

Unrefined Sweeteners: We have found that unrefined sweeteners such as barley and rice malts and maple syrup are more nutritious than white sugar or honey. These unrefined sweeteners contain trace amounts of minerals and other nutrients making them ideal for preparing wholesome desserts.

Sea Vegetables: Sea vegetables are unique foods which can provide a wide variety of nutrients and unusual flavors.

Vinegars: We have found that brown rice vinegar and unrefined malt and cider vinegars are superior in flavor and quality.

Types of Oil: The oils recommended in this cookbook are unrefined olive, corn, safflower, and sesame oils. These oils are rich in polyunsaturates and other valuable nutrients.

Soymilk: Soymilk has been used extensively in the recipes in this book. This relatively new food is an excellent ingredient for use in sauces, soups, and gravies. It is low in fat and sugars, yet rich in protein. There are many varieties of soymilk to choose from in natural foods stores, but the recipes in this book have been developed using the plain (unflavored and unsweetened) variety called Edensoy—produced by the Eden Food Company.

Arrowroot and Kuzu: Arrowroot or kuzu (also known as kudzu) are used instead of cornstarch for thickening sauces. Cornstarch is a very refined food with a high concentration of sugar. Arrowroot and kuzu are naturally derived starches with all the benefits of a thickening agent and none of the health hazards of cornstarch.

Glossary

Arame   A thin black, thread-like sea vegetable similar in texture and appearance to hijiki—often used as a side dish. Arame is rich in iron, calcium, and other minerals. It is one of the most popular of the sea vegetables for the American taste.

Arrowroot Starch   Arrowroot is a tropical perennial with swollen starchy *rhizomes* (underground stems). The starch is in very fine grains which are easily digestible and is thus particularly suitable for children or sick people. Almost the entire world export supply of arrowroot is provided by the island of St. Vincent in the West Indies.

The starch is prepared from the rhizomes by cleaning, peeling, washing, and grating. The grated material is mixed with water and the mixture strained. The filtered fluid is then allowed to settle out in the form of starch grains, and the starch is dried in the sun and then pulverized. This pulverized material is the commercial arrowroot starch. Like cornstarch and kuzu, it is used as a thickening agent in making sauces, stews, gravies, or desserts.

Bancha Tea   Correctly named kukicha, this tea consists of the stems and leaves from mature Japanese tea bushes. This tea is harvested in the autumn when the caffeine level is the lowest in the leaves. In addition, the leaves of this tea are roasted in cast iron caldrons in order to deactivate the tea's tannic acid. Bancha tea aids in digestion and is an excellent conclusion to any meal.

Barley Malt Syrup   A thick, dark brown sweetener made from barley or a combination of barley and corn. Barley malt syrup is used in making desserts, sweet and sour sauces, and in a variety of medicinal drinks.

Bran   Bran (nuka in Japanese) is the fibrous outer portion of whole cereal grains that is often polished off in the refining process. The bran contains considerable nourishment, especially minerals and B vitamins. In making seitan, the bran in whole wheat is only partially washed away during the extraction of gluten from the wheat and water mixture.

Brown Rice   Brown rice is whole, unpolished rice. This is the form white rice originally takes before it is separated from its bran and germ. Brown rice is available in many varieties, including short grain, medium grain, long grain, sweet rice, flakes, and aromatic. Brown rice provides an excellent source of minerals, protein, and vitamins.

Bulgur   Bulgur is a staple food in the Middle East. It is prepared from whole wheat which is cracked, steamed, and then allowed to dry. This grain is very quick to prepare since it has already been cooked, and it is often made into a salad called taboule in which the grain is only soaked, and not recooked.

224

Chestnut Flour.   Chestnut flour is made from ground dried chestnuts. This very fine powder has a sweet taste and is a pleasant addition to cookies and other desserts. You may purchase it in Italian and Oriental markets, Middle-Eastern markets, and some natural food stores.

Chickpea Flour   Chickpea flour is made from ground dried garbanzo beans, also called chickpeas. It is a delicious addition to cream sauces and croquettes, useful for its binding qualities as well as its fine flavor. Chickpea flour is obtainable at Middle-Eastern markets, some natural food stores, and Oriental markets. Another name for it is "Besan" or Gram flour.

Chinese Hot Pepper Oil   This seasoning is made from red chili peppers that are marinated for 48 hours in toasted sesame oil. This aromatic and pungent condiment can add an authentic spicy Chinese taste to your cooked vegetable dishes and sauces.

Couscous   A traditional North African grain made from semi-refined wheat. It is very light tasting and cooks quickly.

Corn Flour   Like cornmeal, corn flour is made from dried corn kernels, but its texture is much finer. It is useful in baked goods, sauces, and batter for deep-frying.

Dulse   Dulse is a reddish-purple sea vegetable used in soups, salads, and vegetables dishes. This sea vegetable is very rich in vitamin A, iodine, and phosphorus. Dulse is a traditional North American and European sea vegetable.

Egg Roll Wrappers   Also called "spring roll wrappers," they are usually square 7″ by 7″, and are packaged about 15 to 18 wrappers to approximately one pound. There are no standard sizes. They are most often made from white flour and have been dusted with cornstarch to keep them from sticking together while in the package.

Gluten Flour   Gluten flour is simply the dried portion of wheat flour which has the bran and starch removed. In baking and seitan-making, it is often mixed with white wheat flour or other flours. Gluten flour can be used to make seitan and when used alone does not require the preliminary steps of washing out the starch.

Filo Dough   This paper-thin dough comes ready-made in packages containing 25 to 50 sheets. It can be refrigerated or frozen. You can purchase it in Middle-Eastern markets and some supermarkets.

Flint Corn   As the name suggests, flint corn is a very hard grain. It makes a rich-tasting and sweet corn meal ideal for tortillas, corn bread, and cornmeal mush. It is also delicious when cooked whole. The flint corn commonly available is yellow or amber and is grown primarily in Ohio.

Flour   Wheat is available in hard and soft varieties. The hard wheats contain higher levels of protein than the soft wheats, and the soft wheats contain higher levels of carbohydrates. Both hard and soft wheats are further classified as being spring or winter varieties. This refers to the season in which they are planted. Wheat is further classified by color—usually as red or white.

The hard wheats, because of their higher *gluten* (protein) content, are the wheats used for making seitan and bread. Generally the hard spring wheats tend to have a bit more gluten than the hard winter wheats.

Because they do not rise as well as the hard wheats, soft wheat varieties are used in making pastries or are blended with the harder varieties for bread baking. Pastry wheat, a white spring variety that is very low in gluten content, is used for crackers, pastry dough, and cakes. Some of this is exported to Japan for making *udon* noodles.

Fu   Fu is a dried gluten product available at most Oriental foods stores. Fu is sold either in thin sheets or thick round cakes. It is made from wheat gluten which has been steamed, formed and dried. Fu is generally used in soups, salads, stews, and vegetable dishes.

Ginger   This spicy, golden-colored root is used when fresh as a garnish or seasoning in many dishes. It is excellent as a seasoning for fish. Dried ginger is a commonly found in many baked goods.

Gluten   Gluten is the stretchy protein portion of wheat. It develops after wheat is mixed with water and is kneaded. Bread flour is measured by the strength, quantity, and quality of gluten in the flour. Gluten is what allows bread dough to trap the gases responsible for making bread rise, and for allowing the dough to stretch and develop into loaves. The majority of the protein in wheat is in the gluten.

Granulated Tapioca   Granulated tapioca is a finer, more quick-cooking version of the larger tapioca. It does not require soaking prior to cooking, and is very useful as a thickening agent for dessert puddings. It is available at most supermarkets.

Kampyo   These dried gourd strips are first soaked and then used to bind vegetable rolls. Kampyo is completely edible and is a source of minerals and fiber.

Kasha   Brown to dark brown in color, *kasha* is roasted buckwheat groats. Kasha is a staple food in Central Asia and Russia and is well-known for its warming qualities and hearty flavor.

Kombu   A broad, flat, dark green sea vegetable that grows in deep ocean water, *Kombu* is rich in essential minerals. It is used in making soup stocks, condiments, and candy, and is often cooked with vegetables and beans.

Kukicha Tea   *Kukicha* tea is made from the twigs and stems of the Japanese tea plant. This tea is extremely low in caffeine and has a very mild flavor.

Kuzu   A white starch made from the root of the Japanese *kuzu* plant. In this country, the plant is called *kudzu*. It can be used in making smooth velvety soups, sauces, gravies, desserts, and also for medicinal purposes.

Liquid Hickory Smoke Seasoning   This seasoning is made from extracting the flavor from smoked hickory chips. There are no chemicals used in the process, and this product also contains zero calories and only a trace of sodium. Made by Wright's, it is a discovery which I was delighted to make. It is available in supermarkets.

Maple Granules   Maple sugar granules are produced by a vacuum drying process from

Dark Amber or Grade B maple syrup. The resulting sugar is milled and screened to separate the fine powder from the granules. The powder is sold to commercial processors and the granules are reserved for home use.

Maple Syrup Maple syrup is the concentrated sap of maple trees. It is very sweet yet has considerably more minerals than other types of refined sweeteners such as honey or cane sugar.

Millet This small, yellow grain is a staple in China and Japan, but grows throughout the world. It is very hearty and can be eaten regularly throughout the year. Millet is generally used in soups, vegetable dishes, or eaten as a cereal.

Mirin Mirin is related to saké (rice wine). Like saké, traditional mirin manufacture begins with a mixture of rice koji, cooked white rice, and water. After a one-month fermentation, however, the resulting white, slightly alcoholic mash undergoes a distillation process that is not part of traditional saké-making. The clear distillate, called shōchu, is mixed with cooked sweet rice—the variety of rice highest in natural sugars—and more rice koji. After three months of additional fermentation, the shōchu is pressed, and the resulting clear liquid is aged for six months to two years in ceramic containers. The thick, sweet, golden liquid removed from the containers is mirin, Japan's answer to fine brandy. Mirin is virtually always used for cooking, while saké is usually served hot as an alcoholic beverage. Cooking quickly evaporates mirin's 13 to 14 percent alcohol content, leaving only its sweet essence.

Many brands of mirin, especially those sold in Oriental markets, are not naturally brewed and are sweetened with added sugar or corn syrup. However, in most cases the mirin available in natural foods stores is a high-quality, naturally fermented product made with slight modifications of the traditional process described above. Even when shopping in natural foods stores it is necessary to read the label carefully to see whether the mirin was naturally fermented, and to check for purity of ingredients (sweet rice, rice koji, and water are the only ingredients in authentic mirin).

Miso A fermented grain or bean paste made from ingredients such as soybeans, barley, and rice. There are many varieties of miso now available. Miso is high in protein and vitamin B_{12}, and is especially beneficial to the circulatory and digestive organs.

Mochiko (Sweet Rice Flour) This high gluten flour is made from very finely ground sweet rice. It can be used as you would use rice flour although these flours are not completely interchangeable. Sweet rice flour has a softer and stickier texture than plain rice flour. Japanese sweet rice flour is less glutinuous than the Chinese variety.

Natural Soy Sauce or Shoyu Natural soy sauce is made from soybeans, wheat, salt, water, and a special starter called koji. It is a very tasty and nutritious seasoning. The best-quality natural soy sauce is naturally fermented over two summers and is made from round soybeans and sea salt that is not highly refined. Natural soy sauce is preferred over the commercial varieties available. (See also **Tamari.**)

Nori These thin sheets of dried sea vegetable that are black or dark purple. Nori is often roasted over a flame until green. It is used as a garnish, wrapped around rice in making sushi, or cooked with tamari as a condiment. Rich in vitamin A and protein, nori also contains calcium, iron, vitamins B_1, B_2, C, and D.

Oil (dark and light sesame, safflower, olive)

Light Sesame Oil. Sesame oil has been used since antiquity. Two basic types of sesame oil are available: light and dark. The light oil is mild and nutty tasting, suitable for a wide variety of uses. Although it is 87 percent unsaturated, sesame oil contains only 42 percent linoleic acid. This factor and other components give sesame oil excellent stability and resistance to oxidation. It is a good choice for salads and sautéing.

Toasted Sesame Oil. Toasted sesame oil (also known as dark sesame oil) is made in Japan from whole sesame seeds that have first been carefully toasted then pressed to extract their flavorful oil. No chemicals are used in the processing and, since this oil contains the natural preservatives vitamin E, lecithin, and sesamol, no artificial preservatives are added. Like other natural unrefined oils, toasted sesame oil should be stored in a cool, dark place.

Safflower Oil. Safflower oil has the highest percentage of unsaturated fats of all the oils (94 percent) and is highest in linoleic acid (78 percent). Since unsaturated fats become rancid more quickly than saturated fats, one drawback of high unsaturation is short shelf life. Safflower oil is best stored refrigerated to retard rancidity. It can be used for deep-frying, though its flavor does not remain stable under deep-frying temperatures.

Olive Oil. Olive oil is unique in that it is the only oil normally available that can be considered cold-pressed. The oil of the Mediterranean, it is produced almost exclusively from the fruit of olive trees grown in that area. The best oil comes from olives that are handpicked just before they are fully ripe. The first extraction is a simple, gentle pressing that doesn't heat the oil much above room temperature. Oil obtained from this first pressing receives no further treatment other than filtering to remove pulp. This oil is labeled "virgin olive oil" and is the only oil that can be labeled as such.

Virgin olive oil comes in three grades: "Extra virgin" has perfect flavor and aroma; "fine virgin" has the same flavor as "extra" but a high acidity; "plain virgin" oil, the grade most often sold in the U.S., is imperfect in flavor and has the highest acidity.

Pure olive oil has excellent stability and can sometimes be stored without refrigeration for over a year, but virgin oils degrade more quickly. Most of the unsaturates in olive oil are in the form of monounsaturated oleic acid, instead of the lighter polyunsaturate linoleic, which amounts to only 15 percent. This results in a heavier and more fatty oil.

Polenta/Cornmeal Cornmeal (known as polenta in Italy) is usually milled from yellow dent corn, but occasionally from flint or flour corn. Cornmeal is used for corn bread and cornmeal mush. It can be combined with wheat flour in bread recipes to produce a slightly crumbly, crunchy sweet loaf.

Rice Malt Syrup A sweet, thick syrup made from brown rice and barley that is used in dessert cooking. This complex carbohydrate sweetener is preferable to simple sugars such as honey, maple syrup, and molasses. It does not have as strong a flavor as some other sweeteners, and therefore is more useful for salad dressings and other sauces where a mild sweetness without overbearing flavor is desired.

Rice Vinegar A mild vinegar made from whole brown rice or white rice.

Saké *Saké*, called "rice wine" in this country, is actually related more to other koji-fermented foods such as amazake, miso, and rice vinegar than to wine or beer. Natural saké contains only rice, water, koji, and yeast. Manufacturing begins with the steaming of rice to make koji. The koji is added to water and cooked rice along with a special strain of yeast. Koji enzymes turn complex rice carbohydrates into simple sugars, which the yeast then ferments to alcohol. After about 60 days most of the sugar has been converted to alcohol and the white mash, called moromi, is ready for pressing, filtering, and bottling. Saké is usually served warm, but can also be used in cooking like dry white wine.

Sea Salt   This type of salt has been extracted from sea water and has been minimally refined contains small amounts of trace elements and has no additives, making it moderately superior to other types of salt.

Seitan   Wheat gluten cooked in seasoned broth, usually tamari, kombu, and water. Seitan can be made at home or purchased ready-to-eat at many natural food stores. Seitan can be enjoyed in many forms, and some people use it as a meat substitute.

Shiitake   These exotic mushrooms are available fresh in some stores, but are more often found dried, imported from Japan. They are used in soup stocks, vegetable dishes, and medicinally. *Shiitake* is effective in helping the body neutralize the effects of excessive consumption of salt or animal fat.

Soymilk   Soy beverages, which are very popular in the Orient, are gaining in popularity in the West. They are made from soybeans and have a flavor and consistency similar to dairy milk. They contain small amounts of calcium and protein. Soymilks are excellent for imparting a delicious creamy consistency to sauces, gravies, soups, custards, and puddings.

Suribachi   This serrated, glazed clay bowl is used with a pestle, called a surikogi. It is useful for grinding and pureeing foods, and making dressings and sauces.

Surikogi   This device is the wooden pestle used with a *suribachi*. It is used to grind and mash vegetables, seeds, and other foods into a powder or paste.

Tahini   A smooth paste made from ground white sesame seeds.

Takuan Pickles   These traditional Japanese pickles are made from the daikon radish. The radishes are mixed with rice bran and salt and pressed under a heavy weight for one to three years.

Tamari   The generic name sometimes given to traditional, naturally fermented soy sauce to distinguish it from chemically processed varieties. Real *tamari* is made without the use of any wheat. It was originally the liquid poured off during the process of making *hatcho* miso, but is now made for its own use as a flavoring in cooking. The difference between these two delicious seasonings is in the absence of wheat in true tamari. However, if a recipe calls for shoyu, an equal amount of tamari can usually be substituted with good results.

   Although shoyu contains about two percent more salt than tamari, it tastes slightly sweeter. The subtle sweetness of shoyu and its alcoholic bouquet are both the result of wheat fermentation. Much of the rich taste and aroma of shoyu is lost during cooking due to evaporation of alcohol, so tamari should be used when longer cooking is called for.

Toasted Sesame Seeds   Prepare by heating sesame seeds in a dry frying pan over a medium heat, and stirring constantly until they begin to pop and are very fragrant. Do not allow them to burn. They are completely toasted when you can reduce them to a powder by rubbing a few gently between thumb and third finger.

Tofu   High in protein, tofu (soybean curd), is made from soybeans and nigari (a coagulant taken from salt water). Tofu is used in soups, vegetable dishes, dressings, and desserts. The mild flavor of tofu makes it adaptable to many seasonings and styles of cooking.

Umeboshi Paste/Plums   These salty, pickled plums stimulate the appetite and digestion and aid in maintaining an alkaline blood quality. Shiso leaves are usually added to the plums during pickling to impart a reddish color and natural flavoring, and are useful on their own as a seasoning agent for many dishes.

Ume Su   Ume su translates as "plum vinegar," however it is actually the brine drawn from kegs of mature umeboshi. Ume su contains all the healthful qualities and nutrients associated with umeboshi, and it is easy and convenient to use. Pleasantly tart and salty, it is a versatile seasoning that's especially refreshing in hot weather. When substituting ume su for vinegar, substantially reduce or eliminate the salt in the recipe.

Wakame   Wakame is a long, thin, green sea vegetable used in making soups, salads, and vegetable dishes. High in iron, magnesium, and iodine, this sea vegetable has a delicate texture. Dried wakame is available from *Eden Foods* in flake form, which requires neither soaking nor cutting. It can be added directly from the package to your soups and vegetable dishes. This type of wakame is especially enjoyed for its delicate flavor and brilliant green color.

Wasabi   A light green Japanese dried horseradish powder that is traditionally used in sushi or with raw fish (*sashimi*). When mixed with a little water it develops a very strong, pungent flavor.

Wheat Starch   The starch remaining from the washing of wheat flour. This starch can be used as a thickener for sauces, soups, and gravies. Additional information on using and storing wheat starch can be found in the recipes and Appendix 1.

Wood Ash   Ash left over from the burning of hard woods (without any paper, varnish, or paint mixed in) can be used for softening the outer hull of corn before cooking. The ash acts as a strong alkaline in much the same way as lime is used in Mexico, but it is far less caustic.

Bibliography

Whole World Cookbook, Editors of *East West Journal*, Avery Publishing Group, Inc., Wayne, New Jersey, 1984.

The Book of Whole Meals, Colbin, Annemarie, Ballentine, New York, 1983.

Laurel's Kitchen Bread Book, Robertson, Laurel, Random House, New York, 1984.

Aveline Kushi's Complete Guide to Macrobiotic Cooking for Health, Harmony, and Peace, Kushi, Aveline, Warner Books, New York, 1985.

Cooking with Japanese Foods, A Guide to the Traditional Natural Foods of Japan, Belleme, Jan and John. East West Health Books, Brookline, Massachusetts, 1986.

Natural Foods Cookbook, Estella, Mary, Japan Publications, Inc., Tokyo, New York, 1985.

Mastering the Art of French Cooking, Vol. II, Child, Julia and Beck, Simone, Alfred A. Knopf, New York, 1983.

A Commonplace Book of Cookery, Grabhorn, Robert, North Point Press, San Francisco, 1985.

Florence Lin's Chinese Vegetarian Cookbook, Lin, Florence, Shambhala, Boulder, Colorado, 1976.

The Thousand Recipe Chinese Cookbook, Miller, Gloria Bley, Atheneum, New York, 1966.

The Gluten Cookbook, Moulton, LeArta., The Gluten Co., Provo, Utah, 1981.

The Joy of Cooking, Rombauer, Irma S. and Rombauer-Becker, Marison, Bobbs-Merrill Co., Inc., Indianapolis, Indiana, 1964.

The Silver Palate Cookbook Rosso, Julee and Lukins Sheila, Workman Publishing, New York, 1979.

Make All the Meat You Eat from Wheat, Shandler, Nina and Michael, Rawson, Wade Publishers, Inc., New York, 1980.

The El Molino Cookbook, Ranhill, June, El Molino Mills, div ACG Co., City of Industry, Ca., 1976.

Good Food from a Japanese Temple, Yoneda, Soei, Kodansha International, Tokyo, New York, San Franciso, 1982.

Index

236